Grandma's Kitchen

by Jason A. Shulman
A Blue Cliff Editions Book

A Fireside Book published by Simon & Schuster, Inc.
New York

Copyright © 1985 by Blue Cliff Editions, Inc.

Produced by Blue Cliff Editions, Inc.
611 Broadway
New York, NY 10012

Project manager: Louise Moed
Editors: Jane Bayer (text), Alexandra Greeley (recipes), Elizabeth
  Lawrence (recipes), Peter Pickow (text)
Cover illustration: Tom McKeveney
Interior design: Tim Metevier
Art assistant: Diane Stevens

A Fireside Book
Published by Simon & Schuster, Inc.
Simon & Schuster Building
1230 Avenue of the Americas
New York, NY 10020

FIRESIDE and colophon are registered trademarks
  of Simon & Schuster, Inc.
Manufactured in the United States of America
10 9 8 7 6 5 4 3 2 1

Library of Congress Cataloging in Publication Data

Shulman, Jason A.
    Grandma's kitchen.

    "A Fireside book."
    1. Cookery, International.   I. Title.
TX725.A1S514   1985   641.59   85-1820
ISBN 0-671-55793-9 (pbk.)

Contents

Acknowledgments

Many people made this book possible. Like the recipes themselves, the creation of this book has been handed from person to person, each of whom garnished it with care and attention.

First there were the interviewers, who gathered the documentation upon which these stories were based: Amy Appleby, Majorie Bair, Linda Knowles, Pamela Kraft, Melanie Menagh, Louise Moed, and Nancy Stevenson. They not only caught the spirit of this book, but tracked down photos and researched endlessly for missing details, and delivered the raw material that made possible the writing and design of this book. Additional interviews were contributed by Lynn Green, Judy Myers, Diane Rosenthal, Alan Saly, Sandy Schulman, Margaret Schwarm, and Arlene Shulman. I thank you all.

I also thank Tim Metevier, whose elegant sense of design created a perfect vehicle for the feelings of this book, and Diane Stevens, who helped paste it down. Jane Bayer and Peter Pickow helped polish the prose; and Alexandra Greeley and Elizabeth Lawrence took recipes, often scantily remembered, or jotted down on scraps of paper, and made them printable and reproducible.

A special thanks must go to Louise Moed, who managed this entire project. The creation of a book like this means the creation of thousands of pieces of paper, each with a desire to go its own way: Louise kept them in line and flowing toward our desired goal. Her astute editorial recommendations became an integral part of the book.

Finally, I must thank the people we interviewed, who allowed us to delve into cherished memories and bring something private and personal to print. Without them—and their grandmothers, occasional grandfathers, uncles, and aunts—this book would have remained a dream.

Preface

My grandmother's house was cool and dark: four rooms in the basement of a tenement that opened into a bright garden.

My grandmother had house plants that thrived in the semi-darkness of the basement: straight, thick-leaved plants that I thought only she could grow. We lived in the upstairs apartment, and many early mornings, I'd walk down the stairs and knock on my grandmother's door. She'd let me in and then disappear for a few moments only to come back with a brown paper bag filled with dark, hard cinnamony cookies that I would crunch all morning: Grandma Cookies.

Whether we knew our actual grandmothers or not, we all know what having a grandmother is like. Sometimes she wasn't our real grandmother: She was the next-door neighbor who watched us while our mothers worked, or she was an aunt in a faraway city whom we looked forward to visiting each year at holiday time. Sometimes the special one was a grandfather, or an uncle. But whoever it was, he or she fulfilled our dream of the true grandmother, loving us unabashedly and uncritically, filling us with the foods that glow in our memories with the most special and delicious tastes.

This book is dedicated to those memories of all the food they fed us: cookies hard and soft, special soups and stews, fish prepared that certain way, breads, cakes, and puddings.

This book is also dedicated to my grandmother, Rose, and to all our grandparents, uncles, and aunts, wherever they may be at the moment.

A Word About the Recipes

Who invents a recipe? Where does it come from?

For the most part, recipes exist as a kind of collective wisdom about something that is good to eat and how it can be made, handed down from one generation of cooks and eaters to the next. Bits and pieces change along the way. One generation, in love with the new process of canning that allows them to have foods out of season, thinks nothing of substituting canned green beans for fresh. Another generation, concerned with health and nutrition, substitutes preservative-free safflower oil for lard.

Properly looked at, each recipe is a little history unto itself: Like an archeologist, one can look at a recipe and see the journey certain ingredients have taken from one country to the next, constantly changing their role and context in each cuisine and culture. We can find those dishes created when times were hard, and food had to go a long way, and those created for the sheer pleasure of mouth and eye. Some were brought by immigrants, and others evolved from native food. Each recipe evokes a bit of time and place.

The recipes our grandmas have given us are no-nonsense directions for enriching our lives with food that is interesting, nurturing, and delicious. The recipes in this book possess the all-important added ingredient of *pleasure*—the pleasure of the circumstances in which they were first encountered; the pleasurable memories of the communion of friends and family around the table; the pleasure of carrying forward a previous generation's involvement with food and family.

The recipes in this volume do not qualify as culinary masterpieces, unique in the world of cooking. You will find no *nouvelle cuisine*, no elegant presentations, calling for special utensils or equipment. But they are all the "specialty of the house." You will find that each grandmother, aunt, grandfather, or friend has added a certain something in the way of ingredients or technique to make that recipe uniquely his or her own. Yetta Handler surprises us with a sweet potato in her chicken soup (see page 2). Lynn Andersen's dessert delights us with—would you believe it—snow! Some of these recipes are your own favorites, and some you probably have never heard of or tasted before.

We have made every effort—wherever possible—to translate to modern measurements such time-honored amounts as "a handful" of this and "a touch" of that. We do not require you to determine if your oven is at the right temperature by sticking your hand in, as some of the cooks described in these pages did. We want you to be able to reproduce these recipes so that they may live again and spread the love with which they were originally created. And we hope this book will encourage you to keep track of your own family's food history, and support you in bringing these joys of the past back into the present. *Bon appetit!*

"What is patriotism

but the love of the good things

we ate in our childhood?"

— Lin Yutang

Yetta Handler's Chicken Soup and Cheese Blintzes

Caren (granddaughter): So many things happen around food in a Jewish family! When Passover came, my grandmother Yetta would wash the whole kitchen from top to bottom and then carry up barrels of special dishware from the basement. She'd cook for days. She'd make a nut cake and a sponge cake—they were always the best desserts. But my favorite thing was the chicken soup with matzoh balls. There are two types of grandmothers—the grandmothers who make the floating kind of matzoh balls and the grandmothers who make the rocks. The rocks you love because your grandmother made them, but the other kind *taste* good!

Clare (daughter): My mother was a fantastic cook. It was extremely important to her that we ate well. There were three children. If one of us wanted lamb chops, one wanted steak, and the other one wanted something else—no problem. She'd dish that out for us. A lot of the dishes she prepared were peasant dishes from Russia, so they were cheap to make—borscht, potato and rice dishes, and blintzes. She always prided herself that her blintzes were thinner and better than anyone else's. She'd start out making cheese blintzes and end up spending hours in the kitchen, making potato blintzes as well!

—*Caren Warhaftig Borowsky and Clare Handler Warhaftig*

1

Chicken Soup

1 large carrot
1 large sweet potato, peeled (or scrubbed and unpeeled) and quartered
1 bunch of soup greens (parsnip or celery tops, parsley, dill)
1 large onion, peeled and whole
1 stalk celery, whole
4 quarts water
3–4 pound kosher chicken*
5–6 whole peppercorns
2 bay leaves
3 tablespoons salt
Matzoh balls (recipe follows)

Place the carrot, sweet potato, soup greens, onion, and celery in a 2–3 gallon soup pot half filled with water. Bring to boil. Add the whole chicken, peppercorns, bay leaves, and salt, fill the pot to the top with water, cover, and simmer for at least 2½–3 hours. Periodically skim off the fat with a spoon.

When the meat falls off the bones, remove the chicken from the liquid. Strain and save the broth, and discard the vegetables. Remove the meat from the bones, cut it into small pieces, and add with the matzoh balls to the broth. Reheat.

Makes 8 to 10 servings.

*Yetta prefers kosher chickens because she feels they give more flavor.

Matzoh Balls

Caren: This recipe comes from my mother-in-law, Beverly Borowsky.

4 extra-large eggs (or 5 large eggs)
½ cup chicken broth, at room temperature
1 cup cold water
1 teaspoon nutmeg
1–2 tablespoons melted chicken fat
½ cup parsley, finely chopped
Dash of white pepper
1 teaspoon salt
3 cups matzoh meal

Separate the egg yolks from the whites. Beat the yolks with the chicken broth until lemony yellow. If necessary, add a little cold water to make it the desired color. Add to this mixture the nutmeg, chicken fat, parsley, and white pepper. In a separate bowl beat the egg whites with the salt until stiff. Grdually add matzoh meal to the yolk mixture. If necessary, add additional water until the consistency is firm but not dry.

Fold the egg whites into the yolk mixture. The consistency should remain firm. Refrigerate for 2–3 hours.

About half an hour before serving time, fill a 3–5 gallon pot with water and a pinch of salt, and bring the water to a boil. Gently shape the dough into soft balls about the size of tennis balls. The shaping will be easier if you cool your hands in cold water. Drop the balls into the rapidly boiling water. Lower heat and simmer the balls until they float to the surface, approximately 10 minutes. (If they are very large, allow them to cook a little bit more after they rise to the surface.)

When done, remove the balls from the water with a sieve or slotted spoon and place in the chicken soup. Serve hot.

Makes about 20 matzoh balls.

2

Cheese Blintzes

Crepe Batter

2 large eggs
1/2 teaspoon salt
1/2 teaspoon sugar
1 teaspoon unsalted butter,
   melted

3/4 cup milk and 3/4 cup water,
   mixed together
1 1/4 cups all-purpose flour

Filling

4 8-ounce packages farmer
   cheese
4 ounces cream cheese, at room
   temperature
2 eggs
1 tablespoon unsalted butter,
   softened
1 tablespoon sugar

1 teaspoon vanilla extract, or to
   taste
Cinnamon to taste
1 tablespoon vegetable oil, for
   frying
3 tablespoons butter, for frying
Sour cream or jam (optional), for
   serving

To make the crepes, beat the eggs, and add the salt, the sugar, and the melted butter. Stir in the milk and water mixture alternately with the flour to make a smooth batter. Let the batter stand for 30 minutes before cooking, then restir it gently.

To make the filling, mix together the farmer cheese and cream cheese, and set aside. Beat the eggs and stir in the butter, sugar, vanilla extract, and cinnamon until well blended. Stir this into the cheese mixture.

Spread a clean kitchen towel on a counter. Grease a 6-inch cast iron skillet lightly but thoroughly with 1 tablespoon butter, and heat it over medium-high heat. Pour a small quantity of the batter into the skillet and swirl it to cover the bottom of the skillet. When the crepe is brown underneath, turn it out onto the towel. This all takes about a minute. Continue making all the crepes in the same manner. You may need to regrease the pan between crepes.

Place one tablespoonful of the filling in the center of each crepe, then fold the crepe into an envelope. (The filled crepes can be placed in a tightly covered container and refrigerated for up to 2 days, or frozen until you are ready to cook and serve them.)

To cook the blintzes, heat the oil and 2 tablespoons of butter in a 10-inch skillet until bubbly. Saute the blintzes, turning on all sides, until golden brown. If necessary, add more oil and butter for sauteeing.

Serve the blintzes plain, or with sour cream or jam.

Makes about 20 blintzes.

Bridget Besso Gushue's New England Boiled Dinner and Raisin-Filled Cookies

I remember my mother cooking New England boiled dinner. It's still my favorite meal. It's a smoked shoulder of pork, boiled in a pot with potatoes with the skins on, carrots, and cabbage. You serve it with mustard. I remember our meals as nourishing; my mother was very nutrition-conscious. We had roast beef, liver, pork chops, and a lot of hash. I get a very warm feeling when I remember meal time, sitting around the table with my two brothers and my sister. Plenty of food. My father would say grace. Sometimes we'd sit around the table afterward just talking, my father telling jokes. Or sometimes he would tell us a story and he'd switch the first letters around. Instead of saying "Mary had a little lamb" he would say "Mary lad a little ham," and we'd be on the floor, laughing.

Then there's my grandmother, Grammy Gushue, ninety-one and still eating heartily. When her appetite goes, she'll be dead! She's been sick most of her life, but thank God her appetite has never failed her! She's from Newfoundland. There are two types of cookies that she always made. One was mincemeat cookies—two layers of dough with mincemeat or raisins as filling. Delicious! And the other was a vanilla wafer with sprinkles on top. Here are Grammy's recipes.

—*Mary Elizabeth (Mef) Ford*

4

New England Boiled Dinner

3–5 pound smoked shoulder of
   pork
4–5 quarts water
1 teaspoon ground pepper or
   several peppercorns

4–6 medium potatoes, whole,
   peeled, or scrubbed and
   unpeeled
4–5 carrots, peeled and quartered
2–3 pounds cabbage, cut into
   quarters, optional
Mustard for serving

Cover the smoked shoulder with the water, add the pepper, and bring to a boil over high heat. When the water boils, lower the heat and simmer for 1½–2 hours. Add the potatoes, carrots, and cabbage, and continue boiling until the meat is tender when pierced with a fork.

With a slotted spoon, remove the meat and the vegetables from the pot and discard the water. Slice the meat, put the slices on a platter, and surround them with the vegetables. Serve with mustard.

Makes 5 to 6 servings.

Ice Cream Wafers

1 cup plus 1 tablespoon
   shortening
⅔ cup sugar
1 teaspoon salt

2 teaspoons vanilla extract
2 large eggs
2½ cups all-purpose flour

Preheat the oven to 375 degrees. Grease two cookie sheets with 1 tablespoon of shortening.

Combine the rest of the shortening, the sugar, the salt, the vanilla, and the eggs, and beat thoroughly. Add the flour and mix thoroughly. Drop level tablespoons of dough on the greased baking sheets. Flatten the cookies with a glass covered with a damp cloth so the dough will not stick to the glass. It helps to work with slightly chilled dough. Bake the cookies for 10 minutes until delicately browned. Cool and serve with ice cream.

Makes about 4½ dozen cookies.

Raisin-Filled Cookies

Dough

½ cup (1 stick) plus 1 tablespoon
   shortening, softened
½ cup sugar
1 large egg

½ cup milk
1 teaspoon vanilla extract
3 (or more) cups all-purpose
   flour

Filling

1 teaspoon all-purpose flour
½ cup sugar

½ cup water
1 cup black raisins, ground

To make the dough, cream together the shortening and sugar. Blend in the egg, milk, and vanilla, in that order. Stir in the flour, adding more if necessary, to make a stiff dough. Chill the dough for one hour.

While the dough is chilling, make the filling. Stir together the flour and sugar in a saucepan. Add the water and ground raisins, stirring carefully. Bring to a boil over moderate heat and cook until thick, stirring occasionally. This should take about 15 minutes. Cool the mixture.

Preheat the oven to 350 degrees. Grease two cookie sheets with 1 tablespoon of shortening.

Roll out the chilled dough on a floured board or cloth to a thickness of about ⅛ inch. Cut into desired shapes (squares, rounds, stars, etc.). Place half the cookies on the cookie sheets, allowing about one inch between cookies. Place a small dollop of filling in the center of each (the exact amount depends on the size of your cookies). Place another cookie on top of each and seal the edges. Bake for 15 minutes, or until lightly browned.

Makes about 3 dozen filled cookies.

Aunt Eva's Maryland Crabs and Crab Cakes

We lived in a very large house with a huge kitchen. We had a very big family, and everyone congregated in the kitchen. You'd go in and you'd say, "Aunt Eva, what are you cooking?" And she'd go, "Aww, I'm not cooking nothin', nothin' at all. It's just some scraps in the pan." Or sometimes she would tell us she was cooking brains, which is a common breakfast food for country people. Every time she would tell me that, I would never believe that a person would eat brains because I would think of brains inside of a head. And lo and behold, that's what she would fix. None of the kids would eat them.

The one thing in the entire world that no one can cook like my Aunt Eva is Maryland crabs. This is Aunt Eva's *crème de la crème* recipe. She's about eighty-two years old and still cooking! If you could see her in the kitchen when she's making them, you'd roll over in laughter! She grabs the live crab with her tongs. Maybe some of us are peeking in, watching her, but no one says a thing. She grabs each live crab and she says, "Come here, you little sucka!" She puts them in the pot and she steams them in flat beer, bay leaf, and garlic. They're just scrumptious. I really shouldn't give this recipe away, you know, or her famous recipe for crab cakes. But they're magnificent! We all loved them, everyone who lived in the house—my grandmother Katy; my Aunt Ethel and her husband, Uncle Jasper; my Aunt Eva; my Aunt Della; my mother, Ruth; Aunt Eva's grandkids, Billy and Ronnie; me; my two sisters; and my brother.

—*Donald Bowman*

6

Maryland Crabs

Don: To prepare this recipe, you will need *live* Maryland crabs from the Chesapeake Bay (they are seasonal, available in late spring and early fall), and a 5–gallon stainless steel or enamel pot for steaming. Aluminum pots may change the taste of the crabs.

1 gallon water
2 bay leaves
¼ cup Old Bay seasoning
1 clove garlic, crushed and peeled

½ teaspoon salt
½ teaspoon pepper
1 dozen large live Maryland crabs
1 can flat beer (previously opened, at room temperature)

Put the water, bay leaves, Old Bay seasoning, garlic, salt, and pepper into the pot and bring the water to a boil over high heat. When the water boils, lower the heat to simmer and, wearing a pair of gloves and using long tongs, carefully place the live crabs in the simmering water, one at a time. Cover and simmer for 20 minutes. If you like your crabs very spicy, add to the water an additional crushed clove of garlic and an extra quarter-cup of Old Bay seasoning.

Add the beer to the pot, cover the pot, and simmer the water an additional 10 minutes. The crabs are cooked when the shells are bright red. Remove the crabs with the tongs and place them on a platter.

Makes 2 to 3 servings.

Don: The traditional Maryland way to eat steamed crabs is to eat over newspaper spread on the table instead of using plates. Use a nutcracker and a nut pick, or seafood fork, for utensils. Turn each crab over on its back (the smooth side down). Lift the lip or flap on the underside with the pick; this will crack the shell. After you remove the shell you will see 5 or 6 soft finger-like structures. These are called "Devil Fingers." *Do not eat them!* Discard them. All the rest of the meat is wonderful, so go at it, picking it out and enjoying yourself. Use the nutcracker to crack the claws and the pick to extract the meat.

Maryland Crab Cakes

1 pound crab meat, shelled and with all cartilage removed (see previous recipe)
1 cup fine, dry breadcrumbs
2 bunches scallions, minced
½ teaspoon salt

¼ teaspoon pepper
1 large egg, beaten
½ cup water
3–4 tablespoons oil for frying
Cocktail or tartar sauce for serving

Mix together the breadcrumbs, scallions, salt, and pepper. Add the beaten egg and water, and stir to make a thick batter. Shred the crab meat very finely, and add it to the batter, mixing well. Shape into patties 2–3 inches wide.

Heat the oil in a 10–inch skillet and saute the cakes until golden brown. Remember that the crab meat is already cooked: you are just cooking the rest of the mixture. This should take only about 3–4 minutes.

Serve with a cocktail or tartar sauce, and accompany with a fresh salad and cold beer.

Makes about 10 cakes, which will serve 5 people.

Kiss's Cold String-Bean Soup and Cucumber Salad

My mother was the best cook in the whole world. It was hard to pin down exactly what her recipes were—a pinch of this or a handful of that. She felt Hungarian cooking was too heavy and greasy, so she would tone it down a little. She made the most wonderful dessert—palacsinta—kind of like a Hungarian crepe suzette. She would make a whole batch and fill them with different fillings, like jelly, chocolate, nuts and raisins, or cottage cheese. Then she'd dribble a delicious sauce over the whole thing. Chocolate was my favorite. This dish took a lot of skill; you had to get the batter very thin and turn it over at just the right moment. It had to cool, but not too much, so that when the filling was put in and you rolled it the crepe wouldn't break up. It had to be rolled very carefully.

I also loved her cold string-bean soup. In the summer nothing was better. She made it with sour cream and onions and string beans and a little flour. At that time they didn't have stringless beans, so my sister and I had to pull the spines off and break the beans into inch-long pieces. That was our job. I loved to hear the snap of the beans as we broke them. There was nothing more delicious after coming home from school on a hot day than that ice-cold soup! My mother learned to make it from *her* mother. I remember my grandmother making it for me when I was a little child in Hungary.

—*Margaret Schwarm*

Cold String-Bean Soup

Margaret: This soup can be served hot, but we always prefer it ice-cold.

½ pound fresh string beans
1 large onion, peeled and thinly
* sliced*
2–3 cups water

Salt to taste
1 cup sour cream
1 tablespoon all-purpose flour

Wash the string beans, snap off the ends, then break them in halves or thirds, depending on the length of the beans. Put the beans and the sliced onion in a medium-sized pot, and add water to cover the beans. Add salt to taste. Bring the mixture to a boil and cook for 5–8 minutes, until the beans are tender but still slightly crisp. Remove from the heat.

While the string beans are cooking, blend the flour gradually into the sour cream, stirring until smooth. When the string beans are ready, stir 1 tablespoon of the cooking water into the sour cream mixture, then stir this mixture back into the string beans, combining thoroughly. Reheat the bean mixture to the boiling point. Remove the pot from the heat and allow the contents to cool. Chill before serving.

Makes 4 to 6 servings.

Cucumber Salad

2 medium cucumbers, peeled and
* thinly sliced*
1 medium onion, peeled and
* thinly sliced*
1 teaspoon salt

1 teaspoon sugar
2 tablespoons vinegar, or to taste
Paprika to taste

Sprinkle the cucumbers with half of the salt, and stir thoroughly. Let them rest for at least 1 hour but preferably 2 hours.

Meanwhile, place the onion slices in a bowl. Add the sugar and the remaining salt. Sprinkle this with the vinegar and let it rest for at least 15 minutes.

Then press the cucumbers between your hands to extract as much of the liquid as possible, discarding the liquid. Place the cucumber slices in the bowl with the onion slices, and mix well. Add the sour cream and mix well again. Add more vinegar or salt, to taste.

Sprinkle each portion with paprika to taste.

Makes about 6 servings.

Grandma Chang's Tsung-yu Bing

We lived with my grandmother until I was eight. She used to do a lot of cooking and was very good at it. One dish she made was a rich stew with pork and heavily salted pickled cabbage in a brown sauce. We went to her house for dinner many years later and she served this dish. I said, "Oh! I like this dish; you haven't made it in a long time!" She thought about it and said she hadn't made it in fifteen years. But the taste of it was so familiar, it was as if fifteen years had been nothing.

My grandmother also made a Shanghai appetizer called tsung-yu bing. It's a pan-fried pancake with scallions and spicy pickled turnip. When it's fried, it gets chewy and the scallions are smooth and fragrant. And you get little crunchy bits of hot, salty turnip. It's delicious!

Although I grew up in Queens, my family was originally from Shanghai. A few times a month the whole family would get into the car and drive into New York City to one of the few non-Cantonese restaurants around in those days. We'd sit around a big round table and eat for hours. I remember as a child trying so hard to control my chopsticks. Everybody used them differently, and each had a suggestion as to what was the best way. Contrary to what everybody thinks, no Chinese is born just knowing how!

—*Dallas Chang*

Tsung-Yu Bing

Scallion Cakes

1½ cups all-purpose flour
⅔ cup water
Pinch of salt
2 cups scallions, finely chopped

Szechuan spicy pickled turnip, finely chopped, to taste, (available in Asian groceries)
1–2 tablespoons vegetable oil for frying

Mix together the flour and water to make a stiff dough, adding more flour or water as necessary. Roll out the dough as thinly as you can. Sprinkle the dough with a few drops of cooking oil and spread the oil over the surface to make it shiny and glistening. Sprinkle the dough with salt. In a thick layer, spread the scallions and then the pickled turnip over the surface.

Starting at one end, roll the dough into a jelly roll-like cylinder. Use a rolling pin to flatten the roll to the width of two fingers. The scallions will pop through in various places.

Add the oil to a 10–inch heavy-gauge skillet and heat the oil until it shimmers. Add the pancake to the hot oil and and cook it, covered, until it browns on the underside. With a large spatula, flip the pancake over and brown the other side, leaving the pan uncovered. Press down with a spatula as it cooks. When the pancake has browned, slide it from the skillet to a plate and slice diagonally into serving pieces.

Makes about 8 servings.

Chinese Stew

3 cloves garlic, crushed and peeled
1 tablespoon butter or shortening
48–ounce can chicken broth
A small amount of raw vegetables such as snow peas, green peppers, dried black Chinese mushrooms, string beans, celery, broccoli, scallions, etc., cut into small pieces. The quantity is optional.
1 cup leftover cooked vegetables, to taste

½ cup leftover cooked meat, to taste
½ cup all-purpose flour
½ teaspoon pepper
½ teaspoon onion or garlic powder
½ teaspoon paprika
¼ teaspoon coriander
¼ cup water

Melt the butter in a small heavy-gauge skillet, and saute the garlic until golden. Then set aside.

Heat the broth in a pot until boiling. Reduce to a simmer, then add the raw vegetables and the sauteed garlic. Cook until the vegetables are fork-tender. Add the leftover vegetables and meat.

In a small bowl, stir together the flour, pepper, onion or garlic powder, paprika, and coriander. Add the water slowly, stirring until the mixture is more liquid than paste. It should be glutinous, but not runny. Hold the bowl over the pot of boiling soup. Tilt the bowl until the dough slides to the rim. Using a chopstick or knife, drop 2–inch pieces of dough into the soup. The dough dumplings will drop to the bottom, and when they float to the top, they are done. These dumplings thicken the soup into a stew.

Makes 4 to 5 servings.

Grandma Sabél's Pizza Dolce

My grandmother's name was Isabella, but people called her "Sabél." She came to America after her family lost their farm in the grape famine. This was around 1896. My grandmother and my great-aunt, who were around fourteen or sixteen, came to the glorious New World, the "land of opportunity," to make enough money to go back and start up the farm again. But they never got to do that. My grandmother got married at nineteen, here in America, to someone from her own town in Italy.

When my father was a year and a half old, my grandfather died. Of *agita!* Indigestion! He was only twenty-four. They had spent the whole day at a wooden picnic table at Manhattan Beach, eating all sorts of Italian foods and drinking wine. Then, on their way home, they stopped at Lundy's, the famous seafood restaurant in Brooklyn, and not only ate clams there, but brought buckets of clams back to the house and continued eating into the evening. Sometime that night, my grandfather died. It's been said you shouldn't eat shellfish with wine. I don't know. It's been said: "Eat clams and die!" But in any case, he died of a heart attack. At that time, there wasn't a term "heart attack," so the death certificate said "Indigestion."

I remember my grandmother's back porch, covered with grape vines. There was this big fig tree in the backyard. And there were yellow jackets drunk with the nectar of the grapes, just humming and not attacking.

Whenever there was a holiday, my grandmother made everything from scratch. I would watch her make fresh pasta, shaping it different ways. We kids would steal pieces of the dough and eat too much—indigestion! Sabél also would make a calzone-type of pie, almost like a square pizza with onion, spinach, anchovies and other things, and dough on top of it. She'd cut a plug in the middle of the pie so she could pull it out to see if it was done. We kids made a tradition of stealing the plug and eating it like an appetizer! Every province in Italy had their own calzone, so this was not the usual calzone as most people know it. It doesn't have ricotta or mozzarella. We used to call it Pizza Dolce, "sweet pizza."

—*Anthony Vulpis*

Pizza Dolce

2½ tablespoons olive oil
1½–2 pounds small white onions
(about 30 small onions)

1 pound pizza dough (recipe follows)
1 can anchovies, drained
1 handful of black raisins

Grease a 12–inch round pizza pan with ½ tablespoon of olive oil. Preheat the oven to 375 degrees.

Peel and slice the onions. Heat 2 tablespoons of olive oil in a heavy-gauge skillet and saute the onions until soft, then drain the onions in a colander. Line the pizza pan with half of the dough. Let stand for 30 minutes.

Spread the onions and the anchovies evenly over the dough. Sprinkle the raisins over the anchovies. Roll out the other half of the dough and place it over the filling. Cut a hole about 1½ inches in diameter in the center of the pizza to allow the steam to escape. Bake for 30 minutes.

Makes a 12–inch pie, 8 to 10 slices.

Pizza Dough

1 cake or 1 envelope dried yeast
1⅓ cups lukewarm water
4 cups all-purpose flour

1 teaspoon salt
2 tablespoons olive oil

Grease a large bowl and set aside.

Dissolve the yeast in ⅓ cup of the water, and let sit until bubbly. Stir together the flour and salt. Add the remaining water and the oil to the yeast mixture and gradually stir it into the flour mixture, making a stiff dough. Turn the dough out onto a floured board and knead it for about 10 minutes. Place the dough in the greased bowl, turn to coat it, then cover it with a clean towel and let the dough rise in a warm place until doubled in size, about 1½–2 hours.

Makes enough dough for 2 pizzas.

Thanksgiving Mustard Onions

Both my grandmother and my mother were working women when I was growing up in Moscow, Idaho. My grandparents owned a photography studio, in which my grandmother hand-colored portraits. My mother was a hospital nurse's aide. Because both of my parents worked, my grandmother would do my hair in the morning and I would go to her studio after school.

I remember that all the best activity and best smells happened in the kitchen of my mother's house. I always thought the kitchen was huge. It was where I did my homework and played with my dolls, and where all the cooking and baking was done, and where my mother gave me "perms" in my teen years. I went back a few years ago and noticed that the kitchen is really very tiny. But it's where the affection was.

The kitchen was my mother's. I was always welcome, but she ran it. After school, even when she was working, there was always freshly baked bread, all deliciously gooey in the middle, and on birthdays and holidays there were always special dishes and desserts cooked only for those occasions. My sixth birthday is one I remember best. I was into storybook dolls then, and my mother baked a cake in the form of a doll dressed in a beautiful ruffled gown.

Every Christmas and Thanksgiving she made a steamed carrot pudding, topped with an incredible sauce that she learned from my grandmother. I remember barely being able to wait for this marvelous dessert, but strangely, I never thought to ask her to make it at any other time. It went with the holidays. Also on Thanksgiving we had to have my grandmother's mustard onions and a very spicy tomato aspic. Now I make the mustard onions every Thanksgiving. It wouldn't be Thanksgiving without them.

Since I've had children of my own and temporarily put my own career aside, I've gotten into duplicating the warm feeling of my mother's kitchen. For years after I left home, my mother sent me "care" packages of cookies, but since my parents are now retired I send *them* cookies!

—*Karen Sterner Bratnick*

Carrot Pudding

1 tablespoon unsalted butter
1 cup carrots, peeled and grated
1 cup potatoes, peeled and grated
1 cup brown sugar
1 cup black raisins
4 tablespoons unsalted butter,
   melted
¼ cup citron, chopped

½ cup walnuts or pecans,
   chopped
2 tablespoons milk
1 cup all-purpose flour
1 teaspoon baking soda
1 teaspoon cinnamon, ground
½ teaspoon cloves, ground
½ teaspoon salt
Ice cream sauce (recipe follows)

With 1 tablespoon of butter, grease a 1–quart pudding mold or large can with a lid. Heat about 2 inches of water in a steamer or kettle fitted with a rack.

Mix together the carrots, potatoes, sugar, raisins, melted butter, citron, nuts, and milk. Sift the flour with the baking soda, cinnamon, cloves, and salt. Stir in the carrot mixture and pour it into the prepared pudding mold or can. The mold or can should be about two-thirds full. Cover the container tightly and steam it for 3–3½ hours. Replenish the water in the pot as needed.

Remove the container from the steamer and allow it to cool for about 15 minutes before unmolding. Serve warm with ice cream sauce.

Makes 8 servings.

Ice Cream Sauce

1 cup heavy cream
1 large egg
¾ cup white sugar
Pinch of salt

⅓ cup (⅔ stick) butter, melted
1 teaspoon vanilla extract or
   brandy

Whip the cream until stiff and set aside. Beat the egg until light, then add the sugar and salt and beat well. Add the melted butter gradually and then the vanilla or brandy. Fold the egg mixture into the whipped cream. Chill and serve it on steamed pudding.

Makes 8 servings.

Mustard Onions

2 pounds white boiling onions,
   peeled and whole, or yellow
   onions, peeled and sliced
½ teaspoon salt
8 cups water
1½–2 tablespoons unsalted
   butter or shortening
1½ tablespoons all-purpose flour

1 teaspoon prepared mustard
1 teaspoon prepared horseradish
   or horseradish-flavored
   mustard
½ cup milk
½ cup water
Salt and pepper to taste

Preheat the oven to 350 degrees.

Cook the onions in salted water almost to cover for about 10 minutes. Meanwhile, over medium heat, melt the butter in a small saucepan and stir in the flour to form a paste. Stir in the mustard and horseradish, then gradually add the milk and water, stirring constantly. Cook this mixture until thickened. Season with salt and pepper to taste, and remove from the heat.

Drain the onions and place them in an ovenproof casserole. Pour the sauce over the onions, cover, and bake for 15–20 minutes. If you wish, remove the lid for the last 10 minutes of cooking to give the dish a little color.

Makes 6 servings.

Grandma Sadie's Banana-Lemon Cookie Cake

My grandmother, Sadie Andersen, had a wonderful kitchen back home in Sturtevant, Wisconsin. I roller-skated and rode my bicycle around in it, and ate huge amounts of cookies in it. I was her only granddaughter, so I could do *anything,* in or out of the kitchen, and she just kept loving me. As for her cooking: To make hamburgers, brown patties fifteen minutes, add water, and then boil for another forty-five minutes. For peas, open a can of Del Monte, add more water, and hard boil for fifteen minutes. For duck, have Grandpa bring one home from the tavern Saturday night, get up early Sunday morning, brown in the oven, then pour water over it, cover; and cook until the leg comes off in your hand when you shake it. For spaghetti sauce, open a can of tomato paste, add salt, water, and hamburger. On a good day, add an onion. And when you make Jell-O, make sure it has a thick crust on top so that you can cover it with whipped cream.

Grandma was a gadabout who wasn't much interested in cooking. But she always had a pot of coffee on the stove and lots of store-bought cookies and coffee cake. The door was always open to visitors. In fact, when things started to get bad for men working on the railroad, and more hobos were to be found down and out, Gram used to make a bacon-and-egg breakfast for those who would knock on her door, though they were never allowed in the house.

As I look back, I seem to remember Grandma being in the kitchen all day long. In those days, it was expected that a woman's job was to put food on the table morning, noon, and night, day in and day out. It's possible that Grandma might have been more interested in cooking if she hadn't always been expected to be doing it. Until I left home, I thought all the food she cooked was the most delicious in the world. Here is one of her recipes that I especially liked as a child, plus one of my own.

—*Lynn Andersen*

Banana-Lemon Cookie Cake

1 package lemon pie filling,
    approximately 3 ounces
1 pound vanilla wafers

6 bananas, sliced into rounds
1 cup heavy cream
2 tablespoons honey or sugar

Prepare the pie filling as directed on the package.

Line the bottom and partway up the sides of a shallow 1–2 quart glass or wooden bowl (a salad bowl works fine) with a layer of cookies. Add a layer of bananas. Pour one-third of the pie filling over the bananas. Add another layer of cookies, a layer of bananas, and a layer of pie filling, and repeat until all ingredients are used up. Refrigerate 1–2 hours to set.

Whip the cream until stiff, then incorporate the honey or sugar. Spread over the top of the cake.

Makes 6 to 8 servings.

Lynn's Snow Cream

Lynn: This dish can only be made in the dead of winter with clean fresh-fallen snow. It's best made when the inside is warm and the night is bright by snowlight. The method is simple: run out (in your bare feet) with a big bowl and scoop up the snow. Run back in, mix flavorings from the following list (or others, as you wish), and stir quickly into the snow.

Flavoring combinations (choose one, or several):

3–4 tablespoons heavy cream or
    nut milk
2–4 tablespoons honey, maple
    syrup, molasses, or sorghum
    molasses
1/4–1/2 teaspoon vanilla extract

1–2 teaspoons carob powder
1/2 cup nuts of your choice,
    chopped
1/2 teaspoon cinnamon, ground
1 teaspoon Pero, Cafix, or instant
    coffee powder

Grandma Kocur's Kolache and Zapraska

For me, memories of growing up in Baltimore are as much about Sundays in Grandma's kitchen on Curly Street, with its wood-burning stove and wringer washing machine, as about anything else. I was her only grandchild for ten years, so it was a special event when I came to visit.

Grandma taught me how to cook, and the way she did it was mostly by the *feel* of things. She would take my hand in hers to feel the consistency of what she was making, so that I could know when it felt right. And she often pointed out the way something should smell, such as "nutty," when it was finished.

Grandma's cooking was a combination of traditional Czech (she was born in the foothills of the Tatra Mountains in what is now Czechoslovakia) with its sweet-and-sour sauces, and American standbys like stuffed turkey and bacon-lettuce-and-tomato on white bread. My favorites were meatballs wrapped in cabbage, her homemade sauerkraut, and hlupe, a ravioli-like dish of meat inside dough. She also taught me how to make the traditional Czech sauce called zapraska, which is a delicious sweet-and-sour gravy to put over string beans, potatoes, and meat.

It was in her big, cozy kitchen that I learned how to vary proportions and timing to fit different conditions—cover the dough with a warm towel if the room is cool, for example, or compensate in other ways if the weather is warm or humid. And she taught me to make certain things like kolache, which is a marvelous coffee cake made with a challah-bread base, and with which one must take lots of time. To this day, no one in the family, including my aunts, can make it as well as I can, which is just the way she did, with lots of time and love.

—*Janet Lawson*

Kolache

Topping

2 pounds walnuts, shelled and
    chopped

½ cup (1 stick) unsalted butter,
    softened
¾ cup sugar

Cake

2 cakes fresh yeast
¼ cup lukewarm water
¾ cup plus 1 teaspoon sugar
½ cup unsalted butter, melted
1¼ cups milk

8 cups (2 pounds) all-purpose
    flour
5 large eggs
2 teaspoons salt

Grease 2 9–inch round cake pans lightly with oil.

To make the topping, chop the walnuts roughly, about the size of fingernails. (If smaller, the walnuts lose a certain quality and flavor.) Place them in a bowl with the butter and sugar. Using your hands, stir the mixture together, and then set it aside while you prepare the cake.

To make the cake, crumble the yeast in the lukewarm water. Add a teaspoon of sugar and several teaspoons of flour to make a thick paste that doesn't roll off the spoon. Set the mixture aside in a warm place and allow it to rise. This should take only a few minutes.

In a saucepan, over medium heat, combine the butter with the milk, and heat until the butter melts but the mixture does not boil. Transfer this mixture to a large mixing bowl and add all but a half teaspoon of the remaining sugar and the salt. Gradually stir in the flour (reserving a little for handling the dough) into the butter and milk mixture with the eggs and the sugar mixture. (Reserve 1 teaspoon of the last egg yolk to make a glaze.) Add the yeast mixture and knead it into the dough. Knead the dough for 10–30 minutes, until the dough pulls away from your hands a little. The longer you knead it, the lighter the texture of the cake.

Make a glaze by mixing together the reserved egg yolk, the reserved sugar, and a tablespoon of water, and set aside.

Place the dough in a large greased bowl, cover with a towel, and set in a warm place. Allow the dough to double in size, from 1–2 hours. Punch down the dough and turn it out onto a floured surface. Cut the dough into 4 equal pieces. Roll out one piece until it is thin and even; the thinner the dough, the nuttier the flavor. Spread the nut mixture over the dough in a layer ½-inch thick. Jelly-roll fashion, roll the dough into a long cylinder and curve it into a horseshoe shape. Lift it carefully into a prepared pan. Repeat with each of the remaining pieces. Two interlocking horseshoes should go in each pan.

Preheat the oven to 350 degrees. Let the kolache rise again for another hour, or until the dough fills the pans. When ready for the oven, brush the tops with the reserved egg yolk glaze, then bake for about an hour. If the tops brown too quickly, cover them with aluminum foil. After removing them from the oven, allow them to cool before slicing into servings.

Makes about 16 servings.

Zapraska

3 tablespoons unsalted butter
3 tablespoons all-purpose flour
1 cup water or meat juice

1 tablespoon white or cider
    vinegar
1 teaspoon sugar

In a saucepan over medium heat, melt the butter until it turns light brown. Add the flour, stirring constantly, until the mixture turns nutty brown. Watch carefully so it does not burn. Gradually stir in the water or meat juice, the vinegar, and the sugar, stirring constantly. Cook until it has thickened and feels bubbly. Serve over meat, potatoes, or vegetables.

Makes about 1 cup.

English Tea and Trifle

My grandmother's name is Jocelyn. She is eighty-three years old. My fondest memories are of sitting with her, drinking tea. We have it out on the veranda, which looks out over the garden. It's a real artist's garden. It has brilliant flowers of different colors. Three ponds go down the hill and in the distance you can see the rest of the village. You get a whole panoramic view of rural England from there.

Usually one of the grandchildren puts the kettle on and Grandmother makes the tea. She drinks only Earl Grey tea, and there's a real ritual to making it. You always serve tea from a big silver teapot. And you also have to have hot water in another pot to add to the tea when it gets too strong. Granny is there to supervise, to make sure you are doing it right. If you do it wrong, she is very unhappy. She's sort of particular, my grandmother. None of her teacups match. They're old Chinese cups and beautifully hand-painted; very, very delicate. I never dropped one, I was pretty darn careful. But she wouldn't have been upset if I had. She doesn't mind about that sort of thing. Breaking things isn't important: making the tea right is.

This brings me to Winnie: She's around seventy, and she speaks the Queen's English, though she probably stopped going to school at age ten. "Maum, yes Maum," she says. She became a maid for one of the big houses, Cleese Hall, I think. She was a scullery maid, but she probably got to help the cook, and I think she got all her recipes when she was in service. Now she takes care of the post office and lives there with her collie dog. She rides a bicycle everywhere. She takes care of my grandmother, comes in and cleans the house, brings her breakfast in bed, and bakes cakes. She makes all kinds of cakes and desserts, but she has a few specialties. Her maple walnut cake is the best I've ever tasted, and she makes wonderful trifle. She makes them all from scratch. In fact, she would never say "from scratch," since that would imply there *was* something else. She denies the existence of premixed cakes.

So we sit there and drink tea and talk about life and listen to my grandmother talk about all sorts of things—what it was like when she grew up; her first, second, third, and fourth husbands; and her boyfriends in between. She led a scandalous life. And we'd eat Winnie's trifle. It has raspberry jam and rum and eggs and cream. We used to go over to the post office and watch Winnie make it. When she cooks, she's chit-chatty, but she's terribly businesslike. She would make one of these cakes whenever the "Americans" were coming over. Winnie's thrilled to think that you like her cake. It makes her very happy.

—*Diana Robinson*

English Trifle

2 sponge cakes, sliced (recipe
   follows), or 2 packages (3–5
   ounces each) lady fingers
1/2 cup raspberry jam, or to taste
1/4 cup sherry or rum, or to taste
6 large egg yolks

1/4 cup sugar
2 teaspoons cornstarch
2 cups heavy cream
1/4 teaspoon vanilla extract
1/4 cup almonds, toasted* and
   slivered, optional

Spread the sponge cake slices or lady fingers generously with raspberry jam. In a 2–quart glass bowl layer the cake slices or lady fingers and sprinkle them generously with the sherry or rum. Set aside.

Place the egg yolks in a bowl, and stir in the sugar and cornstarch. In a saucepan, heat the cream until very hot, but not boiling. Remove it from the heat and cool slightly, then gradually stir it into the egg mixture, blending well. Place the saucepan over a low heat and stir constantly until the custard thickens and coats the spoon. Do not allow it to boil or it will curdle. Stir in the vanilla extract and allow it to cool for a few moments. Pour it over the cake and leave until thoroughly cooled.

Chill for several hours. Sprinkle with toasted almonds just before serving.

Makes 8 servings.

*To toast almonds, heat 1/2 tablespoon of vegetable oil in a heavy-gauge skillet and pan-fry the almonds until slightly brown. Drain them on paper towels.

Sponge Cake

4 large eggs at room
   temperature, separated
1 cup sugar
1/4 cup boiling water

1/2 teaspoon vanilla extract
1 cup sifted cake flour
1 1/2 teaspoons baking powder
1/4 teaspoon salt

Preheat the oven to 350 degrees. Grease and flour 2 9–inch pans.

Beat the egg yolks until very light and lemon-colored. Sift the sugar and gradually beat it into the egg yolks. Gradually add the boiling water, stirring constantly. Allow the mixture to cool, then stir in the vanilla extract.

While the mixture cools, sift together the flour, baking powder, and salt. Stir the flour mixture into the egg yolk mixture, combining well.

Beat the egg whites until stiff but not dry. Fold them into the batter lightly. Pour the batter into the 2 cake pans. Bake for about 30 minutes, or until lightly golden. Remove the cakes from the pan and cool them on cake racks. Then slice the cakes into serving pieces for the trifle.

Makes 2 9–inch cakes.

Walterboro Sandwiches and Cheese Grits

The MacMillans are a family that I sort of sought refuge in. They're real relaxed people and they have lots of children who are about my age, younger and older. They've got a nice farmhouse outside of Atlanta. We're part of this network of people who worked at camp together. So, frequently, the MacMillans will have a big party because somebody's gotten back into the country, or three birthdays come together, or whatever. People come from all over, driving ten hours sometimes, to come to these parties. We party till all hours, and in the morning, when everybody starts stirring, we make a big breakfast with Walterboro sandwiches and cheese grits.

A Walterboro is an open-faced egg sandwich with many added ingredients. It's named for Walterboro, South Carolina, where a couple of our friends moved. Walterboro sandwiches, starting from the bottom up, are: a piece of wheat toast, and then, according to your taste, ketchup and mayonnaise, a couple of tomatoes, a fried egg, and then whatever vegetables are around from the night before. So you end up going through the kitchen like it's a cafeteria, just reaching for different things and piling it on. How do you make the egg for a Walterboro? Well, you smack it on the side of the pan—soon you'll be able to do it without breaking the chickie, though some people like it that way—then you fry it. You always do it in an iron skillet. And you never really clean your iron skillet. You gotta cook flavor into it. Just wipe it out.

Now, you talk about your family traditions: The pan we use is passed down along maternal lines, and to get Mama's skillet is something! I don't have a chance in hell for it; I'm the youngest of five. The way to get it is to get married. Once you get married, then you've started a real life. But this is too big a price for me to pay, just for a skillet!

—*Sam Preston*

22

Walterboro Sandwiches

Sam: These sandwiches are sort of free-form, and the amounts vary according to individual tastes. Each person prepares his or her own sandwich, buffet-style.

Garnish

1 pound fresh mushrooms, chopped

3 large onions, peeled and chopped

4 green peppers, sliced

4 tomatoes, chopped

2 tablespoons vegetable oil

Sandwich Filling

6 sausage patties, cooked

1 pound cheddar cheese, sliced

4 tomatoes, sliced

2 cups green or black olives

6 large eggs

1 loaf whole-grain bread, sliced

Condiments

Ketchup

Mayonnaise

Tabasco

Mustard

Seasonings

Salt

Pepper

Garlic powder

Parsley or other fresh herbs

In a large, heavy-gauge skillet, place the mushrooms, onions, green peppers, chopped tomatoes, and oil, and saute briefly. Turn out onto a serving platter. Place the platter on a buffet table, along with plates of cooked sausage patties, sliced cheese, sliced tomatoes, and olives. Place the condiments and the seasonings on the table.

Fry the eggs to order and toast 1 or 2 slices of bread per serving. Using the toast and egg as a base, have each person build a sandwich from the ingredients on the table.

Makes 4 to 6 sandwiches.

Cheese Grits

Sam: The perfect cheese combination? White and yellow. And you might have some hash browns with it, too—scattered and smothered. That means you scatter them out over the grill instead of cooking them in a big clump, and you let them all get crisp. Then you smother them in onions.

5 cups water

1 teaspoon salt

1 cup regular hominy grits

6 slices bacon, optional

½ cup (1 stick) plus 2 tablespoons unsalted butter

1½ cups cheddar cheese, grated

½ cup milk or heavy cream

Salt and pepper to taste

In a small saucepan, over medium heat, bring the salted water to a boil. Lower the heat and slowly pour the grits into the simmering water. Stir constantly until the mixture is smooth. Lower the heat as much as possible, cover the saucepan, and cook for 30 minutes.

Meanwhile, in a heavy-gauge skillet, over medium heat, fry the bacon until crisp. Remove it from the skillet and drain on paper towels.

Preheat the oven to 350 degrees. With 2 tablespoons butter, grease a 9 × 9–inch baking dish.

When the grits are cooked, remove the saucepan from the heat. Crumble the bacon, then stir into the grits the bacon, butter, cheese, milk or cream, and the salt and pepper to taste. Spoon the mixture into the baking dish, put it in the oven, and bake for 30 minutes. Remove from the oven, and cool slightly before slicing into serving pieces.

Makes 4 to 5 servings.

Swedish Pepparkakor and Roast Pork with Prunes

My mother and father were from Sweden. My father came from a farm and my mother from the city. In the morning, at breakfast, my father would make sure we had clean fingernails, hands, and faces, and if we didn't, we would be sent back to wash. When we sat down, we were never allowed to talk. My mother and father would carry on a conversation and we would sit quietly. I had to keep one hand in my lap and eat with the other. We had to finish everything on our plates. This was quite hard for me whenever we had liver. When I thought we were going to have liver, I'd make sure I had something in my lap I could spit into. I think my mother always knew, but my father—never! When we were finished eating, we asked to be excused and we said our Thankful Prayer in Swedish. And my mother would say, "Don't go far!" We had to do the dishes. However, it wasn't solemn. It was a ceremony; we were celebrating what we had.

My mother prepared an elaborate spread at Christmas and it was fantastic. There would be pressed cold meat that my mother made herself, hogshead cheese, and some kind of a herring, which she would marinate. She'd also serve different kinds of bread, one kind with saffron in it. It was a smorgasbord! She made very thin molasses cookies she learned from her mother, and they were wonderful. We called them pepparkakor. They were so thin you had to roll them out on a marble slab when the dough was ice-cold. My father got mocha and java beans at a wholesale place in Boston. We had our own coffee grinder, so the beans were ground fresh and you could smell it all through the house. When my mother served coffee and cake, she always had sugar tongs for the guests to snip off pieces of lump sugar to sip their coffee through.

My mother would go everywhere to get the right Christmas tree. It would have to be a balsam and would have to be perfect. We decorated it with frosted birds and ornaments from Sweden and Germany. And we used candles, but no lights! And no icicles or "snow"! My mother wanted to see the tree. In those days, you didn't heat the parlor, so the tree would keep for months. I would come home from school, steal in there, and just look at it for hours. I loved it. There would be nobody home. There was this peace about it. And the smell—I think that's what attracted me the most. My mother used to gather the pine needles and toast them on our big black coal stove, and the room would smell of pine.

—*Elsa Philpott*

Pepparkakor

Swedish Ginger Cookies

1½ cups all-purpose flour
1 tablespoon baking soda
1½ teaspoons ginger, ground
1 teaspoon cinnamon, ground
¼ teaspoon cloves, ground
½ cup (1 stick) unsalted butter
   or shortening

¾ cup sugar
1 large egg, beaten
1½ teaspoons light molasses or
   dark corn syrup
10 almonds, blanched

Sift together the flour, baking soda, ginger, cinnamon, and cloves. Set aside. Cream together the butter and sugar until light and lemony. Beat in the egg, then the molasses or corn syrup. Add the flour mixture gradually, beating well after each addition. Wrap and chill the dough for several hours or overnight.

When ready to cook, preheat the oven to 375 degrees. Remove the dough from the refrigerator and place on a lightly floured surface. With a rolling pin, roll it out to about ⅛–inch thick and cut with floured cookie cutters. Transfer to cookie sheets. Roughly chop the almonds and center a piece of almond on each cookie. Bake for 6–8 minutes. Transfer the cookies carefully to cooling racks.

Makes about 7 dozen cookies.

Roast Pork with Prunes

1 pound pitted prunes
4 cups water
4 pounds center-cut pork loin
   roast

Salt and pepper to taste
1 clove garlic, peeled and slightly
   crushed

Preheat the oven to 350 degrees. Soften the prunes in water and set aside as you prepare the roast.

Rub the roast with salt, pepper, and the garlic clove. With a sharp knife, cut slits 1–inch deep at regular intervals across the fat side of the roast. Drain the water from the prunes and insert the fruit into the slits. Place in a heavy roasting pan. Bake for 2½ hours.

Remove the roast from the oven and transfer it to a warm platter. Make the following gravy.

Gravy

Pan drippings
1 or 2 tablespoons all-purpose
   flour
1 cup water

Salt and pepper to taste
Few drops lemon juice
Pinch of dried rosemary

Pour off all the drippings but 2 tablespoons into a measuring cup. Add enough water to make 1 cup of liquid. Place the pan over medium heat and stir the flour into the drippings in the pan. Stir in the salt, pepper, lemon juice, and rosemary. Gradually stir in the water mixture and continue stirring until the gravy thickens. Serve with the pork roast.

Makes 6 to 8 servings.

Mandoo and Chap Chye

mandoo—Korean dumplings. They're thin flour pancakes, filled and then folded over with the edges crimped.

My grandmother used to make namul, a marinated Korean salad made with daikon radishes or Chinese cabbage or bean sprouts or spinach. And most of the meats she made were marinated in your basic stock Korean marinade—soy sauce, a bit of sugar, MSG of course, sometimes sesame oil, and sometimes kochee chang, a kind of hot chili paste—all mixed with a lot of garlic. She also used to make something called duk, which is not duck as in "quack-quack" but pressed rice cake. It comes in a long roll. You can slice it up and put it in soup, or fry it in sesame oil and put honey on it to make a sweet dessert.

My grandfather's name is Song Bong Kim, but we never learned Korean, so we just called him Grandpa. He didn't really speak to us at all, but sat around quietly and smiled a lot. You could tell he was glad to have all the grand-children around. Mostly we would go to visit my grandparents on holidays. They lived right in the heart of the dirt and grime of downtown Los Angeles. They'd be cooking all day, and we'd eat around three o'clock.

I know only bits and pieces about my grandfather's life. He came to the U.S. in 1922, the year my dad was born. Then, in 1948, my grandmother and father came over to the States. My father was twenty-five and had never seen his father. My dad doesn't talk about Korea much. But I do remember him saying that when he was a little boy and they'd be in church, the Japanese soldiers would come into the church and confiscate people's valuables.

When my father and grandmother first came here, they had a little take-out chow mein resturant with my grandfather. And after that the three of them opened a kim chee factory. Kim chee is a pickled cabbage-radish dish. They also used to manufacture

Except for some foods, we were raised completely Westernized. In fact, the thing my grandfather used to love to make for New Year's was fried chicken. My oldest brother was the first American-born Korean in Southern California, so there was still a lot of prejudice at that time. I think that's why my parents disregarded their Korean background. They wanted us to fit in. I hear Korean names, and they sound just about as foreign to me as to anyone else. I don't even know my grandmother's Korean name: Once when I asked my father what her name was, he answered, "Just Grandma."

—Joyce Kim

26

Mandoo

Korean Dumplings

Water to cover
1 tablespoon salt
2 or 3–pound head of cabbage, cut into 6 sections
½ pound beef, ground
½ pound pork, ground
1 cake firm tofu (bean curd), diced
2 large eggs, beaten
2 onions, peeled and chopped
1 tablespoon sesame seeds
2 cloves garlic, very finely minced
Salt and pepper to taste
1 tablespoon sesame oil, or to taste
10–20 egg roll skins (to cut out 20 3-inch rounds), or 20 wonton skins
Flour to dust
Sesame oil to fill frying pan 2 inches*

The traditional method for preparing the cabbage is to place the water and salt in a large pot, add the cabbage, and soak it for two days. A modern alternative is to boil the cabbage for 5 minutes. Then squeeze out the water, and shred the cabbage.

For the filling, blend together the beef, pork, tofu, eggs, onions, sesame seeds, garlic, salt and pepper, and sesame oil to taste.

Lay out the egg roll skins or wonton skins on a lightly floured board. If using egg roll skins, use an empty can to cut out 20 circles about 3 inches in diameter. Place a teaspoon of filling in the center of each round, fold it over to form a pouch, and crimp the edges shut.

In a heavy-gauge skillet, heat 2 inches of oil and deep-fry the dumplings until golden brown, about 5–7 minutes.

As an alternative cooking method, fill a large saucepan with water and bring it to a boil. Drop in the dumplings, one at a time, being careful they do not stick together. You may have to cook them in two batches. Simmer for 10 minutes or until the dumplings float to the surface. Remove them from the pot and serve them immediately.

Makes 20 dumplings.

Editor's note: Oriental sesame oil scorches readily. This can be avoided by substituting vegetable oil for half of the sesame oil used in sauteeing.

Chap Chye

1 8–ounce package bean threads or cellophane noodles
2 tablespoons sesame oil, or 1 tablespoon sesame oil and 1 tablespoon peanut oil (see note in Mandoo recipe)
1 small head cabbage, shredded
½ pound spinach, chopped
1 stalk celery, cut into ½–inch slices
2 medium onions, peeled and chopped
2 carrots, peeled and julienned
⅔ cup dried black mushrooms (available in Asian groceries), soaked in water to soften
Salt and pepper to taste
1 teaspoon sugar
½–1 pound flank steak, cut into ½–inch strips
1⅓ cups soy sauce mixed with ⅔ cup water, for marinating meat
1 teaspoon fresh ginger, finely minced
4 cloves garlic, or to taste, peeled and minced
Soy sauce to taste
1 tablespoon sesame seeds
1 chili pepper, crushed
2 eggs, fried and cut into strips, optional
Scallions, sliced crosswise, to garnish

Soak the cellophane noodles in water until they expand and become soft. While they are soaking, in a large container, marinate the meat in the diluted soy sauce mixture, salt and pepper, ginger, and garlic. Cover with plastic wrap and refrigerate for one hour.

At serving time, in a heavy-gauge skillet, add 2 tablespoons of sesame and/or vegetable oil and saute the cabbage, spinach, celery, onions, carrots, and black mushrooms with salt, pepper, and sugar, until soft, about 10 minutes. Set them aside.

In the same skillet, with added oil if necessary, over medium-high heat, saute the meat in oil until seared and browned, about 5–7 minutes.

Drain the noodles and sprinkle them with the remaining soy sauce, stirring well. Combine the noodles and the vegetables with the meat, stirring well to mix. Saute the mixture quickly over medium-high heat for 3–5 minutes. Remove to serving platter and garnish with the sesame seeds, chili pepper, eggs, and scallions.

Makes 5 to 6 servings.

Banbury Tarts

When I was a kid I lived in San Diego, California, and Christmas was really special. I would wake up in the morning and there would be presents under the tree, and after we'd opened them, we would all drive up to Pomona where my grandmother lived. All our cousins would be there, and there would be more presents.

My grandmother used to make a bunch of pastries. The ones I remember best were called Banbury Tarts. She would spread the dough out in a circle and put the Banbury stuff in the middle, fold the dough over, and press the edges down with a fork all the way around to seal it. The tarts were white with powdered sugar, and that always reminded me of snow—we never got snow in Southern California. My grandmother would make about a million of those tarts and put them on the table around an ornamental angel. Some of my cousins thought the tarts were gross, because when you bit into one, you found it was dark, thick, and gooey inside. But I thought they were just great. They tasted best hot, but usually by the time we got to them, they were cold. My grandmother would only have one batch ready when we arrived. Then she'd get us to help make more. You sort of got drafted. She would put all the raisins, dates, and nuts and stuff together into a big grinder that she'd clamp onto the counter with a vise. And everybody would have a turn cranking it. When the tarts were ready to bake, she'd put them into a big glass baking pan. She always baked them in that pan. It was opaque, but we could sort of see these vague, white shapes in there, and we'd know—Banbury Tarts! They'd come out smelling of warm raisins and spices.

—*David Granger*

Banbury Tarts

Filling

1 pound black raisins
1 cup nutmeats, preferably
  walnuts

1 cup sugar
Juice and grated rind of 1 lemon
1 large egg

Pastry

3 cups all-purpose flour
½ teaspoon baking powder
¾ teaspoon salt

1 cup shortening
½ cup water
Confectioners' sugar for dusting

Grind the raisins and nuts. Add the sugar, the lemon juice and rind, and the egg, mixing thoroughly.

Place the flour in a mixing bowl. Stir in the baking powder and salt. Using a fork, pastry blender, or two knives, cut in the shortening. Sprinkle the dough with the water and mix until it forms a ball. Cover with wax paper and chill for at least an hour.

Preheat the oven to 400 degrees.

On a floured board, roll one third of the dough out to ¼–inch thickness. Use a 2–inch round cookie cutter to stamp out circles for the tarts. Place a teaspoon of filling on each circle, fold it over, and crimp the edge with a floured fork. Place the cookies on a baking sheet and bake for 15 minutes. Dust them with confectioners' sugar when cool.

Makes about 2 dozen tarts.

Peanut Brittle

7 tablespoons unsalted butter
1 cup water
3 cups sugar
1 cup light corn syrup

2¼ cups (1 pound) raw Spanish
  peanuts, skins on
1 teaspoon vanilla extract
1 tablespoon baking soda

With 3 tablespoons of butter, grease well a 10 × 15 baking pan.

In a large saucepan, over medium-high heat, combine the water, sugar, and corn syrup. Stirring constantly, bring the mixture to a rolling boil. If using a candy thermometer, the temperature should be 250 degrees. Remove the mixture from the burner and carefully add the remaining butter and the peanuts. Return the pan to the heat and stir constantly until the mixture begins to brown slightly and reaches a temperature of 290 degrees. The skins of the peanuts will pop open when the peanuts are roasted. Take care not to burn the candy. Remove it from the burner and, stirring rapidly, add the vanilla extract and baking soda.

Carefully pour the hot candy into the well-greased pan, spreading the mixture rapidly with a spatula to make a smooth surface. Let the candy cool, turn it out of the pan, and break it into eating-size pieces.

Makes about 2 pounds.

Grandma Mignerey's Special Cornbread

My grandparents lived on a quiet, tree-lined street in Queens, where I grew up. My mother worked, so I spent a lot of time with my grandmother. My school was right near where she lived, so often during lunch hour, I would go to her house to eat. One of the great things I remember is her special cornbread and corn muffins. They were always a treat. Coming into the house and smelling the cornbread baking would always be a tremendous experience for me.

I liked the smell of it as much as I liked eating it. That smell is one of the mementos of my childhood. If I smell it now (and it's so rare—it seems nobody's making cornbread anymore),

it immediately plunges me back to those times. Whether or not this was true, my grandmother always said she'd made the cornbread just for me, and I would have it either as part of my lunch or for a snack. She served it warm, with a lot of fresh butter sitting on top. I'd have to wait until the butter melted into the cornbread. If she made it when my mother or one of my aunts or uncles was there, they'd say, "Here comes Frank. He'll have one of those muffins!" Sometimes it came with soup. My grandfather was a great soup-eater. In fact, I don't remember him eating anything *but* soup. Other times we would have cornbread and tea. We'd have the tea British style, with a lot of milk and sugar, not like we drink it today, Oriental style, with no milk or sugar.

I loved spending time at my grandparents' house; they always treated me nicely. My grandfather would be puttering around in the basement, and he'd allow me to help him, or he'd show me how to make stuff. And I loved being with my grandmother. She always asked me to tell her stories, and I think that's one of the ways I became a writer, by making up stories and telling them to my grandmother. I would go on for hours, making up adventures that she would listen to and ask me questions about. "And then what would happen?" she would say.

—*Frank Brady*

Cornbread

1 cup yellow stone-ground corn
   meal
1 cup whole wheat pastry flour
1 tablespoon baking powder
½ teaspoon baking soda
½ teaspoon salt
1 cup buttermilk

¼ cup honey
1 large egg
4 tablespoons unsalted butter,
   melted
Kernels of 2 ears of corn, cooked,
   or 1 small can (4 ounces) corn
   niblets, well-drained

Preheat the oven to 350 degrees. With 1 tablespoon of butter, grease a 9–inch loaf pan.

Sift together the corn meal, flour, baking powder, baking soda, and salt. Combine the buttermilk, honey, egg, and the remaining butter. Stir the wet ingredients slowly and gently into the dry ingredients until just combined. Do not overmix. Gently fold in the corn.

Pour the batter into the greased pan and gently smooth the top. Bake for 30–35 minutes, or until the bread is light brown around the edges and firm in the center. Serve warm, with extra butter.

Makes a loaf of 6 thick slices.

Grandma Herskowitz's Borscht and Sweet Noodle Kugel

My grandmother was what's called in Yiddish a *baleboosteh*. That's a term of high praise, meaning a woman who is an excellent cook and housekeeper. Although I heard the word often as a child, it only became meaningful long after she had died, when I began tending my own home and family, and cooking her recipes. As a child, all the things that were spoken of in Yiddish were mysteries to me. We children knew instinctively that what they talked about in Yiddish was the most important—gossip, tales of disappointment and pain. It was the language through which the most secret and shameful things were shared. This world of the grownups, especially the women, was denied us through that expressive but alien tongue. And so my dearest memories of being with my grandmother are not about what I heard, but rather about what I felt and smelled and saw and tasted. In my mind, Grandma and her kitchen are inseparable. They were a welcome mat. Cheerful and soft, smelling of onions and chicken soup and apple strudel. Her life seemed uncomplicated to a little girl.

Grandma was always available to stroke my curls and soothe me. While her hands chopped and sewed and stirred and flicked chicken feathers and stuffed cabbage leaves, the rest of her was totally available to be with me and love me. Many years later, my own young daughter complained about my typewriter; when I did my work, which was writing, none of me was available to her.

In my grandmother's kitchen, everything that was cooked took time and patience. Strudel dough was rolled out on the large kitchen table, oiled, rerolled, and stuffed. Challah dough had to be kneaded over and over again. The large stew pot, which my mother ultimately inherited, always seemed to be simmering. One day it was goulash, another day chicken fricassee, still another day pot roast. Friday nights always meant chicken soup, cooked with "five-cent soup greens" and noodles, matzoh balls, or kreplach. And then there were the kugels—puddings made of potatoes or noodles—and the soups—thick mushroom and barley, vegetable, and borscht. They all involved lots of chopping and stirring. And in between, her sewing machine made intricate, old-fashioned blouses for my sister and me. Her pet name for me was *Zeisela,* "little sweet one." She alone, in my life, cherished sweetness in people, and especially in me. It has taken me four decades to discover and value that sweetness.

—*Marjorie Bair*

Borscht

1 small bunch beets, washed, peeled, and grated
5 cups water
1½ teaspoons salt
3 tablespoons sugar
Juice of 1 lemon
1 cup sour cream
4 potatoes, peeled and boiled

Place the grated beets in a large saucepan. Add the water, salt, sugar, and lemon juice. Bring to a boil and cook gently for 20–25 minutes.

While the soup cooks, warm the sour cream in a saucepan over a low heat.

After 20 or 25 minutes, taste the soup. The flavor should be more sweet than sour. Adjust the seasoning, if necessary. Stir the warm sour cream into the soup.

Place a potato in the bottom of individual soup bowls. Ladle in the soup and serve immediately.

Makes 4 servings.

Sweet Noodle Kugel

4 heaping tablespoons shortening
1 pound wide egg noodles
4 quarts water
2 or 3 large eggs, beaten
5 tablespoons sugar
3 tablespoons black raisins
1 tablespoon chicken fat
1 lemon
1 orange
1 apple, peeled and cored
Prune or peach syrup for serving

Preheat the oven to 350 degrees. Put 1 tablespoon of shortening in a 9 × 12–inch pan in the oven until the shortening melts, then remove the pan from the oven and spread the grease over the bottom and the sides.

In a large saucepan, cook the noodles until barely tender, or *al dente*, then drain. Stir in the eggs, sugar, raisins, the remaining shortening, and the chicken fat. Grate the peel of the lemon and the orange, and the whole apple directly into the mixture, and stir well. Pour into the pan and bake for 1½ hours, or until brown. Serve with prune or peach syrup.

Makes 5 to 6 servings.

Lulu Mabel's Ice Cream and Raspberry Pie

I grew up in a little farm community in Dysart, Iowa; an old rural community. At the center of it was a Methodist church and a schoolhouse for 280 kids. A lot of my family lived in that community, and a lot of them went to that school. The big family gatherings were on holidays. We were "hot" on picnics. We were about fifteen cousins, aunts, and uncles. We'd go to the woods across the field, along with the cattle and pigs. There was a wonderful mudhole where we went wading, but first we'd have to chase the pigs out. I remember one picnic when we were gathering berries, a mean old sow chased us all up a tree!

At picnics we always had potato salad, cabbage salad, brownies, and Jell-O. We always had Jell-O with fruit cocktail and bananas floating on top, which, if you didn't eat them fast, turned brown.

My grandmother had some odd food habits. She often fed me coffee when I was very little. And one of her odd favorites was to mix, in a glass, bread, crackers, raw onions, and warm milk. We also had a tradition of putting popcorn in milk with ice-cubes, with apples on the side. You knew it was ready when the popcorn got kind of soggy to the touch, so you'd have to work your gums a little!

My mother canned lots of stuff. We had an apple orchard, a raspberry patch, and a strawberry bed. We grew our own corn, which was blue. It looked like Indian corn; the seeds were almost black. It came down through the family and had the reputation for being the sweetest corn around. We also made fresh cottage cheese from our cows' milk—and homemade ice cream, done by hand. My father always made the ice cream in the basement. It was a big deal. He got a big block of ice, put it in an old gunnysack, and smashed it up. We used an old-fashioned ice cream freezer. He would start turning, and we would all sit there pushing the ice down with sticks. Then we'd add more salt. When it was done, we'd have chocolate ice cream with fresh strawberries. At the ice cream socials at the church, the women would mix the stuff up, and the men would come in afterwards and do the cranking.

At my own home now, I eat simple, fresh food that would have been thought exotic back in Iowa when I was growing up—stuffed zucchini, for instance. I don't remember when I found out what zucchini was. An aunt who had married a diplomat and lived in Washington was the only person I knew who knew what zucchini was! For the most part though, our farming way of life is gone now. I still feel the loss of it when I go home.

—*Lois Hayward*

Black Raspberry Pie

Crust

2 cups all-purpose flour
1 teaspoon salt
½ cup plus 1 tablespoon lard

2–3 tablespoons cold water
Cream for glazing
Sugar for sprinkling

Filling

6–8 cups black raspberries
1–1½ cups sugar
½–¾ cup all-purpose flour

Dash of cinnamon
½ cup water
3–4 tablespoons unsalted butter

To make the crust, use your finger tips to mix together the flour, salt, and lard until the mixture is the consistency of coarse meal. Keep mixing, and sprinkle several tablespoons of cold water into the mixture so that it forms a ball. Divide the dough in half and, if you have time, cover it with wax paper and chill it.

Meanwhile, to make the filling, mound as many berries in the pie pan as it will hold. Pour the berries into a big bowl, and mix in the sugar, flour, and cinnamon, tossing lightly.

Using a rolling pin, roll out each half of the dough to at least ⅛–inch thickness on a floured board or cloth. Place one crust in the bottom of a 9–inch pie pan and fill it with the berry mixture. Add the water and dot with butter. Place the other half of the dough over the filling, seal, and trim the edges. Cut two or three slits in the top crust to allow the steam to escape. Brush lightly with a little cream and a scant sprinkling of sugar.

Bake the pie for about an hour, or until the filling bubbles up and the crust is golden brown.

Makes 8 servings.

Chocolate Ice Cream

4 large eggs
2 cups sugar
1 teaspoon salt
2 teaspoons vanilla extract

¾ cup unsweetened cocoa
1 cup boiling water
1 quart heavy cream
Milk

Beat the eggs until thick, and slowly add the sugar, beating until the sugar is dissolved. Add the salt and vanilla extract.

Dissolve the cocoa in the boiling water and stir to make a thick paste. Cool slightly, then add this to the egg mixture, blending well. Mix in the cream and pour into an ice cream freezer. If the freezer is not full up to 3 inches from the top, add milk to that level. Freeze, following the manufacturer's directions.

Makes about 1½ quarts.

Aunt Liz's Potato Dumplings and Hungarian Nothing Soup

I thought being Hungarian was wonderful, and I loved all Hungarian foods. I fantasized being a gypsy in a foreign land. It seemed exotic to be something not too many of the other children in the town were.

My aunt Liz created a lot of happiness for me as a child. Liz was my mother's sister. There were three sisters: Aunt Liz, Aunt Mary, and my mother, Ida. My memories of dinner are a feeling of total happiness. Sometimes I would have two or three dinners in a night! I would eat at home, then I would eat at my aunt Mary's house next door. My aunt Mary's expertise was with desserts. I had a different favorite daily—lemon meringue pie, chocolate cake, angel food cake, apple pie, or custard pie.

Then we would go to my aunt Liz's across the street. Everything would smell wonderful. One of my favorite dishes there was Nothing Soup. I loved it because it seemed to be made out of nothing. Nothing Soup consisted of flour, water, salt, and pepper. Sometimes we added egg drops. The soup would turn gray. I know it may sound a bit strange, but I suggest you try it! I loved watching it appear on the stove. When my aunt Liz was cooking, I followed her everywhere, watching all the seemingly secret ingredients being gathered together. The ingredients seemed to have special properties— they looked one way separately, but when they were combined they looked and tasted completely different. I would help set the table and match all the plates and napkins in different color combinations. Sitting down to a beautiful-looking meal made me feel very happy and secure. As a child I felt very special. I would request a certain food, and like magic, it would appear.

—*Pamela Kraft*

Hungarian Potato Dumplings

2 medium potatoes, peeled and
   finely grated
1 tablespoon salt
2 large eggs, beaten with 2
   tablespoons water

2–3 cups all-purpose flour
4 quarts water
2 pounds cabbage
½ cup (1 stick) unsalted butter

In a large bowl, place the potatoes and stir in the salt and beaten eggs. Stir in enough flour to make a soft dough.

Bring a large pot of water to a boil. Drop the dough by teaspoonfuls into the boiling water. Once all of the dumplings are in the water, cook for 2 minutes. Test one by rinsing it under cool water and tasting it. If done, drain the rest and run them under cool water.

Chop the cabbage and, in a large heavy-gauge skillet, saute it in butter until golden in color. Cool. Mix together the dumplings and cabbage, and heat in a large skillet for about 10 minutes.

Makes 6 servings.

Nothing Soup

2 tablespoons unsalted butter
1 tablespoon all-purpose flour
Pinch of caraway seeds, optional

2 cups water
½ teaspoon white vinegar
Salt and pepper to taste
1 large egg, beaten

In a large heavy-gauge skillet, melt the butter and stir in the flour. Lightly brown the flour. Add the caraway seeds and stir in the water, vinegar, salt, and pepper. Bring to a full boil, then lower the heat and simmer for about 5 minutes. Beat the egg and slowly add it to the soup. Do not stir. Serve at once.

Makes 2 servings.

Rizskôk

Rice Cake

1 cup long-grain rice, uncooked
2 cups water (or more) to cover
1 quart milk
Cracker crumbs for dusting
¾ cup (1½ sticks) plus 2
   tablespoons unsalted butter

1 cup sugar
5 large eggs, separated
Grated rind of 1 orange
½ cup golden raisins
Confectioners' sugar for
   decoration

Rinse the rice, place it in a 4–quart pan, and add just enough water to cover. Bring to a boil, then drain the rice in a colander. Put the rice back in the pan and stir in the milk. Cook over medium heat until the rice is tender, about 15 minutes.

Preheat the oven to 350 degrees. With 2 tablespoons of butter, grease a 10–inch angel food cake tube pan. Dust with cracker crumbs.

In a large mixing bowl, cream together the butter and sugar. In a separate bowl, beat the egg yolks until thick and lemon-colored, then stir them into the butter and sugar. Add the mixture to the warm rice along with the grated orange rind and raisins. In a clean mixing bowl, beat the egg whites until stiff and then fold into the rice mixture. Pour into the prepared pan and bake for 50 minutes. Cool for 20 minutes, then remove from the pan. Sift confectioners' sugar over the cake.

Makes a 10–inch tube cake.

Rose Glazer's Cheese Kreplach and Potato Latkes

What I loved about her cooking were the dairy dishes. She couldn't cook meat at all, she just dried it out. But her dairy was absolutely delicious. When I was young, I used to love going over to her house because she used real butter. My mother used only margarine, and it was like heaven for me to have real butter. It's funny because now it's a complete switch. My mother uses butter and my grandmother uses margarine. My mother got into more natural foods and my grandmother started watching her cholesterol.

My grandmother was born in Russia, and during the Revolution she saw her father killed by the Bolsheviks. There was shooting in the streets, and her father went to close the shutter. Someone saw him and just shot through the window and killed him, right there in the house. She told me that in those days she would see people hanged from the trees in the streets. It was an everyday sight.

According to her, she was a great adventurer. She had a great operatic voice, but she gave up singing when she married my grandfather. She had escaped from Russia to Rumania. Many of the people she crossed the border with were killed. She never was able to get back into her country, and she lost contact with what was left of her family. When I see my grandmother cooking in the kitchen, it's hard to believe she had such an adventurous youth.

I remember the yellow formica kitchen table and my grandfather sitting at the head of the table with his schnapps. The men and women would play gin at night—the men in one room and the women in the other. There was a window in the apartment that my grandmother would hang her wash out of. All the women would be leaning their heads out, speaking Yiddish to each other. It all had a very romantic feel to me.

She used to make her own gefilte fish and creamed herring. She made kreplach and blintzes, knishes, noodles and cheese, and latkes. The latkes were wonderful. She would grate fresh potatoes and add matzoh meal and serve them with fresh sour cream or cold applesauce. Sometimes I even had both.

I used to go over and watch her cook, and she would give me tea while I watched. My mother would never, ever give me tea, but at my grandmother's, we would get tea in a glass with sugar in it. It was wonderful.

—*Arlene Harris Shulman*

Cheese Kreplach

3 large eggs
1½ cups all-purpose flour
Pinch of salt
1 cup farmer cheese
1 cup pot cheese

3 quarts water
1 teaspoon unsalted butter for
　boiling water
Melted butter for serving
Sour cream for serving

In a large mixing bowl, beat 2 of the eggs until light and fluffy. Gradually add the flour and the salt while stirring the mixture. Turn the moist dough out onto a floured board and knead lightly until it is smooth and pliable. If necessary, add additional flour slowly while kneading. If the dough still feels moist, sprinkle a small amount of flour on it. Test the dough for stickiness by rolling out a small piece.

Form all of the dough into a ball, and with a floured rolling pin, roll it out to form a circle ⅛–¼ inch thick. Lightly flour a 2–inch round cookie cutter or the rim of a drinking glass, and cut out circles of dough. Repeat the procedure until all the dough is used up. Keep hands dry by rubbing them in flour.

In a separate bowl, combine the remaining egg with the pot cheese and the farmer cheese, and blend well. Place 1 teaspoon of the cheese mixture in the middle of each dough circle and fold it over to form a half-circle. Moisten the edges, then pinch them together to form a seal. Join the tips of the crescents to form a circle. Pinch up around the edge of the dough to form a little cup.

In a large saucepan, bring the water to a boil, and add 1 teaspoon of butter to the water to prevent sticking. Add the kreplach, and gently boil until they float to the top. Remove them with a slotted spoon, drain, and then serve them hot with melted butter or sour cream poured over the top.

Makes approximately 25 kreplach.

Latkes

Potato Pancakes

2 large potatoes, peeled
1 medium onion, peeled
1 large egg, beaten

2 tablespoons matzoh meal or
　all-purpose flour
Salt to taste
2–3 tablespoons oil, or more if
　necessary

Peel the potatoes, then place them in a bowl of cold water to prevent them from turning brown. Grate the potatoes finely one at a time into a large mixing bowl, then grate in the onion. Put the grated vegetables in a colander to drain, and when the excess moisture is gone, place them back in the mixing bowl.

Stir in the egg, matzoh meal or flour, and salt.

In a heavy-gauge skillet, over medium heat, add oil and heat until it begins to bubble. With a tablespoon, spoon the potato mixture into the oil, fry until golden, then turn and brown the other side. Remove them from the skillet and drain on paper towels.

Makes 4 to 6 servings.

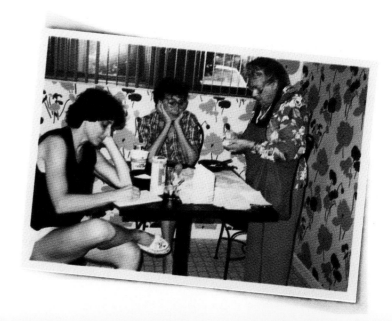

Mabel Funnell's Cottage Pudding

It was always a great treat to stay overnight at Grandma Funnell's. I would sleep in the tiny, narrow back bedroom of her Victorian house, which had in it the only window that looked out into the backyard. In the yard were several old apple trees full of character and charm, and beds of rhubarb.

When we stayed overnight at Grandma's, we would always have pancakes and maple syrup for breakfast. My grandmother cooked them directly on the hot griddle of her coal stove. How she managed to get the right temperature for everything on that stove is a miracle to me. But I never saw a single batch of cookies come out of that oven burned.

My grandmother, who came from England, was always calm and methodical in the kitchen. She needed lots of space and order. It was a great big kitchen, and the walk-in pantry was half the size of the living room. She kept the icebox in there, and an old-fashioned coffee grinder that was always a treat for us children to turn. She made very good pies and yeast biscuits. I recall helping many times to peel the apples for a pie, and her showing me how to peel the whole apple in one long string of peel. She taught me to throw the peel over my left shoulder onto the floor and then quickly turn around to discover what letter of the alphabet it looked like: That letter was supposed to be the first initial of the man you would marry!

On Sunday nights, our family went to Grandma Funnell's for supper. It was always a casual meal of leftovers from the Sunday dinner roast or chicken fricassee, along with several kinds of homemade relishes, conserves, and her fresh yeast rolls. After supper the children would dry the dishes and put them away in the pantry with its shelves filled with blue onion pattern and white ironstone platters and cups and saucers, some of which I was lucky to inherit years later.

Grandma Funnell was a warm and kind person, not at all reserved or stoical. When I was little, she knitted a green suit for my teddy bear, which was two feet tall. It had a little jacket with matching pants and brass buttons. I still have it. She always had toys and books there for us to play with when we visited. Our favorite was *Little Black Sambo*. Little did I dream then that one day I would grow up, marry a man from India, and go and live in that country.

—*Ann Kortright Banerji*

Cottage Pudding

2 large eggs
¾ cup whole milk or light cream
1 cup sugar
1 tablespoon unsalted butter

1½ cups all-purpose flour
2 teaspoons baking powder
½ teaspoon salt
Sauce for serving

Preheat the oven to 400 degrees. Grease an 8 × 8–inch pan with 1 tablespoon of butter.

In an 8–ounce measuring cup, break the eggs and then add enough milk or cream to make a total of 8 ounces of liquid. Pour the mixture into a large mixing bowl, add the sugar, and beat until smooth. Add the flour, baking powder, and salt, stirring until smooth. Pour the mixture into the baking pan and bake for 25–30 minutes.

Makes 4 servings.

Lemon Sauce

½ cup sugar
1 tablespoon cornstarch
1 cup boiling water
2 tablespoons unsalted butter

1½ tablespoons lemon juice
Pinch of nutmeg, ground
Pinch of salt

In a small saucepan, over medium heat, combine the sugar, cornstarch, and water. Boil, stirring constantly, for 5 minutes or until the mixture thickens. Remove from the heat and stir in the butter, lemon juice, nutmeg, and salt. Serve hot or cold.

Makes 1 cup.

Chocolate Sauce

¾ cup sugar
1 teaspoon cornstarch
2 tablespoons cocoa

½ cup boiling water
1–2 tablespons unsalted butter
½ teaspoon vanilla extract

In a small saucepan, over medium heat, combine the sugar, cornstarch, cocoa, and water. Boil, stirring constantly, for 5 minutes or until the mixture thickens. Remove from heat and stir in the butter and vanilla extract. Serve hot or cold.

Makes ½ cup.

Tomatoes St. Jacques

4 small tomatoes
3 teaspoons salt
1 teaspoon paprika, or to taste
½ pound fresh large white mushrooms

1½ tablespoons unsalted butter
½–1 cup cream sauce
4 tablespoons Parmesan cheese, grated

With a sharp paring knife, carefully cut out the tops of the tomatoes at the stem end, and with a teaspoon carefully scoop out the seeds. Combine the salt and paprika, and use half of the mixture to season the inside of the tomatoes. Set aside.

With a damp paper towel, wipe off any dirt clinging to mushrooms, and when they are clean, with a sharp paring knife, peel the caps. Then cut the caps and stems into small cubes. In a 10–inch heavy-gauge skillet, over medium heat, saute the mushrooms for 3–4 minutes. Add the cream sauce and the remaining salt and paprika to the mushrooms, mixing well.

Preheat the oven to 350 degrees.

Fill each hollowed tomato with the creamed mushrooms, and set them into a baking pan, or individual ramekins if you prefer. Sprinkle each tomato with 1 tablespoon of Parmesan cheese, then bake them for 12 minutes.

Makes 4 servings.

Cream Sauce

2 tablespoons unsalted butter
2 tablespoons all-purpose flour

1 cup milk or heavy cream
Salt and pepper to taste

In a saucepan, melt the butter over low heat, and when bubbly, whisk in the flour, stirring constantly. When the two are well blended, gradually stir in the milk or cream, adding extra liquid if the sauce seems too thick. Use a whisk and stir constantly until the sauce is smooth and thick.

Makes 1 cup.

Venezuelan Arepas and Besitos

I grew up in the western part of Venezuela, the Oriental Plains. My village, Pariaguan, had 7,000 inhabitants. It was surrounded by a kind of oasis, called a *morichal*, full of splendid, tall palms with exquisite, meaty fruit. We went there for picnics and to learn how to swim. We were five brothers and two sisters: I am sixth of seven. My father was a young and handsome man who owned a big pharmacy, which became the center of town. My grandfather was a doctor and a kind of inventor: He invented the wireless telegraph about the same time Marconi did. We lived in a large colonial house with big trees—mangoes and papayas—in the courtyard. Five maids also lived there with their families. My great-aunt Maria Elena was in charge of the family. I lived in that house until I was six years old. There were great amounts of food served because there were so many people.

The day would begin with the smell of coffee. We ate at a big round table which seated thirteen or fourteen people. My great-aunt always walked around the table checking to see if we were eating correctly. We were not to eat with our hands! Every day at breakfast there were three or four guests. Our meal was meat, liver, eggs, empañadas with cheese and meat inside, coffee and milk, and my favorite, arepas, which are hot corn griddle cakes in a round shape. The maids would wake at five in the morning to boil corn for the arepas. They were brought to the table in a big basket, smelling of fresh corn, and served with fresh, white butter.

At around four in the afternoon, we would have *merienda*—a snack—on the patio, under the grape vines. The maids brought us all kinds of sweet things. My favorite was besitos—"little coconut kisses"—which were painted red or brown with vegetable dye and served with brown cane sugar. One besito just fit in the mouth. It came with a hot drink—watered coffee—just for kids, called guarapo. We would have this after school. What a beautiful, poetic, deeply nourishing time my life was then! My great-aunt was lovely and sweet, but cried too much. At six I taught all the maids to read and write. Food was the center of life. I still dream of that place.

—*Dora Gomez-Pierrakos*

Arepas

Dora: Arepas are the Venezuelan national bread. Made from corn, they are a legacy from the native Indian culture. Arepas are eaten hot at any time of the day, although they are most often found at breakfast. For light dinners we prepare them as "tostadas," slicing them in half and filling them with cheese, meat, seafood, or beans.

5 quarts plus up to 1 cup water *1 pound corn meal*
2 tablespoons unsalted butter *2½ teaspoons salt*

Preheat the oven to 350 degrees. Bring 5 quarts of water to a boil. With the butter, grease a baking sheet.

In a large mixing bowl, place the corn meal and add the salt and enough of the extra cup of water to form a workable dough. Divide the dough into 2–inch balls. Place a ball on wax paper and flatten it with your hands to form a circle about 1½ inches in diameter. Repeat with the rest of the dough. Drop the arepas in the boiling water, 5 or 6 at a time, and cook for about 10 minutes, or until they float to the surface. They should have a hard crust. Remove with a slotted spoon and place on the baking sheet. Place in the oven for 5 minutes to create a shiny crust. To see if they are ready, take one out and tap it. It should sound hollow.

Makes about 2 dozen arepas.

Besitos de Coco

Coconut Kisses

1½ cups brown sugar *1 pound shredded coconut*
2 cups water *¼ cup all-purpose flour*
12 whole cloves *¼ teaspoon baking soda*
2 tablespoons unsalted butter

In a large saucepan, place the brown sugar, water, and cloves, and bring to a boil, cooking for 18–20 minutes, or until syrupy. With a slotted spoon, remove the cloves. Set the syrup aside to cool.

Preheat the oven to 375 degrees. With butter, grease a baking sheet.

In a large mixing bowl, place the shredded coconut and stir in the flour, baking soda, and cooled syrup. Drop teaspoonfuls of the mixture onto the baking sheet, leaving about two inches between cakes.

Bake for 20–25 minutes.

Makes about 3 dozen besitos.

Goulash and Cherry Soup

The kitchen was the center of my grandmother's world and her opportunity for creative output. She was the queen of her domain, and she took great pride in it. My mother wasn't allowed in the kitchen, but I was the favorite grandchild, and she liked me to help. Every Sunday was baking day. Every Sunday she would bake four pies or one large marble cake, or yeast cakes with plums or peaches.

She was born in 1896 and came here from Berlin in 1939, just before the War. She left with my mother, who was then fifteen, on one of the last boats out of Germany. She worked in a bra factory, sewing bras and underpants. She would rush home at about two-thirty, fix herself a cup of hot water and lemon, or tea, and, by three-thirty, start cooking dinner for the family. She was always busy cooking and cleaning. I always looked forward to my grandmother's coming home because the house would begin to take on the smells of the kitchen. What I loved best was when she cooked salami or sausage with eggs and fried potatoes. She used lots of onions in her cooking. My favorites were fried potatoes with onions, red cabbage soup, and cherry soup.

I would sit there while she cooked. When I was little, I sat on the counter. She smelled like her aprons and her cooking. I used to love to lean against her. I remember falling asleep in her arms in the synagogue.

My grandmother always encouraged me to pursue my talent. She felt this country was a place of opportunity, and she helped me financially through school, though she had very little money for herself.

—*Irene Koenig*

44

Goulash

1 pound lean beef
1 pound lean veal
¼ cup vegetable oil
½ cup onion, peeled and chopped
2 tablespoons green pepper, diced
1½ teaspoon salt
1 teaspoon paprika
¼ teaspoon pepper

½ teaspoon marjoram
1 teaspoon caraway seeds,
    optional
1 28–ounce can stewed tomatoes
2 cups potatoes, diced
1 cup carrots, diced
Dumplings (recipe follows)

Cube both the beef and the veal. In a heavy-gauge skillet, over medium heat, heat the oil, and add the meat, browning it evenly on all sides. Add the onion and green pepper, and saute until lightly browned, stirring occasionally. Add the salt, paprika, pepper, marjoram, and caraway seeds. Cover and simmer for 40–45 minutes, until the meat is tender. Add the potatoes and carrots, and cook 20 more minutes, or until the vegetables are tender. Add a little water if necessary to thin the goulash. If desired, add dumplings to the goulash to steam during the last 15 minutes of cooking.

Makes 4 to 6 servings.

Dumplings

1½ cup all-purpose flour
2 teaspoons baking powder
½ teaspoon salt

1 tablespoon shortening
¾ cup milk

Into a large mixing bowl, sift the flour. Add the baking powder and salt, and sift again. Blend in the shortening with a fork or pastry blender, then add the milk. Drop the dough by the tablespoonful onto the surface of the simmering goulash. Cover the skillet and steam for 15 more minutes.

As an alternative, you can cook the dumplings separately in a closely-covered steamer and add them to the goulash at serving time.

Cherry Soup

20–ounce can pitted sour cherries
3½ cups water
½ cup red wine
1–2 tablespoons sugar, or to taste
2 tablespoons lemon juice

½ teaspoon vanilla extract
2 tablespoons cornstarch
¼ cup cold water
Yogurt or vanilla pudding to
    garnish

In a large saucepan, combine the cherries (juice and all), the water, wine, sugar, lemon juice, and vanilla extract. Bring to a boil, then lower the heat and simmer for 15–20 minutes. Dissolve the cornstarch in the cold water and slowly stir it into the hot soup. Continue to simmer the soup, stirring constantly until the soup is clear. Cool and serve dressed with a dollop of yogurt or vanilla pudding, if desired.

Makes 8 servings.

Bhabiji's Spiced Chicken in Yogurt

My grandmother was born in West Pakistan in a town called Quetta. Now West Pakistan is just called Pakistan. Quetta is on the border of Pakistan and Afghanistan in a beautiful area up in the mountains. We had a good life there. My grandmother was born in 1899 and she died in 1980, at eighty-one. Up until the end of her life, she had no problems. She had beautiful teeth and beautiful skin color. She used to walk two miles every day, even when she was eighty-one. She was very healthy because of the food, the mountain air and spring water, and a beautiful mental attitude. She was very positive, very spiritual too. She used to get up at four o'clock and pray for an hour or two every morning. I used to join her later on, and she taught me how to pray. My brother and I would sit on her lap and she would say, "This is how you pray."

She was quite a woman. During the Partition she took part in the fighting itself, defending her household. She used a shotgun. She let fly! My grandfather almost got murdered on the street during the Partition. They used their wits to get away. It wasn't easy. They swapped their home for one a hundred miles away, in Poona. I was born in Poona, and I grew up with her.

She was always trying to fatten me up. Sometimes she would go into the kitchen and prepare things especially for us. One particular dish was made of whole wheat flour and was like a pancake. You would fold it over, like a half-moon, and stuff it with sugar and a bit of spices. It was delicious. She used to make this thing called kookie, but it's not like an American "cookie." It's made of flour, barley, onions, a bit of spices, and green and red chilies. It's eaten piping hot, right off the *tava,* a kind of wrought iron stove. You serve it with melted butter and sour cream. We used to have it on Sunday mornings. She also made lassi. It's made from curds. You take yogurt curd and churn it around with water. It is like a yogurt drink. You can make it either with rose water or salt water. We used to have it in the summertime. And she also made fresh ice cream with milk and sugar and honey. It was the best I ever tasted.

My grandmother was also quite a gardener. She grew tomatoes, potatoes, onions, and beautiful roses and flowers. We had twelve mango trees, one papaya tree, two guava trees, an evergreen, and an absolutely huge aloe vera plant in the center of the garden. It was about three and a half feet tall. After about ten years it finally bloomed, and it had a large center stalk with a beautiful flower. My grandmother would cut off the leaves and use them for medicinal purposes, like to relieve burns. She enjoyed gardening. She made pickled mango, pickled onions, pickled cucumbers, carrots, and chilies, right from the garden. You name it, she did it. They would last for years, and I used to go crazy over them. She was a warm, loving grandmother and like a mother to me. A very dedicated and beautiful person. And very godly.

—*Mark Popli*

Spiced Chicken in Yogurt

2½–pound chicken
3 cloves garlic, peeled
1 teaspoon ginger, ground
¼ cup vegetable oil or ghee
   (clarified butter)
1 large onion, peeled and thinly
   sliced
1 teaspoon salt
3 cups water

1½ cups unflavored yogurt
1 bunch fresh coriander or
   watercress, chopped
¼ green pepper, sliced
½ teaspoon turmeric, powdered
1 teaspoon garam masala
   (available in Indian groceries),
   or curry powder

Rinse the chicken, pat it dry, and cut it into serving pieces. Mash the garlic into a paste and stir in the ginger.

In a 10–inch heavy-gauge skillet, over medium heat, heat the vegetable oil or ghee, and brown the onion. Add the garlic-ginger paste and cook over low heat for 5 minutes. Add the chicken pieces and saute until brown. Add the water and simmer until the chicken is tender, about 30 minutes, and so the liquid has reduced to 4 tablespoons of gravy. Stir in the yogurt, the coriander or watercress, the sliced green pepper, the turmeric, and the garam masala. Bring to a boil, remove from the heat, and serve immediately.

Makes 4 servings.

Carrot Halvah

A few strands of saffron
2 teaspoons warm water
1 pound carrots
6 cups milk, or a mixture of 4
   cups milk and 2 cups light
   cream
1½ cups sugar

1 ounce (about ⅓ cup) black
   raisins
4 tablespoons unsalted butter
¼ cup almonds, blanched and
   slivered
Seeds of two green cardamoms,
   coarsely ground, optional

Soak the saffron in the warm water. Peel and grate the carrots as finely as possible.

In a large saucepan, over medium heat, bring the milk to a boil and add the grated carrots. Simmer, stirring occasionally, until the mixture is very thick and creamy, about 20 minutes. Add the sugar and raisins and continue to cook until the mixture is very thick. Add the butter and saffron and continue cooking until the halvah is a rich golden color. Pour it into a dish and sprinkle it with the almonds. Chill. Garnish with the coarsely ground seeds of the cardamoms, if you wish.

Makes 5 to 6 servings.

Rosie Fugitt's Chicken Casserole with Homemade Egg Noodles

Grandma Rosie was my adopted grandmother. She was from Aurora, Indiana, like my mom. Both of my grandmothers were gone by the time I was five and Rosie was like family. You see, Rosie Fugitt was my maternal grandmother's best friend. They lived next door to each other all their lives. She was born before the turn of the century (in 1887, I think), so she was very old when I knew her. She was very

much a family woman and we all felt very special when we were with her. I suppose that's why we gravitated toward her and adopted her as a grandmother. When we were first introduced to her, she told us to call her Grandma Rosie. She signed her letters, "Love, Grandma Rosie," and that's what we called her.

I have a picture of her kitchen in my mind. It was very small. It had all gas appliances—nothing fancy—and a lot of cabinets that always seemed to be full of goodies. There was no formal dining room. She had a butcher block table in the center of the kitchen, and that's where we ate. Rosie made homemade egg noodles. She had a lot of recipes she used with the noodles, and I've picked out the best one, the chicken casserole. That's what she made for us the most. She was a great cook and she spent a lot of time in the kitchen doing things for us. If you haven't had a dish made with scratch-made noodles—well, I can't tell you how delicious it is! She always did her most to make us feel welcome, and her cooking was part of that.

Some years back, we stopped in Aurora on my way East to visit colleges. Rosie was still as sharp as a tack. She couldn't exert herself too much, but she could still cook. She lived with her daughter Ruth. I think that Ruth has now moved in with one of her daughters, so you can see how things have cycled around. Time marches on.

A lot of Americans these days discard their elderly relatives when they become a "burden." But Rosie lived in her own house until she was past ninety, and her daughter took care of her. Rosie was basically a housewife. She had great-grandchildren and grandchildren and children. She died when she was ninety-six.

—*Anders Lars Thompson*

Chicken Casserole

1 5–pound stewing hen
Water to cover
Salt and pepper to taste
2 stalks celery
1 large onion, peeled
½ cup bread crumbs
1 tablespoon unsalted butter,
    melted

1 medium onion, peeled
Homemade noodles (recipe
    follows)
Milk
1 pound sharp cheddar cheese,
    finely grated
3 large eggs, well beaten

In a large stock pot, place the stewing hen and enough water to cover. Add salt and pepper to taste, a stalk of celery, and the large onion. Bring to a boil, lower the heat to a simmer, cover the pot, and let it cook until the meat falls from the bones, about 2 hours. (A pressure cooker is ideal for this task, and much faster.) Remove and discard the celery and onion. Remove the chicken, cool it slightly, and pick the meat from the bones, cutting it into small pieces. Discard the bones, and strain the broth.

Preheat the oven to 350 degrees. Mix the bread crumbs with the melted butter and set aside.

Bring the broth to a boil, adding the remaining celery and onion, and reduce the broth slightly. Remove the celery and onion, add the noodles, and cook until the noodles are tender, about 5–7 minutes. Add enough milk to the reduced mixture to make it creamy, then slowly add the cheese and eggs so the eggs don't cook and scramble. Mix well. Stir in the chicken. Pour the mixture into a shallow casserole. Cover with a thin layer of buttered bread crumbs. Bake until the crumbs are brown and the casserole is heated through, about 30 minutes.

Makes 6 servings.

Egg Noodles

3 large eggs
¼ cup water

3 cups all-purpose flour

Beat the eggs and water together slightly. Gradually add enough flour to make a *very* stiff dough. With a rolling pin, roll the dough very thinly to ⅛–inch thickness on a floured board, using plenty of flour on the rolling pin and the board to keep the dough from sticking. Let the dough dry for a bit—about 15 minutes. (If it dries too much, it will become fragile.) Gently roll the sheet of dough into a cylinder. Cut across the roll to make long strips. The cuts should be fairly close together—the closer the cuts, the thinner the noodles. Each strip should then be unrolled and cut into segments about 2 inches long. Finally, allow the noodles to dry completely. Use immediately or store in a plastic bag in the freezer.

Makes about ¾ pound.

Grandma K's Chili Sauce and 1796 Sugar Cakes

My grandparents lived for thirty or forty years in a house they had built themselves in Detroit. Their whole yard was shaded by old trees. We had dinner with them every Sunday after church. It was a formal Sunday dinner with a white linen tablecloth, white linen napkins, and napkin rings. My grandmother had a pantry in which she always set things out before bringing them to the dinner table. My great-aunt would pour the milk a half-hour ahead of time so that it would "take the chill off," because cold milk wasn't good for young people. The cream would rise to the top.

Sunday dinner always meant a roast—pork, beef, chicken, or turkey. If it was beef or pork, it was served with Grandma's recipe for chili sauce. She always made homemade biscuits and her own crabapple or currant jelly to go with it. She would go to the market in the fall and buy produce and put it up into jelly or chili sauce or mustard pickles.

For dessert, we sometimes had plum pudding. My grandmother learned to cook from her mother, who was from Cornwall, England, and I'm sure her mother had made that pudding in Cornwall, so she kept up the tradition. My grandmother also did all her own home canning and baking. We'd sometimes have a home-baked cake for Sunday dinner that she had made on Saturday. When dinner was finished, the men would retire to the living room, and the women—after the dishes were done—always went upstairs and had woman-talk. We would sit and hear what had gone on during the past week, and would stay together all afternoon. We would go home around four, or sometimes after a light Sunday supper.

—*Mary Lou Duncan*

Chili Sauce

8 quarts ripe tomatoes
8 large onions, peeled
3 sweet red peppers
4 green peppers
4 or 5 hot chili peppers
1 bunch celery
1½ cups packed brown sugar

3 cups white vinegar
3 tablespoons salt
1 tablespoon cinnamon, ground
1 tablespoon allspice, ground
1 tablespoon nutmeg, ground
1 tablespoon ginger, ground
1 tablespoon cloves, ground

Chop the tomatoes, onions, peppers, and celery. If you wish, you can put them through a grinder or food processor instead. In a large saucepan, over medium heat, combine all the vegetables and bring them to a boil. Cook them gently until the vegetables are tender, about 15 minutes. Add the sugar, vinegar, salt, and spices. Simmer uncovered for 1–3 hours, or until thick. Pack in sterilized pint jars and seal according to manufacturer's directions.

Makes 15 pints.

1796 Sugar Cakes

½ cup (1 stick) unsalted butter
1 cup sugar
1 large egg
2 cups all-purpose flour, sifted

½ teaspoon baking soda
½ teaspoon cream of tartar
1 teaspoon vanilla extract
Granulated sugar for dipping

Preheat the oven to 350 degrees.

In a large mixing bowl, cream together the butter and sugar, then beat in the egg. Sift together the flour, baking soda, and cream of tartar. Gradually add this to the butter mixture and stir in the vanilla extract. Between your hands, roll teaspoons of dough into small balls. Place the balls on ungreased baking sheets. Dampen the bottom of a glass with water, dip in sugar, then flatten the cookies. Bake for 6 minutes, or until the edges are lightly browned.

Note: These cookies can be decorated before baking with candied fruit, colored sugar, nuts, or small candies if you wish.

Makes about 4 dozen cookies.

Date Cookies

1 cup packed brown sugar
¾ cup lard or shortening
1½ cups cake flour
1 teaspoon baking soda

½ teaspoon salt
¾ cup sour milk or buttermilk
1½ cups rolled oats, uncooked
1 pound pitted dates

Cream the sugar and lard or shortening until light. Sift together the flour, baking soda, and salt, then add the milk and oats alternately with the flour mixture to the sugar mixture, mixing well after each addition. Chill the dough for about 30 minutes.

Preheat the oven to 350 degrees.

With a rolling pin, roll out the dough to about ⅛-inch thickness on a lightly floured board. With a cookie cutter, cut the dough into 2–inch rounds. Place a date in the center of half of the cookies. Use the other half for the top, to make cookie sandwiches. Press the edges gently to seal. Place on baking sheets and bake for about 10 minutes, or until lightly browned.

Makes about 3 dozen filled cookies.

Mae's Egg Custard and No-Flop Raisin Cake

Oh, my Lord, in her day, my grandmother was the Pearl Mesta of upper Manhattan! She brought her family up in upper Manhattan and the South Bronx. She'd always be giving parties and hiring little bands of musicians, which I guess was affordable in those days. She was having a dinner party, with a string quartet, on the night Pearl Harbor happened. Everyone in the family remembers the strange opposites of the lovely ambiance of Mae's posh evening and the announcement that the United States had gone to war. The evening broke up with all the men going off to enlist.

I think that her primary idea of motherhood was to have plenty of food and to get plenty of it into her kids. She made a very old-fashioned, instantaneous equation between good wholesome home cooking and success in every other area of endeavor. I remember how if I was worried about something, like an exam, her solution would always be, "Have a good meal," or, "Let me make you a sandwich," or, "Let me boil you a ham." She was big on the good, hearty boiled dinners that you would associate with an Irish heritage.

Her own mother was an Irish immigrant whose husband had been a New York City policeman, injured in the line of duty and paralyzed for life. My grandmother's mother had to open a boarding house. That meant that she had to prepare meals for something like twenty people nightly. My grandmother naturally learned by the example of her own mother some invaluable lessons about domestic engineering, homemaking, and stretching resources. She was brought up in a brownstone, and there was a small yard in back of the house, which my great-grandmother used for planting a vegetable garden. No meal was ever without homegrown vegetables. And my great-grandmother churned her own butter, and even imprinted each pat with a rosebud stamp before it could be presented at her table! There is no question that my grandmother's expertise in the kitchen, her own flawless assuredness when it came to "just knowing" when a batter consistency was right, or when a rice pudding was ready to be taken out of the oven, were talents consolidated by years of fond and attentive apprenticeship under her own mother.

She has always been a very social creature. That's how I think of her, a belle of Old New York! I can't have a conversation with her without her saying, "How's your love life?" One of her philosophies, which I hold dear, is one of "it's all-rightness." Her way of seeing adversity is suffused with a sense of things never being as bad as they might appear. Another of her philosophies is summed up in the advice she liberally gives to all the womenfolk in the family: "Wear a hat." A lady is enhanced immeasurably by a hat, she contends, and many of our family's favorite photographs bear witness to how well my grandmother both selected and wore hats in years past.

—*Charles Michael Geyer*

Egg Nutmeg Custard

1 quart milk
4 large eggs
1 cup sugar

Pinch of salt
1 tablespoon nutmeg, ground

Preheat the oven to 375 degrees.

In a large mixing bowl, stir the milk, eggs, sugar, and salt together well. Pour the mixture into ovenproof custard cups, filling the cups three-quarters full to allow room for the custard to rise. Sprinkle evenly with nutmeg. Fill a large shallow pan half-full with water and set the cups in the pan. Place the pan in the oven. After 1 hour insert a dry knife through the crust of one of the custards. If any of the mixture adheres, cook for an additional 10–15 minutes.

Makes 5 to 6 servings.

Raisin Cake

2 tablespoons unsalted butter
2 large eggs
1½ cups sugar
2½ cups all-purpose flour

5 teaspoons baking powder
2 cups black raisins
2 cups milk

Preheat the oven to 375 degrees. With the butter, grease, and then flour a 12–inch round cake pan.

In a large mixing bowl, beat the eggs well, then gradually add the sugar and milk, stirring well. In a separate bowl, combine the flour and baking powder. A few spoonfuls at a time, add the flour to the egg mixture, then fold in the raisins. Pour the batter into the prepared pan and bake for 1 hour. During baking, do not open the oven door or the cake will "flop." Remove the cake from the oven, cool it slightly, then remove it from the pan and serve.

Makes 4 to 6 servings.

Two-Ocean Plum Pudding

Before the turn of the century, my great-grandmother, living on East Seventy-first Street in New York City, had a cook who was previously employed by the Lord Mayor of London. The cook's name was Bridget, and she had brought several original English recipes with her. The one that was the family's favorite was for plum pudding, or as Bridget called it, Christmas Pudding. We came to call it Two-Ocean Pudding, but more about that later.

Besides its rich taste, the work that Bridget had to put in to make the pudding just right was something the children could really appreciate. For example, before the Dromedary Company marketed candied orange peel and citron, we had to do the candying ourselves. We bought orange peel and large pieces of citron. Then we diced them into half-inch squares and candied them. When we finally completed the preparations and assembled the ingredients, it took a strong arm to mix everything well.

Each year at Christmas, we children and grandchildren could hardly wait for the pudding to be ready to eat, since we had been helping to prepare it for a month beforehand. The pudding was first put into containers and steamed to cook it. Then it would have to be steamed again, for most of the day, before it was ready for us all to devour at Christmas dinner. My great-grandmother had to do the final steaming Christmas Day on the laundry stove, because the cooking stove was full of pots and pans simmering with the rest of the Christmas dinner.

Even during World War II we tried to keep up the tradition of Christmas Pudding because it was such an important part of the celebration for my family. In 1945 I was in the Navy, stationed in Tsing Tao, China. My mother mailed the plum pudding right before she received the letter telling her I was coming home. I took a rather slow boat. When I left, I told my buddies on the ship that they were welcome to any of the food packages that came for me after I left—I had the feeling my mother had sent the traditional pudding along. Somehow the pudding was intercepted, probably by the postmaster who knew my change of address, and sent back to the States. So the pudding travelled all the way to Tsing Tao and back home again. My poor buddies never got a chance to sample it, but I ate it myself, that very same pudding, home in New Jersey. And that is how the pudding got its final name. It had traveled across the Atlantic from the Lord Mayor's kitchen in London to New York. Then it traveled all the way across the Pacific to Tsing Tao and back. Hence, Two-Ocean Pudding!

—*Charles Menagh*

English Plum Pudding

2¼ cups (1 pound) brown sugar
3¼ cups (1 pound) black raisins
3¼ cups (1 pound) golden raisins
3¼ cups (1 pound) currants
3 cups (1 pound) mixed candied
   orange peel, lemon peel,
   citron, and cherries (available
   as a mixture)
¾ pound beef suet, ground

8 large eggs
1½ cup brandy
1 cup all-purpose flour
1 teaspoon salt
1 teaspoon nutmeg, ground
¾ teaspoon cinnamon, ground
⅛ teaspoon mace, ground
Hard sauce (recipe follows)

In a very large mixing bowl, combine the sugar, raisins, currants, candied fruit, and ground suet, and stir well. Then add the eggs and one-half cup of brandy, and when these are well blended, add the flour, salt, nutmeg, cinnamon, and mace. Spoon this mixture into four 1–quart crocks or pudding molds, and cover tightly with foil. Place the molds on a trivet in a large stock pot filled with 1–2 inches of boiling water, and boil for 4–5 hours. Replenish the water as necessary to keep the level constant. The puddings should be above the water, not in it.

Keep the steamed puddings tightly covered in foil in a cool place for a month before serving. When ready to serve, steam the puddings for 1 hour to reheat and soften. Turn each pudding out onto a serving platter. Serve flambéed with brandy: heat one-quarter cup of brandy for each pudding, light it with a match, and carefully pour over the pudding. Serve with hard sauce.

Makes 4 puddings of 8 servings each.

Hard Sauce

½ cup (1 stick) unsalted butter,
   softened

1 cup confectioners' sugar, sifted
2–4 tablespoons brandy, rum, or
   whisky

Cream together the butter and sugar. Add the brandy or other spirits slowly, beating until fluffy and smooth. Chill until ready to serve.

Makes about 1½ cups.

Herbed Pigeon Casserole and German Fruit Tarts

My husband, Doug, and I were stationed in France during the Korean War. The Air Force was there to build an American base in Château Neuf. When we got to France, there were no facilities at all, not even quarters for us to live in. We ended up staying with another American couple who had found shelter, and "finding shelter" meant living with a farmer. It was a typical French farm. The farmers lived in the main house. The old farmhouse had been turned into a chicken coop, so we converted and restored it and lived there. It had brick floors and wood stoves. We put in a kitchen, and a flush toilet—which was a luxury—and lived there for two years. Looking back, I'd say we had a wonderful time.

The farmer we stayed with hunted every weekend, and Doug had a gun, so he hunted with the farmer all the time. In France the farmers shoot and eat every kind of bird. They shoot anything that flies. One day Doug shot the mayor's homing pigeon. Thank God I spoke French and was able to make amends. It was pretty bad for Franco-American friendship for a while! In France they believe in letting the game hang for up to ten days, to get the right gamey flavor. Americans don't do that, and that was the big controversy: to cook it right way or to let it age.

I learned all about cooking from my mother. She was a German, raised in Belgium, who married a Dutchman. She taught me how to make a roux, and how to cook with beer instead of wine. I was the eldest child, and I just always cooked. She knew all the basics of French cooking. All the things Julia Child teaches us nowadays, I learned at home from my mother. And many of these recipes had been passed down through our family. My mother made a wonderful tart. It's a classic German recipe, but this is truly the original version, passed down in my family. My family in Holland still makes it. I grew up having this tart on birthdays and holidays and other special occasions. I remember when I was first living in the States and I needed the recipe, but thirty years ago you didn't just pick up the phone and make a transatlantic call to get a recipe. I couldn't wait for her to send it to me.

When you have a birthday in Europe, in Holland, or Germany, all your family and friends come over. You throw your own party. Starting at ten in the morning, people come with little presents, and you hold court all day. My mother would be ready in the morning with coffee and some of these tarts. She would make them out of prunes or strawberries or peaches. And flowers are cheap in Europe so people would bring them and you'd end up with twenty vases of flowers all over the house. It's a very nice custom.

—*Victoria Weber-Gordon*

Herbed Pigeon Casserole

4 wild pigeons (squab), available
    at specialty butchers
3 sprigs fresh thyme or ½
    teaspoon dried thyme
1 bay leaf
3 sprigs parsley
Salt and pepper to taste
8 tablespoons unsalted butter

1 tablespoon flour
1 cup chicken broth, or ½ cup
    chicken broth and ½ cup
    white wine
12 small whole white onions,
    peeled
2 tablespoons shallots, minced
½ cup Madeira wine, optional

Preheat the oven to 375 degrees.

Tie the thyme, bay leaf, and parsley into a small square of cheesecloth to make a bouquet garni.

Season the cavities of the pigeons with salt and pepper. In a Dutch oven or ovenproof casserole, heat 4 tablespoons of the butter, then add the pigeons and brown them on all sides. Add the shallots and stir 1 minute. Add the flour and turn the birds several times until well coated. Add the broth, white wine, and the bouquet garni. Cover the casserole, and put it in the oven. Turn the oven down to 325 degrees. Baste and turn every 10 minutes until done (when the juices run clear), probably less than 30 minutes, depending on the size of the pigeons.

While the pigeons are in the oven, in a heavy-gauge skillet, heat 2 tablespoons of butter and brown the onions. Add to the casserole during the last 10 minutes of cooking.

Remove the pigeons and onions and arrange on a serving platter. Cook the liquid in the roasting pan on high heat to reduce it to 1 cup. Add salt and pepper to taste and the Madeira wine, if desired. Cook at full boil for 1 minute. Turn off the heat and add the remaining 2 tablespoons of butter. Ladle the sauce over the pigeons, or serve separately in a gravy boat.

Makes 2 servings.

German Fruit Tarts

⅔ cup (1⅓ sticks) unsalted
    butter
1¾ cups all-purpose flour
¾ cup sugar
1 large egg, lightly beaten
Pinch of salt

4 cups sliced fresh peaches,
    strawberries, or other seasonal
    fruit
½ cup sugar, optional
½ teaspoon almond extract,
    optional
1 cup heavy cream

Place the flour in a mound on a large pastry board. Cut the butter into small pieces and sprinkle evenly over the flour. Then mound the flour and butter, make a well in the center of the flour, and add the egg. With your fingers, work the flour and butter in from the edges and blend into the egg, making sure that the egg does not flow out. Repeat this process, gently kneading the ingredients until you form the dough into a ball. If the dough is too soft to roll out, wrap it in plastic wrap and refrigerate for 1–2 hours.

Slice the fresh fruit and, if desired, sprinkle it with one-half cup of sugar and the almond extract.

Preheat the oven to 400 degrees.

With a rolling pin or your hands, flatten the dough to fit a 10–inch tart shell. Transfer the dough to the pan and fit it into the pan. Prick with a fork. Bake for 7–10 minutes, or until lightly golden in color. If you want a soft shell, cook 5–7 minutes.

Whip the cream until it forms soft peaks. Fill the shell with the fruit and serve with whipped cream.

Makes a 10–inch tart.

Grandfather's Linzertorte

Food was scarce in my childhood because of the War. Our relatives in Switzerland used to send packages to us in Germany. Twice a year they would mail us coffee, tea, cocoa, and maybe some chocolate. My grandmother kept all of this in a cabinet, and I always loved to open the door of that cabinet because it smelled so good! We made those special foods last a whole half a year. I think that in a way it's too bad that now everything is available so easily, because that special feeling is gone forever.

My grandfather was a cultural historian. He wrote about Beethoven, Mozart, Goethe, the age of romanticism, and the age of classicism. He even wrote his own memoirs, which are very interesting. He was a lot of fun. He would clown around with us. If I wanted money, I didn't go to my grandmother but to him. He was much more a pal. We called my grandmother Mutter, which means "mother." She was the hostess, the "queen bee," and she would sit in a particular chair, receiving guests. She was very charming and good at making conversation. She was very well-read, and critiqued and edited my grandfather's writing. I remember that she was incredibly sensitive to noise: All of the kids had to tiptoe around and not make any sudden sound. To this day, when a door slams, I still think, "Oh no! Mutter!"

When my grandfather's birthday came around, people would come over to visit in the morning before lunch. The town celebrities would show up—the mayor, a journalist—and we'd have vermouth or cognac, and something to eat, like these ham crescents. People would bring flowers or little presents, sit around for an hour, and then go. My grandmother would make his favorite cake, Linzertorte. She'd make two of them, one as the official birthday cake (everyone would get a piece of that one) and one that was all Grandfather's. Nobody could touch that one except him. He would eat it in the middle of the morning, between breakfast and lunch. It kept for a long time and became better when it sat for a while. That's because the jam spreads slowly through the dough. It's a very simple but delicious recipe. To give it a "traditional edge" you have to have a nut grinder like Grandma's. I don't like food processors. They seem very cruel to food. Too fast, too loud.

—*Verena Schleicher Shapiro*

Linzertorte

Verena: This torte should be made two weeks ahead of time to allow the flavors to develop. Wrap it loosely and keep it refrigerated, then bring it to room temperature before serving.

1 cup all-purpose flour, sifted
1 teaspoon unsweetened cocoa
1/2 teaspoon cinnamon, ground
Pinch of cloves, ground
Pinch of salt
1/2 cup (1 stick) salted butter, cut into small pieces
1/2 cup sugar

4 ounces almonds (about 2/3 cup), ground
1 small egg
1 tablespoon Kirsch or brandy
3–4 tablespoons raspberry jam
1 egg yolk, lightly beaten, for glazing

Place the flour in a mixing bowl. Add the cocoa, cinnamon, cloves, and salt, and stir well. Using a fork, two knives, or a pastry blender, cut the butter into the flour until the mixture forms small balls the size of peas. Add the sugar, ground almonds, and egg. Knead into the dough and gradually add the liqueur, working as quickly as possible. Let the dough rest for 1 hour.

Preheat the oven to 350 degrees. Roll out half of the dough between 2 pieces of wax paper to a thickness of 1/8–1/4 inch, a little thicker than pie dough. Fit the dough into a 9–inch pie pan. Cut off any excess dough and set aside. Spread the jam over the dough.

Roll out the other half of the dough as above, and cut it into 3/4–inch wide strips. Criss-cross the strips over the torte. Brush the egg yolk over the lattice. Bake the torte for 45 minutes.

Makes a 9–inch torte, 6 to 8 servings.

Crescents

1½ cups all-purpose flour
1/4 cup unsalted butter
1/2 cup sour cream*
1 teaspoon salt

1 large egg yolk
Ham or mushroom filling
(recipes follow)

*For fewer calories, yogurt can be substituted for some or all of the sour cream.

In a large mixing bowl, sift the flour with the salt. Cut in the butter until the mixture forms balls the size of peas. Mix in the sour cream and/or yogurt. If the dough is too moist, add more flour; if too dry, add more sour cream or yogurt. Form the dough into a ball, then let it rest for 1 hour.

Preheat the oven to 350 degrees.

With a rolling pin, on a floured surface, roll out the dough 1/16–inch thick. Cut it into 4 × 4–inch squares or circles 4 inches in diameter. Place a spoonful of the filling in the middle of each piece, fold over in half, moisten the edges, and press the edges to seal. Brush the crescents with egg yolk, and place them on baking sheets. Bake for 20–25 minutes, or until golden brown.

Note: The crescents can be baked half-way and then frozen for future use.

Makes 1 dozen crescents.

Ham Filling

1/4 pound ham, boiled and sliced   1/3 cup parsley, chopped

Dice the ham, and mix it with the chopped parsley.

Mushroom Filling

4 medium mushrooms
1 onion, peeled and chopped

1 tablespoon unsalted butter
Salt and pepper to taste

Dice the mushrooms. In a heavy-gauge skillet, place the mushrooms and onions, add the butter, and saute the mixture for 2–3 minutes, adding salt and pepper to taste.

Noodles Anna and Christmas Fruitcake

My grandmother's name was Anna McGuinness. She was born in County Cavan, Ireland, in 1875, and then lived at 779 Tenth Avenue in New York City. She met and married a plasterer, my grandfather, John. They had five children, one of whom was my mother Julia. Grandmother was known to have the patience of a saint, and when tragedy struck, she took it well. Here's an example. Her son was hit by an automobile. When they came to tell her, they told her to sit down in a chair—that they had bad news for her. And when they were finished telling her that her son's leg had been amputated, she said, "Is that all? I thought he was dead." I always admired her for that. This was her favorite child. And you know, that child went on to lead a very healthy life, and I think that healthiness came from her attitude, right from the beginning. These people were tough that grew up on the West Side. They really knew hardship. They came over in those boats, God help them.

The family was very close-knit. Everybody lived near each other on Tenth Avenue. Everyone came up to my grandmother's to eat; she cooked for her daughters and all the grandchildren. She baked her own bread every morning when she got up at five o'clock to get her husband off to work. Irish soda bread was always a big treat. And she made her own pot cheese with sour milk wrapped in cheesecloth and hung to drip. She was very meticulous about her cooking, and she wore a full apron that covered her dress completely and tied up around the neck. Some of the dishes that Grandma McGuinness served her family were roast leg of lamb, corned beef and cabbage, and oxtail soup. When she cooked cabbage, she cooked it in fried bacon and its drippings. Many weeks before Christmas my grandmother baked her fruitcake. She said it tasted much better if it was marinated long before eating. So the Christmas cake was made in August, when all the fresh fruit was in season. My grandmother would dry the fruit herself. And she would pour brandy over the fruitcake every week until it was ready for the holidays. It was very, very good. I've used her recipe, and my sister, Pat, says it's as wonderful as my grandmother's was.

I think that people in this country ate better one or two generations ago than they do now. Fresh vegetables and fresh fruits were all we knew. We didn't grow up in this "frozen" era. My grandmother shopped once a week for her big shopping, but for perishables she shopped every day. Everything was fresh from the market. Fresh. She bought her meat from a German butcher, groceries from an Irish storekeeper, vegetables from the Italian market, and the bakery was run by a German family. All of these people were first-generation immigrants.

—*Dolores McCarthy*

Christmas Fruitcake

1 cup light molasses
½ cup water
11 ounces black raisins
11 ounces pitted prunes, diced
11 ounces pitted dates, diced
8 ounces packaged coconut, shredded
8 ounces sweetened banana chips (available in health food stores)
½ cup mixed candied fruit, diced finely
½ cup dried figs, diced
1½ cups pecans, chopped
1½ cups walnuts, chopped
2¼ cups all-purpose flour

1 cup (2 sticks) plus 2 tablespoons unsalted butter or shortening
1½ cups sugar
6 large eggs
1 tablespoon orange rind, grated
1 teaspoon salt
1½ teaspoons cinnamon, ground
1¼ teaspoons nutmeg, ground
¾ teaspoon allspice, ground
½ teaspoon cloves, ground
¼ teaspoon baking soda
½ cup orange juice
1 cup brandy for moistening the baked cake
Apricot glaze (recipe follows)

In a large saucepan, over medium heat, blend together the molasses and water, and bring to a boil, stirring constantly. Stir in the raisins, prunes, and dates, and bring to a boil once again. Reduce the heat to low and simmer for 5 minutes. Remove from the heat, stir in the coconut, banana chips, and candied fruit. Set aside to cool.

Preheat the oven to 275 degrees. With 2 tablespoons of butter or shortening, grease two 9 × 5–inch loaf pans and line with greased wax paper.

Toss the pecans and walnuts with one-quarter cup of flour.

Cream the butter until smooth and light. Gradually add the sugar, beating constantly. Beat in the eggs one at a time, then stir in the orange rind. Sift together the remaining flour, salt, cinnamon, nutmeg, allspice, cloves, and baking soda. Add this to the butter mixture alternately with the orange juice. Stir in the fruit mixture and the nut-flour mixture. Pour into the prepared pans and bake for about 3 hours.

Store the fruitcakes in airtight containers for about a month, seasoning once a week with a few tablespoons of brandy.

Spread the apricot glaze over the cakes several hours before serving.

Makes two 3½–pound cakes.

Apricot Glaze

1 cup canned apricots
¾ cup sugar

⅓ cup boiling water

Force the apricots through a fine sieve. Add the sugar and boiling water, and cook, uncovered, until the mixture is as thick as jam. Cool and spread over the fruitcake.

Makes about 1⅓ cups, enough for 3 cakes.

Noodles Anna

1 large onion, peeled and cut into 16 pieces
2 tablespoons bacon fat
1 large green pepper, chopped
1 10¾–ounce can concentrated tomato soup
1 leg bone from a roast leg of lamb
1 bay leaf, broken in half

1 teaspoon salt
¼ teaspoon pepper
2 cups cooked leftover lamb, cubed
1 pound wide egg noodles, cooked
Grated pecorino Romano cheese for sprinkling, optional

In a 10–inch heavy-gauge skillet, heat the bacon fat and add the onion. Saute until golden brown. Add the green pepper and stir for 1 minute, then add the soup, lamb bone, bay leaf, salt, and pepper, and bring to a boil. Stir, cover, and simmer for 1 hour, then remove the bone and the bay leaf. Stir in the meat and heat for 10–15 minutes, or until the meat is heated through, then add the noodles and stir. Serve immediately with cheese to sprinkle.

Makes 6 servings.

Garnett Ashby's Spoon Bread and Chicken Souffle

My father was in charge of breakfast on Sunday mornings, and we almost always had spoon bread. Spoon bread is almost like a souffle made with yellow corn meal and eggs. It rises a lot. The outside is kind of crispy and the inside is moist and delicious. I guess they call it spoon bread because it's so mushy that you can eat it with a spoon. You eat it with butter and pickled artichokes or green tomato pickle as a condiment on the side. My father would buy the pickle at the church fair. My grandmother always made good breakfasts, and my father probably got this recipe from her.

My father always got up at four-thirty in the morning to run. On Sundays, when he'd come back from his run, he'd wait until we were all awake. He'd just putter around, drinking coffee and reading the Sunday paper. And when we'd all finally gotten out of bed, we'd go downstairs and fight over who was going to help. It was very prestigious to be the one who helped! He assigned each of us jobs so we wouldn't fight. It was always, "Now you get the eggs out of the refrigerator, and you beat them, and you can beat them when she's tired." My mom liked our Sunday breakfasts because she didn't have to cook, and it kept us kids occupied.

My father is very relaxed in the kitchen. He's not one of those authoritarian cooks. And he's not precise at all, but it always tastes good. I'm sure he had spoon bread when he was a little boy. He grew up in Jacksonville, Florida. It's more like the Old South than some other Florida cities. Nothing bothers him in the kitchen. He never loses his temper if anything comes out wrong. He gets rattled about other things, but not about cooking. He just sips coffee and keeps everything under control.
—*Elizabeth Ashby Frew*

Spoon Bread

2 cups water
1 cup yellow corn meal
1/4 teaspoon salt
3 tablespoons unsalted butter

4 large eggs, beaten
1 cup milk
Butter for serving

Preheat the oven to 350 degrees. With 1 tablespoon of butter, grease a 1½–quart souffle dish.

In a large saucepan, add the water and bring to a boil. Sprinkle the corn meal and the salt into the boiling water, stirring constantly. Remove the corn meal from the heat and cool slightly. Add the remaining butter, stirring until it is melted, then add the eggs and milk. Stir until smooth. Pour the mixture into the prepared souffle dish and bake for 45–50 minutes. Serve with butter and pickled artichoke or green tomato pickle (see the recipe for pickled tomatoes on page 121.)

Makes 4 servings.

Chicken Souffle

1 tablespoon unsalted butter
7–ounce can chicken, or 1 large chicken breast, boned, skinned, and cut in half
6 cups of water to poach chicken breast

1 10¾–ounce can cream of mushroom soup
1 teaspoon curry powder
6 large eggs, separated

Preheat the oven to 350 degrees. With the butter, grease, and then flour a 2–quart souffle dish.

If using a chicken breast, in a medium saucepan, over low heat, simmer the water, then add the chicken breast halves to poach for 10 minutes. Set aside to cool.

Meanwhile, in a large bowl, place the soup and stir in the curry powder. In a separate bowl, beat the egg yolks until light, then stir them into the soup mixture. In a separate mixing bowl, beat the egg whites until stiff but not dry. Mince the chicken finely and stir it into the soup mixture, incorporating well. Gently fold the egg whites, half at a time, into the soup-chicken mixture. Pour the mixture into the prepared souffle dish and bake until puffed and firm, about 45–50 minutes.

Makes 4 servings.

Bagala Polo and Domeh Kalam

In Iran, the family is the most important thing. Whole families will live together under one roof, each family having its own set of rooms, like an apartment. There is usually one entrance, a central courtyard with a fountain in it separating the different sets of rooms, and a communal kitchen. Grandma's apartment was the closest to the front door because she got the most visitors. Seven, eight, or nine people came to visit her each night. Over there, it's a pleasure to get old. The older you get, the more respect you get. When grandma became too old to cook, my mother would cook for everyone. But whoever cooked, the first plate would always go to Grandma. Grandma was always there anytime you had a problem. She was the one sitting and listening. She was very, very smart. She would just listen, and give you tea.

Iranians cook not just to eat. There is an art to it, and cooking is considered a pleasure. My mother and my grandmother were proud of their cooking. Traditionally, the kitchen was the smallest room in the house. This is changing now, and new houses are more European, with larger kitchens. Even though the kitchens were very small, the stoves and ovens were large. Housewives in Iran were always prepared to feed many people. My mother usually cooked for twenty to twenty-five people. She would cook in a very, very big pan over a traditional Iranian stove, which is sort of like a camping grill, with an open fire underneath and charcoal over the pan so that the heat would circulate all around the food.

In Iran, it is the custom to eat two big meals a day, together with your family. Lunch is the main meal, and you are never allowed to touch anything until all the cooking is done. Also, the table had to be very colorful, with different colored tablecloths chosen to complement the colors of the foods.

One of the most important holidays was New Year. The table would be set with seven items, for a tradition called *Hafte Seen,* which stands for the first Persian letter, *seen,* and the Farsi word for seven, *haft.* The items would be: *sekeh,* a coin; *samanuy,* a dish made of flour, coloring, and sugar; *sabzi,* a green vegetable; *sonbol,* a hyacinth; *seer,* garlic; *senjed,* a dried fruit; and *serkeh,* vinegar. We would also put out the Koran, the Islamic holy book, and a bowl of goldfish, which represented life and were considered good luck. New Year's, which we call *Noh Ruz,* is a time to make up any differences you have had with your neighbors throughout the year. The tradition is that no matter how mad you are at each other, on New Year's you make up. The younger people go to the older ones to make up, and friends pick up the younger enemy and take him or her to the older enemy's house.

In Iran, one of the best joys of life is food. And I would give anything to go over there again and have my mother cook for me!

—*Mohammad Karimian*

Bagala Polo

Rice with Lima Beans and Potatoes

Serve this dish with the fried fish that follows.

1 gallon water	2 tablespoons vegetable oil
1/4 cup salt	1 or 2 large potatoes, sliced
2 cups long-grain rice, uncooked	1/8–inch thick
24 ounces frozen lima beans	1 bunch fresh dill, chopped

In a large saucepan, place the water, then add the salt, and bring to a boil. Add the rice and cook for 10 minutes, or until tender but still firm in the center. Pour the rice into a colander, drain, run under cold water, and drain again. Stir the lima beans and dill weed into the rice.

In the same saucepan used for the rice, add the oil and warm it, swirling the pan to coat the bottom with the oil. Arrange the potato slices over the bottom, and pour the rice mixture over the potatoes. Over this, add 4 layers of paper towels, or a heavy bath towel folded to fit. Cover the saucepan with a tight-fitting lid and cook over low heat for about 45 minutes, stirring occasionally.

Makes 6 to 8 servings.

Fried Fish

1 cup all-purpose flour	2 1/2–3 pounds ocean perch or
1/4 cup corn meal, optional	other fish fillets
1/4 cup curry powder	3 tablespoons vegetable oil or
1 teaspoon pepper	unsalted butter for sauteing

In a mixing bowl, combine the flour, corn meal (if using), curry powder, and pepper, and roll the fish pieces in the mixture.

In a heavy-gauge skillet, over medium heat, warm the oil or butter and saute the fish on both sides until crisp. Serve with the bagala polo.

Makes 6 to 8 servings.

Domeh Kalam

Stuffed Cabbage Leaves

11 cups water	1/2 cup long-grain rice, uncooked
Pinch of salt	1/2 cup parsley, chopped
1 large head cabbage	1/2 teaspoon cinnamon, ground
1/4 cup yellow split peas	1/4 teaspoon pepper
1 pound beef, ground	1/3 cup vegetable oil
1 onion, peeled and chopped	2/3 cup lemon juice

In a large pot, bring 8 cups of salted water to boil. Core the cabbage and add it to the boiling water. Cover the pot and cook the cabbage until tender, about 25–30 minutes. Drain well, remove the leaves, and cut off the tough part of any leaf.

In a saucepan, add 1 cup of water and the peas, and bring to a boil. Cook for about 30 minutes.

In a large mixing bowl, combine the beef, onion, rice, parsley, cooked peas, cinnamon, and pepper. Place a tablespoon of the meat filling in the center of a cabbage leaf, fold the ends in, and roll the leaf up. Repeat with the remaining leaves and filling. Place any torn leaves in the bottom of a 4–quart pot. Pack the rolled leaves on top of the torn leaves. Pour in 2 cups of water, the lemon juice, and the oil. Cover the pot and cook over low heat for 35–40 minutes. Serve hot or cold.

Makes about small 50 rolls.

Grammy's Potato Schupnudel and Panakuchen

Grammy used to live in Bethlehem, Pennsylvania, and we'd drive to see her on weekends. Sunday breakfast was a big part of our being together. We would go to mass first, and then come home and have a big brunch with eggs, bacon, muffins that Grammy baked, and panakuchen. We kids called the panakuchen "roll-up pancakes," and we loved them because we could roll them up and eat them with our fingers. Every time we came to visit we'd say, "Grammy, will you make roll-up pancakes?"

Cooking was her favorite thing to do. She didn't read or write English, so it was hard to get her to write the recipes down. And when you tried to get her to *tell* the recipes, she'd say, "Oh well, just a handful of this," or "Oh, just a little bit of milk." And you'd try to pin her down to a cup or a teaspoon, and she'd say, "Just this much!" My mom learned just by watching, and then she would write it down, since she was familiar with measurements.

I'm sure Grammy got her recipes from *her* mother. Grammy's mother was a German, living in Austria-Hungary, and that's where Grammy grew up. There were eight or nine children, and I think Grammy was the youngest. When she was eighteen years old, her parents arranged her marriage to my grandfather. He had had a wife and a son, but the wife had died, and they needed somebody to cook and clean and take care of the little boy. My grandfather already had plans to come to America, so my grandmother came with him under his first wife's passport. This was in 1920. Because it was arranged so quickly, she didn't bring a lot of things with her to America, just her cooking things and her jewelry.

Now my grandmother lives with us. Grammy doesn't do all the cooking anymore, since she had her stroke, but sometimes she supervises us in the kitchen—we make something, and she tells us how to do it. One of my favorites is schupnudel. I first had it at her apartment in Bethlehem, and we have it on holidays. Grammy has a very heavy accent, and I remember her saying, "Aaah, vir gon ta hef schupnudel!"

My grandmother is precious to me and I adore her. She has some really cute sayings, like sometimes she will pat you on the shoulder and say, "Eat, eat. How are you going to keep it up?"
—*Martie Ripson*

66

Potato Schupnudel

Martie: My grandmother served schupnudel as a dessert with sliced peaches.

2 potatoes, boiled, peeled, and
  minced
Salt to taste
2 cups all-purpose flour
1 large egg

A few tablespoons water
½ teaspoon salt
½ cup plain breadcrumbs
5–6 tablespoons unsalted butter
  or shortening

In a large mixing bowl, combine the potatoes with salt to taste. Stir in the flour and egg. Mix thoroughly with your hands. Add enough water to bind the dough and shape into a long loaf. Cut the dough into slices and roll into cylindrical shapes about the size of a finger.

Fill a large saucepan with water, add the salt, and bring to a boil. Poach the potato sticks in the water until they rise to the top, approximately 10 minutes. Drain them well on paper towels.

Brown the breadcrumbs in the butter, and then sprinkle them over the potato sticks.

Makes 12 potato sticks.

Panakuchen

Roll-Up Pancakes

2 cups all-purpose flour
1 large egg, lightly beaten
Scant 2 teaspoons sugar
3 cups milk

3 tablespoons butter, or more if
  necessary
Jelly, marmalade, or
  confectioners' sugar for filling

Beat the flour, egg, sugar, and milk together to make a thin batter.

Over medium heat, warm a 6–inch heavy-gauge griddle or skillet until very hot, then add butter to keep the pancakes from sticking. Ladle 3 tablespoons of the batter into the skillet, tipping it so the batter coats the bottom. Allow the batter to brown slightly, then turn and brown the other side. Keep the pancakes warm until ready to serve.

Spread the pancakes with jelly or marmalade or sprinkle with confectioners' sugar. Roll them up and eat them with the fingers (kids love this part!).

Makes about 18 pancakes.

Mary Adams McLean Taylor's Scottish Shortbread

My grandmother came over to this country from Scotland when she was twenty-five years old. She settled in Westchester, and that's where I grew up. She died when she was eighty-six. She was already an old lady when I knew her, but she was always on the ball. She had the most marvelous Scottish accent, and she could turn it into a really thick brogue when she wanted to. She would come out with things like, "The old dog's for the hard road and the pup's for the pavement."

She was poking fun at us because we were young and lazy—the old generation had had it hard and we pups had the soft life. "You are lazy, lousy, and elaborate," she would say, and laugh when she said it. She arrived here in this country in 1923, on the same day that President Harding died. She would say, "I took the breath out of President Harding!"

She was Granny, never Grandma or Grandmother. That was too formal. But she was a very proper lady. I never saw her wear a pair of pants in my life. She would even wear stockings to the beach! She was constantly drinking tea. We had to boil the water until it was rolling and the kettle was whistling, or else she wouldn't drink it. Sometimes I would try to cheat and make it quickly. I'd make the tea before the water had boiled fully, and bring it to her. But she would notice, of course, and say, "Boil it again." Her closest friends called her "T," not only because her last name began with it, but because she drank so much of it.

She loved her food—good food, nothing junky. She was very traditional. There are three treats I remember her making. One of them was Yorkshire Pudding. It would come out of the oven puffy and raised high, and everyone would dive for it and try to eat it before it got flat. Another one was shortbread at Christmastime. She'd use her knuckles to press it down into the pan, and you'd see her knuckle marks baked into the shortbread. It was so buttery and sweet. She used to make pans and pans of it and cut it into squares. Then she'd wrap them up for presents. The other treat was scones. She'd bake the whole dough in a cast-iron pan, and then cut it into triangles. We'd eat them hot, and butter would run down our chins. It was oh, so good. I just loved it.

—*Rania Bratberg*

Scottish Shortbread

1 pound (4 sticks) plus 1
  tablespoon unsalted butter,
  softened
6 tablespoons confectioners'
  sugar

6 tablespoons superfine sugar
6 tablespoons cornstarch
6 cups all-purpose flour

Preheat the oven to 325 degrees.

In a large mixing bowl, combine 1 pound of butter, the confectioners' sugar, the superfine sugar, and the cornstarch. Stir in the flour, 2 cups at a time. Mix the last 2 cups in with your hands, working the dough in with your fingers. Press into a large roasting pan greased with 1 tablespoon of butter. Prick the entire surface with a fork. Bake for 45–50 minutes. Remove and immediately cut into squares or rectangles. Cool and store in an air-tight tin.

Makes about 48 pieces.

Griddle Scones

2 cups all-purpose flour
2 teaspoons cream of tartar
1 teaspoon baking soda

2 tablespoons unsalted butter
¾ cup buttermilk
½ cup currants, optional

In a large mixing bowl, stir together the flour, cream of tartar, and baking soda, then cut in the butter until the mixture resembles coarse crumbs. Stir in the buttermilk to make a dough. Knead briefly in the bowl, then roll out on a floured board into a circle about 12–14 inches in diameter—to fit into a heavy-gauge skillet.

Heat the skillet over low heat. Cut the dough into wedges and cook over low heat, turning to cook all sides. This should take about 15–20 minutes.

Makes about 12 scones.

Myrtle Orloff's Pork Pie and Chocolate Roll Candy

We met Myrtle because her husband, Alexis, worked with my father. Alexis had escaped from Russia when the Revolution started. Myrtle's sister was a concert pianist and met Alexis in Europe but later broke up with him. When Alexis came to America, he just showed up on Myrtle's doorstep in Chicago because he didn't know anyone else in the States. Later they got married, and Alexis went to work with my father in a tool-and-die company. Myrtle went on to sell Model T Fords in the late 1920s. She was probably the first woman car salesman.

Myrtle was not my grandmother in the literal sense, but in every other sense she was the best grandma I ever had. She sometimes cooked for me and my family and played games with us and told us stories. We always called her Grandma. I remember her kitchen because she had an enormous stove on which she cooked for the entire family, including her mother and her aunt. Her aunt was hard of hearing and had one of the old-fashioned hearing aids with a funnel that you had to speak into.

Dinner at Myrtle's was extremely formal. I had to dress up in knickers, because that was the way little boys were supposed to dress back then. But Myrtle herself was never, never stuffy or formal. She never sat down to eat, but would continually run back and forth, getting food from the kitchen and bringing it to the table. It was at that table that I learned how to butter my bread before eating it, and what table manners were. After the meal all the men would go into the next room, and I would stay with Myrtle, bringing her all the dishes from the table to wash and put away.

Myrtle seemed forever young. She was a seamstress, a photographer, and a golfer. She laid the floor in my mother's house. She did plumbing and bricklaying, and used to fix her own cars. She even built an FM radio one time. She taught me so many things as a little boy, especially how not to be afraid to try things and to fix things. Today she lives in Cambridge, Massachusetts, and still works as a volunteer for local hospitals.

—*Arthur Knowles*

Pork Pie

Filling

2 pounds lean pork shoulder,
  bone in
1 medium onion, peeled and
  chopped
1 carrot, chopped finely

2 or 3 medium potatoes, peeled
  and diced
1 bay leaf
1 clove garlic, peeled and minced
Salt and pepper to taste

Pie crust

1 cup all-purpose flour
1 teaspoon salt

1/3 cup shortening
1/4 cup water

Trim the fat off the meat, then, after carefully slicing the meat from the bone, cut the meat into 1/2–inch cubes. Reserve the bone.

In a large saucepan, over medium heat, place the cubed pork, the bone, the onion, and the carrot. Cover with water, bring to a boil, then lower the heat and simmer until the pork is tender, about 45 minutes. Add the diced potato, bay leaf, and garlic, and cook for 20 minutes more, or until the potatoes are tender. Discard the bone and pour off most of the water, leaving about one-half inch in the bottom of the saucepan. Season with salt and pepper.

Preheat the oven to 350 degrees.

Meanwhile, prepare the crust. Combine the flour and salt in a bowl, and cut in the shortening until the dough resembles cornmeal. Sprinkle with enough water to form a firm dough and mix well.

Roll out two-thirds of the dough on a floured board to a size sufficient to cover the bottom and sides of a small casserole. Roll out the remaining piece to fit over the top. Line the casserole with dough, pour in the meat mixture, and cover with the remaining dough. Bake for about an hour, until the pie crust is brown. Serve warm in the casserole.

Pork pie is delicious served cold and sliced instead of sandwiches.

Makes 4 to 6 servings.

Chocolate Roll Candy

1 tablespoon unsalted butter,
  softened
1/2 pound sweet chocolate

1 large egg, beaten
1/2 cup blanched almonds,
  chopped

With the softened butter, grease a flat dinner plate.

Melt the chocolate in a double boiler, and slowly add the egg, beating until smooth. Remove from the heat, stir in the nuts, and spread the mixture on the buttered plate. When cool, roll into two rolls, 1½ inches in diameter. Let stand until firm. Cut into thin slices.

Makes one-half pound of candy.

Appleanna Bread

1/2 cup plus 1 tablespoon
  shortening
1½ cups sugar
2 large eggs, at room
  temperature
2 cups all-purpose flour
1 teaspoon baking soda

1 teaspoon baking powder
1 teaspoon cinnamon, ground
1 teaspoon salt
2 very ripe bananas, peeled and
  mashed
2 cups apples, peeled and finely
  chopped
1 teaspoon vanilla extract

Preheat the oven to 350 degrees. With 1 tablespoon of shortening, grease, and then flour a 9 × 5–inch loaf pan.

Cream together the shortening and sugar until light. Beat in the eggs. Sift together the flour, baking soda, baking powder, cinnamon, and salt. Beat the dry mixture into the shortening mixture. Stir in the mashed bananas, the apples, and the vanilla extract. Pour the batter into the prepared pan and bake for 1 hour, or until a knife inserted in the middle comes out clean.

Makes one 9 × 5–inch loaf.

Catherine Ward's Irish Soda Bread

My grandmother, Catherine Ward, came over from Ireland when she was sixteen. She met my grandfather at a dance when she was about eighteen. In Ireland, each county would have a dance. So there would be a Leitrim dance, or a Galway dance, or a Dublin or Wicklow dance. This tradition was carried on in the Irish churches in New York. My grandparents met at a Leitrim dance. My grandfather went to all the different dances because he didn't like the Galway girls. My grandmother, being a Leitrim girl, would only go to the Leitrim ones, because a lady didn't go checking out those Kerry or those Cork boys. So they met at the dance, and the rest is history.

My grandmother's brothers were all guerrilla fighters in the IRA. Her uncles were constantly on the run, so she had a hard time of it. And then, coming over here with the Depression, they had a hard life.

The Troubles ended in 1921, but even after British rule was officially lifted, Ireland was still a very poor country. There wasn't much to eat in those days—cabbage, potatoes, and soda bread. It's a heavy bread, made with soda instead of yeast. It's usually made in a sort of patty, shaped like that because originally it wasn't cooked in a bread pan, but over an open fire. A few years ago, when I went back to Ireland with her to visit our relatives, they made the bread for us. Just the same bread. They don't have open fires anymore, so they cooked it in the oven. But at my great-aunt's they're still using a turf-fire stove, in which the fuel is turf, or peat. It gave the bread a special flavor. We went to visit my grandmother's house. It's an old thatched cottage, and it's pretty run-down now. The whole house is permeated with the smell of peat. It's a sharp, pungent, earthy smell. My grandmother didn't want to go back at first. I think she was afraid that it would destroy her dreams, to see everything changed and new. But she was all right, except for the day we went to visit her house in the little village she grew up in and we saw her parents' graves.

The soda bread is very much what she is. Not coarse, but not at all flowery or fancy. It's a stick-to-your-ribs bread, a whole meal. Her hands are very, very soft, but they're the kind of soft that comes from years of being in water, and hard work. They're firm, but they're soft from use. And that's just the way the bread is.

—*Delia Marshall*

Irish Soda Bread

2 cups all-purpose flour
1 cup whole wheat flour
1 tablespoon wheat germ
1 tablespoon baking powder
1 teaspoon baking soda
1 teaspoon salt

¼ cup packed brown sugar
½–1 cup currants
1–2 teaspoons caraway seeds
1½ cups buttermilk
2 large eggs
5 tablespoons unsalted butter, melted

Preheat the oven to 350 degrees. With 1 tablespoon of butter, grease a loaf pan.

In a large mixing bowl, sift together the flours, wheat germ, baking powder, baking soda, and salt. Stir in the brown sugar, currants, and caraway seeds. In a separate bowl, combine the buttermilk, eggs, and the remaining butter. Add to the dry ingredients, stirring to mix until well moistened and almost smooth. Pour into the prepared pan and bake for 1–1¼ hours. The bread is easier to slice if allowed to cool, but it's crumbly and delicious when spread with butter and eaten warm.

Makes a 9 × 5–inch loaf.

Barmbrach

2 cakes or 2 envelopes dried yeast
¼ cup warm water
¾ cup packed brown sugar
2 teaspoons salt
½ cup (1 stick) plus 2 tablespoons unsalted butter, melted

1½ cups milk, warm
4 large eggs, lightly beaten
6 cups all-purpose flour, or more as needed
½ teaspoon nutmeg, grated
2 cups currants or black raisins
1 large egg for glaze
2 tablespoons water

With 2 tablespoons of butter, grease two 5 × 9–inch loaf pans.

In a small mixing bowl, sprinkle the yeast over the warm water and leave until dissolved and bubbly. Meanwhile, in a saucepan, gently warm the milk. When bubbles form around the edge, pour the milk into a large mixing bowl and in it dissolve the sugar, salt, and melted butter. Stir in the yeast mixture and eggs. Gradually add the flour, nutmeg, and currants or raisins, beating until smooth. Add enough of the flour to form a soft dough that comes away from the sides of the bowl. Turn the dough out on a floured board and knead until smooth and elastic. Return the dough to the bowl, cover loosely, and let rise in a warm place until doubled in bulk, about an hour.

Punch the dough down, divide in half, shape into loaves, and place in the greased pans. Cover and let rise again until doubled in bulk.

Preheat the oven to 350 degrees.

When the dough has doubled, bake for 30 minutes. To make the glaze, mix together the egg and cold water. Brush over the loaves during the last 5 minutes of baking.

Makes 2 5 × 9–inch loaves.

Mary Rotundo's Friones and Gnocchi

My Italian grandmother had a very large family. Family, food, and love were her life. I remember once when I was two years old, my mother caught me drinking wine, and my, she had a fit.

My grandmother was there and said, "Leave her alone. A little wine's not going to hurt her!" That's probably the reason I have such a good tolerance for wine now. I started early, thanks to my grandmother!

She used to cook all kinds of wonderful things. My mother said that when she was growing up, she could always tell if her mother was sick or not by whether or not she could smell wonderful bread and pies being baked. It was such a big family that my grandmother would have to make a slew of pies for one meal. She had eleven children, and my grandfather was always bringing people home to eat, too. I guess thirteen people wasn't quite enough to keep him happy.

My grandmother was born in Italy and came here when she was a little girl. We grew up with both my grandmothers, in the little town of Gouverneur, New York, which is way upstate. My Italian grandfather went upstate first and opened up a store, which grew into a car dealership and a hotel and an airport. I was often at the hotel, and I was around food a lot. If the chef wasn't there, my mother and my grandmother and my aunt would fill in.

The meals were gigantic. There'd be several kinds of pasta with different sauces. There'd be a chicken dish, or calamari, in a tomato sauce, and potato salad Italian-style, which is not mayonnaise-based but olive oil based—it's wonderful! And an unusual dish that was a strange conglomeration of fresh beans, potatoes, and eggs—like an omelet. There was wine at every meal.

The cooking my grandmother did in a normal day was what most people would call a holiday meal. So at holidays, she really had to go crazy. One special thing she made for the kids was loaves of bread in different shapes. They could be animals or, at Christmas, wreaths. There was food around me in one form or another all during my childhood. My grammar school was right near the hotel, and I'd come home and go into the kitchen. I was so small that I used to have to pull myself up on the ice cream freezer and then drape myself into it with my legs totally up in the air. I used to make ice-cream sandwiches out of two graham crackers with about three tons of ice cream in between. It was really great having my grandparents' hotel to go to after school. But that was a long, long time ago.

—*Barbara Hendra*

Friones

Dough

5 pounds all-purpose flour
1 teaspoon salt
1 dozen large eggs
1½ cups milk

5 tablespoons unsalted butter
3 cakes fresh yeast
1 teaspoon vegetable oil

Filling

48 ounces ricotta cheese
6 large eggs
⅓ cup fresh parsley, chopped

¼ cup grated Romano cheese
1 teaspoon salt
¼ teaspoon pepper

To make the dough, in a small saucepan, heat the milk until warm enough to dissolve 4 tablespoons of butter and the yeast. Set aside.

In a large mixing bowl, sift together the flour and the salt, then make a nest in the flour. Add the eggs, one at a time, mixing with your hands. Then add the milk slowly, gradually mixing in the flour from the sides of the nest. Knead the dough until smooth and elastic. Bless the dough! Brush with the vegetable oil. Cover with a clean dish towel and let rise in a warm place until doubled in bulk, about 1 hour.

Heat the oven to 350 degrees. With 1 tablespoon of butter, lightly grease a baking sheet.

Meanwhile, to make the filling, in a large mixing bowl combine the ricotta, eggs, parsley, Romano cheese, salt, and pepper.

Punch down the dough, divide into fourths, turn out each section onto a floured board or cloth, and roll it out into a large circle. Place the filling on one side of the dough, fold over the other half, and press the edges closed. Place the loaves on the baking sheet and bake for 45–60 minutes, or until brown. Cut into slices and serve.

Makes 4 loaves.

Gnocchi

6–8 potatoes, peeled
3–4 cups all-purpose flour, sifted
1 or 2 large eggs
1 teaspoon salt

5 quarts water
Spaghetti sauce to taste
Romano cheese to taste

In a large saucepan, boil the potatoes, then rice them into a large bowl. Stir in the eggs and flour, mixing well. Add only enough flour to make the dough soft and smooth, yet still sticky. Divide the dough into 4 pieces and roll each one out on a floured board into a long cylinder one-half inch in diameter. Cut off 1–inch lengths from the cylinders. Place each piece against the inner curved part of a fork and press each against the prongs to create a crescent shape with a ridged surface on one side.

In a large pot, bring salted water to boil. Drop about 12 gnocchi at a time into the boiling water and cook until the pieces rise to the top, about 3–5 minutes. Remove them with a slotted spoon, drain them, and place them in a bowl. Add your favorite spaghetti sauce and sprinkle with Romano cheese.

Makes 8 servings.

Great-Aunt Bonnie's Chicken-Fried Steak

I'm from Texas and the women on my mother's side of the family were wonderful cooks. They were all big women—not fat, but large, powerful; what Texans call "big-boned." I'm amazed when I see pictures of them as young women, because no one today has hands as large as theirs. My grandmother, Beulah, died before I was born, but my great-aunt Bonnie is still living, and some of my best memories of kitchens and food center around her.

It seemed that something was always frying. My brother and I do sound effects of cooking in Texas: *Plop! Chhhuuuuuuuuuuuu!* That's the sound of food hitting hot grease, in case you didn't recognize it. Everything was breaded. I don't think I had broiled or baked food until I got to college. I thought everyone ate the way we did at Aunt Bonnie's.

Most of the food was grown in the garden or on the farm, including the meat. A cow you got to know one week might end up as dinner the next. You were always eating something named Flossie, or Bossie. Chicken-fried steak, fried okra, fried potatoes, fresh tomatoes from the garden, green beans Aunt Bonnie'd canned herself, and maybe peach cobbler and homemade ice cream for dessert—that was a typical Sunday meal. Afternoons following these meals were incredibly lazy. I get sleepy just *thinking* about all that food!

It amazes me to think about how many people Aunt Bonnie used to cook for on Sundays. Sometimes as many as forty people would show up at some point in the day. One time she confessed to me that as much as she loved to see company come, she was always happier to see them go. (She was very practical about it all.) She put so much care into the food, but always got a little uncomfortable when you made a big fuss about it.

My memories of eating ice cream with Aunt Bonnie are more private, more special. Aunt Bonnie, my brother, and I spent lots of time around a big bowl of ice cream. In the spring we'd pick an afternoon to help her move heavy furniture for spring cleaning. We'd do a room, have a bowl of ice cream, do another room, have another bowl of ice cream. My mother died when I was eight, and Aunt Bonnie is one of the few people around who knows all the family history. My brother and I used to use this time around ice cream to ask questions about our mother, to find out what she was like as a girl, and things like that.

I don't cook very much, but every once in a while, I get the urge for real Texas food. I get out some of her recipes. It's a good way to remember things. It helps me remember how far I am from home.

—*Tim Powers*

Chicken-Fried Steak

1 pound round steak
1 cup milk
1 cup all-purpose flour

1½ cups vegetable oil
Salt and pepper to taste
Cream gravy (recipe follows)

With a wooden mallet or the flat side of cleaver, pound the steak well to tenderize it, then cut it into cubes. Pour the milk into a shallow pan and season with salt and pepper. Dip the pieces of meat in the milk mixture and then dip them in the flour.

In a heavy-gauge skillet, over medium-high heat, warm the vegetable oil until very hot. Drop the pieces of meat in the hot oil, and fry on both sides until golden brown. Drain on paper towels, then arrange on a serving platter and cover with gravy.

Makes 3 to 4 servings.

Cream Gravy

2 tablespoons meat drippings
1 tablespoon all-purpose flour

1 cup milk
Salt and pepper to taste

Pour off all but 2 tablespoons of oil from the skillet. Add a heaping tablespoon of flour, and stir well over low heat. Gradually add the milk, stirring constantly, until the mixture thickens. Season with salt and pepper to taste.

Makes 4 servings.

Fruit-Flavored Homedone Ice Cream

3 large eggs, well beaten
1 cup sugar
13½–ounce can evaporated milk
13½–ounce can sweetened
  condensed milk

Half a 3–ounce box fruit-flavored
  Jell-O
1½ pints heavy cream
Milk to fill

In a large mixing bowl, mix together the eggs, sugar, evaporated milk, condensed milk, Jell-O powder, and heavy cream. Pour the mixture into the container of an ice cream freezer. Fill with milk and freeze according to the manufacturer's directions.

Makes 8 servings.

Grandma Lehotan's Poppy Seed Cakes

The most interesting thing about Grandma's kitchen was her stove. This was one of the delights of my youth. My grandparents lived on a farm in Vassar, Michigan, and my grandmother had this huge stove that was made of blue porcelain and stainless steel. My grandfather got it for her when they were in Illinois, and they kept it with them all their lives. The stove used wood and coal, and you really had to be a craftsman to use it. It served two purposes: it heated up the kitchen and it cooked the food. It had a gauge that went from one to twelve, and if you stoked it properly, you could control the drafts to get the proper oven temperature. It was a huge, fantastic thing, and it created the heat and food that made the kitchen the focal point of my grandmother's house. Everybody gathered there. There were always three kettles of water steaming away on the stove. The water moistened the air and kept it warm. They didn't have running water when I was younger, so the hot water was also used for washing up. It was just beautiful. Theirs was a real working farmhouse. They had outhouses until I was a teenager. I think it was a two-holer. And they really did have a Sears catalog there—to read or use!

Almost all of Grandma's food was fresh from the farm. She baked twice a week—breads and cakes. I especially loved her poppy seed cakes. For years she used to bake and can her own meat. She slaughtered her own chickens. She made her own ketchup and her own dill and bread-and-butter pickles from the garden. Their farm was also a dairy farm, and their main crop was potatoes. My grandmother was a very religious Catholic. We always had fish on Fridays and we always said grace before the meal. One of the traditions we had at her house was that there were always two tables because there were so many of us. In the dining room there was the main long table, and that was for the parents and grandparents and one or two of the older cousins. All the other cousins sat at the table in the kitchen, and we all served each other.

The walnut crescents and the poppy cakes go way back in my grandmother's family. She brought these Slovak recipes over with her when she came to America. Before World War I, what is now Czechoslavakia was primarily two separate states, Bohemia and Slovakia. The Czechs in Prague, the capital of Bohemia, tended to be intellectuals and artisans. The Slovaks were mostly farmers. Slovakia is very mountainous. My grandmother grew up on a farm near the town of Siroki. She came here when she was sixteen and lived with her sister in Detroit until she met my grandfather—who was from her hometown. All her life, she kept in touch with her Slovak relatives. She was a very warm-hearted person. In the picture I gave you, she has just arrived in this country.

—*Janet Andrew*

Poppy Seed Cakes

12 tablespoons (1½ sticks)
  unsalted butter
2 cups lukewarm milk
½ cup sugar
2 teaspoons salt

1 cake fresh yeast
2 large eggs
½ cup shortening
4 cups all-purpose flour
½ cup poppy seeds

With 2 tablespoons of butter, grease a large bowl.

In a second large mixing bowl, mix the milk with the sugar and salt. Crumble in the yeast and stir until dissolved. Stir in the eggs, shortening, and flour. Knead until the dough is soft and elastic. Place it in the greased bowl, and turn it to coat. Cover with a clean kitchen towel and place in a warm spot for 2 hours, or until doubled in bulk.

Punch down the dough and allow it to rise again for 45 minutes.

Preheat the oven to 350 degrees. With 2 tablespoons of butter, grease 2 baking sheets.

Roll the dough out into a rectangle on a floured board. Spread the remaining butter over the top of the rolled dough. Sprinkle with the poppy seeds. Cut into ½–inch strips and roll each one into a spiral, jelly roll style. Place on the greased baking sheets and bake for 45 minutes, until golden brown.

Makes about 4 dozen.

Walnut Crescents

4 cups all-purpose flour
1 cake or 1 envelope dried yeast
1 pound unsalted butter
Pinch of salt
1 cup sour cream
1 teaspoon vanilla extract

3 large eggs, separated
½ cup walnuts, chopped
1 pound dates, chopped
1 pound (4 cups) confectioners'
  sugar

In a large mixing bowl, combine the flour, yeast, butter, and salt, using a fork as if you were making pie dough. In a separate bowl, beat together the sour cream, egg yolks, and vanilla extract. Stir into the flour mixture, mixing well. Work the mixture with your hands until it is stiff enough for your fingers to leave marks. Divide in two, form into rolls, and wrap in wax paper or plastic wrap. Refrigerate overnight or for at least several hours.

When ready to bake, preheat the oven to 375 degrees.

Beat the egg whites until stiff. Add the chopped walnuts and dates, mixing well.

Sift half of the confectioners' sugar on a board. Remove half of the dough from the refrigerator and roll it out on top of the sugar to about ⅛–inch thickness. Cut into elongated triangles, spread each with 1 teaspoon of the nut mixture, and roll into crescents. You have to work quickly before the dough softens. Place on ungreased cookie sheets and bake for 15 minutes. Repeat with the other half of the dough. Cool on wire racks.

Makes about 5 dozen crescents.

An English Grandmother's Italian Meatballs

My grandmother was born in England, in Newcastle-upon-Tyne, so she's a Geordie, which is the nickname for the people in Northern England. Her father's favorite poet was Robbie Burns, and she was named after Burns's poem "Jessie." My grandmother's brothers were the famous Five Smith Brothers, "Mr. and Mrs. Smith's Five Little Boys." They were a very famous singing group in England. My grandmother cooked in two styles, English and Italian. Her own mother taught her the English recipes, and she got her Sicilian cooking from her mother-in-law, who taught her how to cook to please her husband. She used to make a magnificent Christmas Eve fish dinner, with delicious fried fish, octopus, and squid—Italian-style—called calamari.

We always went to my grandparents' on Christmas Day. We'd have a big dinner and rush over to the tree, which was always loaded with presents. Every part of the house was decorated, and you could smell her nice Snow Cookies baking in the kitchen. That's a shortbread cookie with sugar on top. And she made fabulous desserts. She used to make trifle, a layered custard pudding with jam inside. It's authentic English. And she did a Yorkshire pudding that she got from her mom. She was famous for her sfingi, which are like zeppoli—deep-fried dough with powdered sugar. They were hot and delicious. They melted in your mouth. She also made her own cannolis.

Sometimes she would make her own steak and kidney pie. I used to help her in the kitchen. She would let me help with the hors d'oeuvres and salads, but only she could do the spaghetti sauce. She made her own sauce by the gallon, and she was very fussy about it.

Everyone wanted to eat a lot at my grandmother's table, and she encouraged a lot of good, hearty eating. Even my grandfather, who was a doctor, used to say, "You've got to be chubby!" My grandmother would laugh and serve you up some more.

We called my grandmother Nana. She lives with my parents now, and I get to see her a lot. Nana has been all over the world and she sure knows how to tell a good story—in a proper British accent, of course. She's one strong lady. And she's been a wonderful character in my life and a great influence on me. I've always felt close to Nana, since I was a little girl. And I think that's made me a better cook and a better wife. Between my grandmother and my mother, I've learned a lot in the kitchen. I'm a pretty good cook myself!
—*Suzanne Andersen*

Italian Meatballs and Sauce

Sicilian Tomato Sauce

1½ pounds neck of lamb, cut
    into small pieces
¼ cup olive oil
6 cups onions, peeled and
    chopped
2 cloves garlic, crushed and
    peeled
2 tablespoons sugar
3 tablespoons dried basil leaves
1½ tablespoons oregano

2 teaspoons salt
1 teaspoon garlic salt
¼ teaspoon pepper
Pinch of garlic powder
1 bunch parsley, chopped
1 cup Italian red wine
2 28–ounce cans Italian-style
    tomatoes
3 6–ounce cans tomato paste

Meatballs

2 pounds beef, ground
¼ pound veal, ground
¼ pound pork, ground
6 large eggs
¾ cup Italian seasoned
    breadcrumbs
¼ cup Parmesan cheese, freshly
    grated
1½ cups onion, peeled and finely
    chopped

2 tablespoons parsley, finely
    chopped
2 cloves garlic, crushed and
    peeled
1½ teaspoons salt
½ teaspoon black pepper
½ cup olive oil for browning
2 pounds spaghetti or macaroni
    shells, cooked

To make the sauce, in a large heavy pot or Dutch oven, over medium heat, brown the lamb in the olive oil. When browned on all sides, add the onions and garlic. Saute until the onions and garlic are golden brown. Stir in the sugar, basil, oregano, salt, garlic salt, pepper, and garlic powder. Cook, stirring for about 2 minutes, then stir in the parsley, wine, tomatoes, and tomato paste. Bring to boil, reduce the heat, cover, and simmer for 70 minutes.

While the sauce cooks, make the meatballs. In a large mixing bowl, combine beef, veal, and pork. Work in the eggs, and then add the breadcrumbs and Parmesan cheese, combining thoroughly. Add in the onion, parsley, garlic, salt, and pepper. Shape into balls. In a large heavy-gauge skillet, heat the olive oil and brown the meatballs. When browned on all sides, drain on paper towels. Add to the tomato sauce and cook for an additional hour. Serve with spaghetti or macaroni shells.

Makes 8 to 10 servings.

Marjorie Dwyer's Sausage Stuffing and Banana Bread

I remember my grandmother's banana bread. In fact, I remember helping her make it. She would give me special jobs. She had a little antique jar with a crank on it, and I would put the nuts in it. It had these little teeth that would break them up, and they'd go into the bottom of the jar, and you could screw off the cap and pour them into the batter. She got the jar from her mom. I guess it was just an old-fashioned nut grinder, but we called it a nut jar and I really loved it. When I made banana bread with Grandma, I had to make sure to stir it lightly. If you stirred it too much, it would get too wet, and Grandma would look over at me and say, "Now stir it lightly—it can work out better by itself." She lived in Chicago, and we were about two hours from her. She would always make banana bread when we were coming. The whole house would smell wonderful. One time, my mom was baking a banana bread at our house. As I arrived home from school, the whole house smelled like Grandma's, and so I thought she was there for a surprise visit.

She was always baking, all the time. She'd have coffee cake or cookies or Irish soda bread. She'd add a lot of fresh fruit and cinnamon and spices to her cakes. Many of her recipes required nutmeg, and she loved to use fresh nutmeg and grate it herself. I'd help Grandma in the kitchen at Thanksgiving and Christmas. She would sew up the turkey with a needle and thread. And she always had really good stuffing. She'd put sausages and raisins in it to give it her special flavor. We would crumble up the bread the night before and lay it on the counter and let it dry out. Then she'd season it. It's much better than croutons you'd buy in a box.

She was very into coffee cake and tea. She used to "hot the pot." She liked her tea nice and hot, so before she made tea in a pot, she'd first pour boiling water in so that the ceramic would get hot. Then she'd pour it out again and brew tea. That's a real tea-lover! Whenever we had coffee cake with her, the grownups would all have tea, and she'd let me have "Teaunk." It's the funniest thing because "Teaunk" was mostly milk, but she'd add a little tea in it to make me feel special. That way, I could drink tea too, like the adults. She was always thinking of things like that to make us feel comfortable and make our visits with her extra special.

My grandmother grew up in Chicago. She lived in the house that her dad built during the Depression, so she's got a lot of memories around her. She's still living there now.

—*Sarah Caitlin Krier*

Banana Bread

½ cup (1 stick) plus 1 tablespoon
   shortening
1 cup sugar*
2 large eggs at room temperature
1 cup mashed ripe bananas
   mixed with 1 teaspoon lemon
   juice

2 cups all-purpose flour
1 tablespoon baking powder
½ teaspoon salt
1 cup nuts, chopped

*If you wish, you can reduce the sugar by up to a half.

Preheat the oven to 350 degrees. With 1 tablespoon of shortening, grease, and then flour a 9 × 5–inch loaf pan.

Cream together the shortening, sugar, and eggs. Stir in the mashed bananas. Set aside.

Sift together the flour, baking powder, and salt. Quickly and lightly stir this into the banana mixture. Do not overmix. Pour into the prepared pan and bake for 1 hour. Cool on a wire rack.

Makes one 9 × 5–inch loaf

Sausage Stuffing

1 large loaf day-old white bread,
   or a combination of white and
   whole wheat, sliced
1 pound pork sausage (bulk,
   sage-flavored is nice)
1 medium onion, peeled and
   finely chopped
3–4 stalks celery, finely chopped

¾ cup black raisins, or a mixture
   of golden and black raisins
¾ cup walnuts, chopped
1 large egg
1 11–ounce can chicken broth
½ teaspoon sage
½ teaspoon salt, optional

If the bread is on the fresh side, let the slices sit exposed to the air overnight, or pop the slices in a 250 degree oven for 10 minutes. Find a helpful little kid in the family to tear the bread into little cubes, leaving the crusts on the bread. You should end up with a large mixing bowlful of stale bread cubes.

In a heavy-gauge skillet, cook the sausage, crumble it, and remove it to a smaller bowl lined with paper towels to absorb the fat. In the same skillet, saute the chopped onion and celery until tender and transparent.

Toss the cooked onion, celery, and sausage into the bread mixture. Add the raisins and walnuts. Beat the egg lightly and thin with a little chicken broth. Add salt and sage to this liquid, and then add this liquid to the bread mixture. Use more chicken broth, if needed, to keep the mixture just moist enough to be sticky but not mushy. The stuffing is now ready to be lightly packed into the neck and body cavity of a turkey.

Makes stuffing for a 10 to 15–pound turkey.

Uncle Alan's Curried Goat and Rice and Peas

Uncle Alan lives in Jamaica. He is an international lawyer, so he travels a lot. We usually get to see him at least twice a year, since he likes to stay at Mom's house when he's in New York. He says it's more comfortable. I guess the curried goat dish got to be known as "Uncle Alan's Curried Goat" because of the time he came to stay with us and decided he wanted make a West Indian dinner. We hadn't had goat for a long time, so our mouths were watering! Goat is sort of like lamb, but tougher, so it needs several hours of steaming it down until it's tender. Well, we all forgot that West Indian men like their food *hot*. Uncle Alan had put a lot of pepper in the mixture while he was cooking, and then added hot sauce on top. Everyone's tongue was burned, and we all were drinking water continuously! Now, everytime I see a plate of curried goat, I reach for the water!

Another dish he used to make was rice and peas. My mom would make it too. Rice and peas is always served in a traditional West Indian home on Sundays and holidays. When I was a child, I remember helping my mom grate the coconut to get the milk, and washing the peas to remove any dirt and twigs. To get the milk from the coconut, you squeeze the grated coconut vigorously, and then strain the liquid you get from that into a bowl. You repeat the process several times, until the moment you combine the coconut milk and water and peas, and boil them until they are ready. Some people add a piece of salt pork, but we don't. We make it just like that. Delicious!

—*Beverly Ffolkes Bryant*

Curried Goat

5 pounds goat meat, including
*   ribs and neck (ask your*
*   butcher to prepare the meat)*
Salt and pepper to taste, plus 1½
*   tablespoons pepper*
Paprika to taste
5½–6½ cups water

4–5 tablespoons curry powder
3 onions, peeled and chopped
1 green pepper, chopped
3 tomatoes, chopped
3 large potatoes, peeled and
*   cubed*

Season the goat meat with salt, pepper, and paprika to taste. Place in a large pot with 3–4 cups of water, cover, and simmer over very low heat for 3 hours or until the meat is tender. Then add the green pepper, tomatoes, potatoes, onions, curry powder to taste, and 1½ tablespoons pepper. Add 1½ cups of water to the mixture. Cover and simmer until the potatoes are soft.

Makes 12 servings.

Rice and Peas

1 cup black-eyed peas (also
*   known as cow peas) or pink*
*   kidney beans, dried*
Ham knuckle, optional
2 cups water
2 cups coconut milk from
*   one-half grated coconut, or*
*   from 2 cups packaged*
*   coconut, shredded*
*   (instructions follow)*

1 small onion, peeled and diced
1 or 2 stalks scallion, finely
*   chopped*
Thyme to taste
Salt to taste
2 cups rice, uncooked

Cover the peas or beans in water and soak overnight. In the morning, discard the water. (If using a ham knuckle, place it in a large stock pot and cover it with cold water, and boil it for approximately one hour. Then discard the water.) In the same stock pot, place the peas or beans in 2 cups of water with the ham knuckle and cook over medium heat. When the peas or beans are slightly tender, after approximately 10 minutes, add the coconut milk, onion, scallion, thyme, and salt.

The black-eyed peas will take a total of 45 minutes, and the beans 1¼ hours to cook. When you can easily mash one pea or bean between your fingers, add the rice and cook until the rice is done, about 30–35 minutes.

Coconut Milk

The coconut milk used in this recipe is not the liquid found in the coconut but is extracted from grated coconut. To do this, follow either of these methods:

(1) Grate the interior of half a coconut. Cover the shreds with 2 cups of boiling water, cool for a few minutes, and then squeeze the coconut until the water is milky. Strain in a sieve, capturing the coconut milk.

(2) Put 2 cups of packaged coconut shreds, or the grated interior of half a coconut in a blender with two cups of boiling water and process. Strain to remove all the solids from the coconut milk.

Omi's Lentil Soup and Nutty Cake

We all call my grandmother Omi. She's from the part of Rumania that used to be Hungary; it's very near Transylvania. She moved here with her mother and father when she was five. Omi lived down the block from us and would cook for us whenever she got the chance. My brother and I went over quite a lot. She'd always lure us to her house with different delicious foods, like goulash. I love Omi's goulash. The meat is always well-done and flaky, with a lot of dark sauce and whole vegetables, especially onions.

Omi loves to eat good food. She's very particular about how she likes it prepared, too. She even puts salt on her bread. She is an excellent salad-maker, and she eats lots of fresh fruits and vegetables to "stay healthy." She tells me stories of the days when her family ate from their own garden. The black radish is her favorite vegetable, and she always wants me to taste dishes that she's made with that in it. She is partial to all kinds of roots—parsley and celery roots in particular. If you'll notice, in her lentil soup recipe, she calls for six sticks of celery with the leaves *attached*. That's how she gives the soup a distinctive, celery flavor.

My grandmother's philosophy in the kitchen is "quick and simple." But she can whip up the most fantastic and even elaborate meals out of thin air. And she always remembers exactly how you like things—how much butter on your toast, or how much of a helping to serve you. She can tell by looking at your face how hungry you are and what it is you'd love to eat.

Omi and I are the best of friends. I think the reason why is because she's so "with it." Whatever the latest mood or the latest fad is, she understands, and she wants to share in the excitement. My friends always remark on how youthful her spirit is. They're often surprised when she comes out with lines like "I dig it" or "You lucked out!" I'm always so proud to be with her. Being with Omi always means having a wonderful time.

—*Charles Altschul*

Lentil Soup

Ham Stock

4 pounds smoked ham, shank portion
2 gallons water
2 large onions, peeled and halved

6 stalks celery, with leaves attached
1 teaspoon paprika
3 cloves garlic, peeled
A few bay leaves

To make the stock, in a large stockpot, place the ham and 1 gallon of water, and bring to a boil. Pour off the water to avoid oversalty stock. Replace with the remaining gallon of water, bring to a boil once again, and add the onions, celery, paprika, garlic, and bay leaves. Lower the heat and simmer for 2 hours, until the ham is quite tender. Strain the stock and refrigerate. When chilled, skim off and discard the fat that has risen to the surface.

Makes about 8 cups of stock.

Soup

1 cup dried lentils

6 cups ham stock

To make the soup, combine the lentils and ham stock, and simmer for 1½–2 hours, stirring occasionally.

Makes about 4 cups of soup.

Nutty Cake

Cake

2 tablespoons unsalted butter
6 large eggs, separated
1¾ cups superfine sugar

2 cups filberts (hazelnuts), finely ground
½–¾ cup ground Zwieback
1 teaspoon rum

Filling

½ cup (1 stick) unsalted butter
¾ cup sugar
5 ounces (5 squares) sweet or semi-sweet baking chocolate

1 large egg yolk
3 tablespoons raspberry preserves
1 cup walnut halves

Preheat the oven to 375 degrees. With 2 tablespoons of butter, grease the bottom of a 9-inch springform pan.

To make the cake, in a large mixing bowl, beat the egg whites until stiff. Add the sugar gradually and carefully, a few teaspoons at first to keep the egg whites from softening. Beat in the egg yolks one at a time. Fold in the ground filberts, the Zwieback, and the rum. Pour the mixture into the greased pan and bake for about 45 minutes. Remove the cake from the oven, and let cool slightly before removing the rim; let cool thoroughly before removing the bottom.

To make the filling, in a large mixing bowl, cream together the butter and sugar. In a small saucepan, over low heat, carefully melt the chocolate, cool slightly, then slowly add to the butter mixture. Beat in the egg yolk.

Cut the cake in half. Cover both halves lightly with raspberry marmalade and then with the chocolate mixture. Place one half of the cake on top of the other and cover the cake with the remaining chocolate mixture. Decorate with walnut halves.

Makes one 9-inch round cake.

Grandma Mimi's Chewy Oatmeal Cookies and Buckwheat Pancakes

My grandmother lives at home with my mother and me. When I was in college a few years ago, she used to tell me that she never thought she'd make it to see my graduation. But she's done much more than that. She's ninety-four years old and just as fit as a fiddle. She still has her driver's license, and she plays bridge with the other ladies in our town and wins pennies from ladies much younger than herself. She still does lots of cooking at our house, and I'm lucky to be able to learn from her now. We call her Mimi, and we love her very much.

The best thing about visiting Mimi when I was a little girl was her chewy oatmeal cookies. I remember getting tins of them when I was at summer camp. My cabinmates were absolutely crazy about them, so I had to write home for another tin. My mother recently figured out how many calories there are in a batch of my grandmother's oatmeal cookies. When she told my grandmother that there were 5,366 calories in one batch, my grandmother asked, "Does that make them taste worse, or better?" I think it makes them taste even better!

Mimi likes her food very well done. She has that philosophy about fruit. She won't touch a banana until it's really flecked with brown, and she won't open a canteloupe until it is almost squishy. You'll sometimes see a melon in the refrigerator with a note that says "Mimi," pinned on with a pearl-handled hat pin. You don't touch that melon!

Everyone was always begging Mimi for her buckwheat pancakes. You need a small amount of cultured starter to make them, so she kept a little container of batter from the last batch in the refrigerator to make more. When I used to eat those pancakes, I'd think that some of the molecules of that batter must be from batches she'd made decades ago! They have a really distinctive, tangy flavor.

My grandmother attended Slippery Rock College in Pennsylvania in the 1920s and got her teaching degree there. It was a coed college, but the male and female students were required to walk on different specified sides of the street, and even had different doorways to the school buildings. My grandmother loves to talk about her college days, and she is very proud that Slippery Rock has become a well-known football school. She still has a school pennant on the wall in her room!

—*Amy Appleby*

Chewy Oatmeal Cookies

4 cups *quick-cooking* oats
2 cups *brown sugar*
1 cup *vegetable oil*
2 large *eggs, well beaten*

1 teaspoon *salt*
1 teaspoon *vanilla extract*
1 cup *black raisins*

In a large mixing bowl, combine the oats, brown sugar, and oil, and let stand overnight.

When you are ready to bake, preheat the oven to 375 degrees.

Stir the eggs, salt, vanilla extract, and raisins into the oat mixture, mixing well. Drop the dough by tablespoonfuls 2 inches apart onto ungreased cookie sheets. Bake for 8–10 minutes.

Makes 4 dozen cookies.

Buckwheat Sourdough Pancakes

Sourdough Starter

½ cup *unseasoned breadcrumbs*
1 cup *milk, scalded*
1 cake, *fresh, or 1 envelope dried yeast*

½ cup *lukewarm water*
1¾ cups *buckwheat flour*

To make the sourdough starter, in a mixing bowl, soak the breadcrumbs in the scalded milk, then cool to lukewarm. In a separate bowl, dissolve the yeast in the warm water. Stir the yeast into the breadcrumb mixture, mixing well. Add the buckwheat flour, stirring well. Cover loosely and allow to stand for forty-eight hours. Remove one cup of the starter and store it in a tightly closed container in the refrigerator for future use. Use the remaining 2 cups of starter to make pancake batter (recipe follows).

Makes about 3 cups of starter.

To refresh the starter: The night before making pancakes, empty the refrigerated starter into a large mixing bowl. Add 1½ cups of warm water and 2 cups of flour. Mix thoroughly. The starter will be thick and lumpy, but will be thin and lively by the morning. Cover the bowl with a kitchen towel and leave it in a warm spot overnight. In the morning, remove one cup of this starter and store it in a tightly covered container in the refrigerator for future use. Use the remaining 2 cups of starter to make pancake batter.

Pancake Batter

2 cups *sourdough starter*
1 tablespoon *baking soda*
1 tablespoon *light molasses, or more, to taste*
1 teaspoon *salt*

1 large *egg, beaten*
2 tablespoons *vegetable oil*
Vegetable oil for greasing griddle or skillet

Gently blend together until smooth 2 cups of starter, baking soda, molasses, salt, egg, and 2 tablespoons of oil. The soda will cause a foaming action and the batter will increase in bulk. Allow the batter to rest for a few moments.

Meanwhile, heat a griddle or heavy-gauge skillet, and lightly brush it with oil. Drop the batter by spoonfuls on the hot surface and bake until brown on both sides.

Makes 16 to 20 pancakes.

Grandma Hepford's Oyster and Chestnut Stuffings

Woodland Studio 4828 Woodland Ave.

My grandmother lived in a large old house outside of Philadelphia. She had a large kitchen with a white porcelain sink and a wooden drainboard. There were cupboards above and cupboards below where she kept her spices and other goodies. And there was a separate pantry that led to the back door. That's where she kept her icebox. We ate breakfast in the breakfast room, and had all our other meals in the dining room proper. Every day my grandmother would sit at the phone and call the market for her day's menu. Everything she made was made with fresh fruits and vegetables.

My grandmother made a fantastic Brown Betty and a Floating Island to beat the band. Those were big favorites in the family. And if there was ever any rice left over from dinner, I got served it for breakfast, cold, with milk and sugar. That was a special treat, and I'm pretty sure it's a Pennsylvania custom.

My grandmother was an excellent cook, but she was not raised to cook, by any means. She had to learn all that after she was married. She tells me that *her* mother had three kitchens—on the different levels of her townhouse in Philadelphia. My great-grandmother descended only once in her life to the first of these three kitchens to see what was going on. Cooking just wasn't her job.

My grandfather used to get me to eat bread and butter by buttering the bread and then taking a knife and drawing little squares on it that he'd say were little houses. Then he'd sprinkle it with sugar. Otherwise I wouldn't touch it. My grandfather would say grace before meals. He was the son of a lay minister, so of course the grace went on interminably. Grace we had. Never a meal without grace!

I do a lot of cooking, and I use my grandmother's recipes, especially for the holidays. These dressings, as with many traditional American recipes, were at one time considered normal, mainstay flavors, at least in that part of the country. But these days, when someone takes the time to prepare one of the more traditional recipes, the flavors seem unusual, very original, and decidedly delicious.

—*Shirley Moulton*

Oyster Stuffing

Shirley: The Philadelphia dressings for turkey are very different from dressings made in other parts of the country. In New England, they usually use a bread dressing—except in Boston, where, because of the Irish influence, they often use a potato dressing. In the South, it's always cornbread. But Philadelphians are particular to the oyster and chestnut dressings. This tradition goes back a long time.

3 cups soft breadcrumbs
1 tablespoon parsley, chopped
1 teaspoon salt
1/4 teaspoon pepper
A few drops onion juice
21 oysters, shucked
1/4 cup oyster liquor
2 tablespoons unsalted butter

In a mixing bowl, combine the breadcrumbs, parsley, salt, pepper, and onion juice. Clean the oysters of any bits of shell, then add them to the crumb mixture. Heat the oyster liquor, add the butter, and stir until melted. Pour over the crumb mixture and mix thoroughly. Cool completely, then use it to stuff poultry.

Makes about 4½ cups.

Chestnut Stuffing

2 cups chestnuts, boiled and
   peeled
8 cups water
Butter to taste
Salt and pepper to taste
1 cup soft breadcrumbs
1 teaspoon salt
1/4 teaspoon pepper
3 tablespoons unsalted butter
1/4 cup hot milk

In a saucepan, place the chestnuts, cover them with 4 cups of boiling water, and simmer for about 3 minutes. Drain and spread the blanched nuts on paper towels. Let them dry overnight.

The next day, in a saucepan, add the chestnuts and cover with 4 cups of lightly salted boiling water. Cover the pan and simmer for 10–15 minutes. Drain, peel, and mash the chestnuts to a paste, or grind them finely. Season to taste with butter, salt, and pepper.

In a mixing bowl, combine the breadcrumbs, salt, and pepper. In a small saucepan, melt 3 tablespoons of butter in the hot milk, and pour over the breadcrumb mixture. Add the chestnut mixture and mix thoroughly. Cool completely, then use it to stuff poultry.

Makes about 3 cups.

Kitty's Chopped Liver

We called her Nana, but Papa and all her friends called her Kitty, and she was famous, at least in our family, for her wonderful chopped liver.

When I was a little boy, my grandmother lived in an apartment that was not too far from where we lived in Brooklyn. I used to go there by myself when I was about ten or eleven. I'd ride over there on my bicycle to visit, and I'd sit in Nana's kitchen. The building had been built in the late forties, and her kitchen had a very forties look. It was painted all mossy green. She had a big chrome dinette set in the kitchen, with a red formica top that matched the red strip around the perimeter of the linoleum on the floor.

On holidays, I remember Nana cooking at our house. She would come over at Passover and help my mother prepare the Passover *seder*. The house would be all dressed up and the table set with the silver and beautiful china and flowers. Nana would come dressed for the holiday, but she would put on an apron and start making her famous chopped liver. The chopped liver was traditionally served in our family before the *seder* as an appetizer. It was served on small plates, along with gefilte fish, on a bed of lettuce. There were also large platters of fruits and nuts out for the guests to have as they arrived, and we would have some wine before we began. We had a large group—maybe sixteen people in the immediate family.

Nana would put a lot of extra rendered chicken fat into the chopped liver because she said it made the liver nice and creamy. Rendered chicken fat is called schmaltz in Yiddish, and that's how we get the word "schmaltzy"— meaning sentimental. It's just all buttered up and almost overrich. She used a lot of salt too, which made it all the more delicious. I've cut down on the salt and fat somewhat in my version of the recipe.

Nana's baked spaghetti was another favorite side dish. She would serve it with a steak or hamburger. It's one of the dishes my mother still makes often, and I make it too. The best thing about it is that it's even better reheated. If you make a batch of it, you'll enjoy it for the next few days.

I have many memories of Nana cooking for us, caring for us, singing to us. I remember vividly when she and Papa would come home from a little neighborhood restaurant called the Savoir Tearoom. She had a bracelet with all kinds of charms on it, and I would hear the sound of it, even in my sleep. She'd rattle her bracelets, and I'd come out and say hello and then go back to sleep. She used to sing "Humoresque" to me, and I learned to play the piano in her living room. I have her piano now, and I cherish it. I'm sure these memories will stay with me always.

—*Andrew Rubenoff*

Chopped Liver

1 pound chicken livers
1 large onion, peeled and
 chopped
5 tablespoons schmaltz (recipe
 follows)

4 large eggs, hard-cooked
½ cup griebenes (see schmaltz
 recipe)
1 head iceberg lettuce
White pepper and salt to taste

In a large heavy-gauge skillet, saute the onion in 2 tablespoons of the schmaltz. In a mixing bowl, chop the eggs and add the onions. Add 3 tablespoons of schmaltz to the skillet and, over medium heat, saute the livers until browned but not dry. Remove the livers, cool them, then blend them into a coarse paste. Gradually add them to the eggs and onion, chopping well after each addition. Stir in the griebenes. The consistency should be that of fine-curd cottage cheese. Pull the leaves off the head of lettuce, and rinse and dry them well. Line each salad plate with lettuce leaves. Serve the chopped liver at room temperature on individual beds of lettuce. Sprinkle with white pepper and salt.

Makes 6 to 8 servings.

Schmaltz
Rendered Chicken Fat

Fat and fatty skin from 2 or 3
 chickens

1 onion, peeled and chopped

In a heavy-gauge skillet, over a low heat, add the fat and the skin, cut into pieces about an inch long. When the skin starts to brown, add the onion. Continue cooking, stirring occasionally, until the onion is lightly browned. You will now have liquified chicken fat and bits of crispy skin, called "griebenes." In order to separate the griebenes from the fat and keep it crispy, strain the mixture through a fine strainer or cheesecloth, then cool and refrigerate. Use the schmaltz for flavoring mashed potatoes, chopped liver, or for frying meat dishes.

The griebenes can be used as a flavoring too, such as in the preceding chopped liver recipe. Use according to taste: the more griebenes, the crunchier the chopped liver will be.

Makes about 1 cup schmaltz and 1 cup griebenes, depending upon the size of the chicken.

Baked Spaghetti

½ pound pasta shells or rotelli
½ pound spaghetti
8 cups water
1 tablespoon salt
1 13–ounce can tomato soup
Milk to fill the can

½ cup (1 stick) unsalted butter
½ pound (2 cups) cheddar
 cheese, shredded
¼ cup Romano cheese, freshly
 grated

In a large saucepan, add the water and salt, and bring to a boil. Then, add the pasta and cook for about 8 minutes, or until *al dente*. Drain in a colander.

Preheat the oven to 350 degrees.

Into the same saucepan, add the soup and milk, stirring well. Over low heat, stir in the butter and cheeses, and when well combined, stir in the pasta. Pour into a 10 × 15–inch baking dish. Bake for 45–60 minutes, or until the top is lightly browned. Cut into squares and serve immediately.

Makes 8 servings.

Moravian Christmas Cookies and German Potato Salad

The nice thing about my grandmother's German potato salad is that it can be served hot or cold. We always took it with us on picnics. It travels well in a half bell pepper, and because there is no mayonnaise in it, it won't spoil in the sun. That was fun for us kids because it was in its own vegetable container. We never had a picnic without fried chicken and my grandmother's potato salad.

My grandparents lived in a Moravian community in North Carolina. They still have Moravian churches down there, and they always have these cookies at the reception afterwards. I always got them at Grandma's. We'd bake all kinds of Christmas cookies there, but we had to have these German-Moravian molasses cookies. My grandmother would store them in tins. They keep very well because they are not moist cookies. Now they have reconstructed Moravian settlements in Old Salem, North Carolina, and they package and sell a version of these cookies there as an authentic Moravian item. They've gone commercial on that recipe.

Traditionally, the Moravians would start baking for Christmas the day after Thanksgiving. They'd do their fruit cakes that early too. They would bake for the church, and they would bake for the neighbors, and they would bake for the family. They would just bake and bake and bake.

We used to go down to see my grandmother at Easter or Christmas. She lived on a farm. I was a real city kid from Washington, D.C. Once she sent me out to the chickens to get some eggs. She gave me a little basket and told me how to get them. Now, I thought that eggs only came from stores, but I went out and I got six eggs, and on my way in I dropped one on the kitchen floor. I went and told my grandmother that I had spilled it. I thought we could pick it up again, and it would be all right. The family got a real laugh out of that!

My grandparents were artisans and farmers, so we don't have a lot of heirlooms and silver. But we do have this little kerosene lamp—just an ordinary glass kerosene lamp that went with my great-grandparents in a covered wagon all the way from North Carolina to Indiana and then back. They made the journey to help resettle one of their farmer sons. In those days, *nobody* made that kind of a journey and then came all the way *back*. The lantern is my grandmother's treasured heirloom. I guess it's sort of a symbol of the tenacity and sheer stubbornness of our people.

—*Linda Gottwald*

Moravian Christmas Cookies

2 cups blackstrap or other dark
   molasses
1 cup shortening
1 cup dark brown sugar
2 teaspoons baking soda

1 tablespoon cloves, ground
1 teaspoon cinnamon, ground
1 teaspoon allspice, ground
4 cups all-purpose flour
4 tablespoons unsalted butter

In a large saucepan, over medium heat, warm the molasses, shortening, and sugar, stirring occasionally, until the shortening melts and the sugar dissolves. Remove from the heat and stir in the baking soda, cloves, cinnamon, and allspice, mixing well. Stir in the flour one cup at a time. The dough should be very stiff. Wrap it in wax paper or plastic wrap and chill for at least 3 hours, preferably overnight.

The next day, remove the dough from the refrigerator and let stand at room temperature until soft enough for rolling out.

Preheat the oven to 350 degrees. With the butter, grease several cookie sheets.

With a rolling pin, roll out the dough 1/16–inch thick on a lightly floured board. Cut the dough into stars (a traditional Moravian Christmas shape) or other shapes with cookie cutters. Place on the greased cookie sheets and bake for 8 minutes. Allow the cookies to cool on the sheets before transferring to a rack, as they are very delicate.

Makes 4 to 5 dozen cookies.

German Potato Salad

4 large eggs
14 cups water
5 medium baking potatoes,
   peeled
3/4 cup celery, thinly sliced
1/2 cup green pepper, chopped

1 large onion, peeled and thinly
   sliced
1 teaspoon salt
1 teaspoon black pepper
2½ teaspoons apple cider vinegar
3 sprigs fresh parsley, chopped

In a saucepan, over medium heat, add 6 cups of water and the eggs, bring to a boil, and cook until hard, about 12 minutes. Put the eggs in cold water and peel. In a saucepan, add 8 cups of water and the potatoes, bring to a boil, and cook until soft, about 20 minutes. Drain and reserve one-third cup of the potato broth, mash the potatoes coarsely, and stir into the potato broth. Stir in three of the eggs, well mashed, the celery, green pepper, and onion. Stir together the salt, pepper, and vinegar, and pour over the potato mixture. Arrange in a serving dish, then slice the remaining egg and sprinkle it over the potato salad. Garnish with the parsley and serve immediately, while still hot.

Note: To take the salad on a picnic, chill and pack into halved, seeded green peppers.

Makes 6 to 8 servings.

Grandma Rose's Grated Salad with Sweet and Tart Dressing

My mother's mother was born in 1899 in Russia. No one seems to know exactly where, so we just say "central Russia." She was a teenager when she came here, and she got a job as a seamstress in a coat factory on the east side of Manhattan. She had come over alone. Later she got married and moved to the Bronx near the Grand Concourse where the train goes by. She had three children—my mother and two other girls. I remember her house: My sister and I would hang out the window to watch the train go by, and it looked like you could touch it, it was so close. The train was up on the rails above the ground then, and it would go right by the window.

My grandparents also had a house in the country for a while. All the floors were wood, and my grandmother was always having to take splinters out of my feet. I remember that real well! She would take them out with a needle and a tweezer. The roads there were paved with tar. On a hot summer's day the tar would get hot and bubbly on top of the road. Then, when it would rain and cool off, little bubbles would form on top of the road, and we would pop them all over the place and get covered with tar and get into trouble!

My grandmother always took a lot of vitamins, and she always made what I considered "strange" food. She was the first one to get me started on drinking coffee. In the morning she would get up and have a big glass of coffee that would be one-third milk. My sister and I would each get a glass and we would savor it because we thought it was something special, and we felt very adult. Along with that she used to make a concoction of large-curd cottage cheese, brewer's yeast, and molasses, all mixed together. She would put it on toasted pumpernickel bread and serve it along with the coffee. That was strange, but I really enjoyed it as a kid, and I even have it once in a while today.

She was always working and cleaning. She never really stopped, so the times we would sit down to eat would make up most of the time we spent together. She used to make a special noodle kugel and a great salad with grated vegetables. They had a hard time getting me to eat vegetables when I was a kid, and the only way I would eat them was the way she used to make them, all grated up with a great dressing on them. Overall, Grandma was very conservative, very hard working. She didn't take a lot of time out for fun, fun for the sake of fun. But any spare time she had she spent with family, doing whatever she had to do. It was good enough to be with the whole family; that was her treat. Her family was her life and her world. Even though she never did anything spectacular, or what the world would consider special, I always considered it an adventure to be with Grandma.

—*Stephen Barrett Roth*

Savory Noodle Kugel

1 8–ounce package uncooked egg
   noodles
8 cups water
¼ cup vegetable oil
3–4 tablespoons sugar
4 tablespoons (½ stick) unsalted
   butter
⅓ cup boiling water
8–10 ounces large curd cottage
   cheese

8–10 ounces farmer cheese
8 ounces sour cream
3 large eggs, beaten
1 medium white onion, peeled
   and finely chopped or grated
3–4 sprigs fresh parsley (lower
   stems removed), finely
   chopped
Salt and pepper to taste

In a large saucepan, add water and bring to a boil. Add the noodles, cooking according to package instructions. Drain in a colander.

Preheat the oven to between 325 and 350 degrees. Add the vegetable oil to a 9–inch square baking pan, and coat it well.

In a large saucepan, melt the sugar and butter in the boiling water and add to the noodles. Allow the butter to melt thoroughly. Turn the mixture into a large bowl and stir in the cottage cheese, farmer cheese, sour cream, eggs, onion, parsley, salt, and pepper, using your hands to mix it really well. Pour into the prepared baking pan and bake for about 45 minutes, until the top is moderately brown and crispy. Allow to cool thoroughly and turn out from the pan. Cut into squares with a serrated knife. Reheat the individual portions and serve.

Makes 6 to 8 servings.

Sweet and Tart Vegetable Salad

Salad

¼ small head iceberg lettuce,
   shredded
½ small head red cabbage,
   shredded
4 stalks celery, diced

1 large onion, peeled and diced
1 green pepper, halved and
   seeded
4–6 large carrots, scraped

Dressing

1 cup fresh lemon juice
1 cup olive oil
¼ cup honey
3 tablespoons red wine vinegar

Salad herbs, such as oregano,
   marjoram, tarragon, thyme,
   and basil, to taste
Salt and pepper to taste

In a large bowl, place the lettuce, red cabbage, celery, and onions. Then grate into the bowl the green pepper and carrots. Serve onto salad plates.

Blend thoroughly the dressing ingredients, and dress each serving of salad, saturating well.

Makes 4 to 6 servings.

Barbara Kissel's Easter Strudel

I lived with my grandmother when I was small. We had the biggest kitchen table you ever saw; it could seat twelve people. We had a couch in the kitchen, and it became our living room and dining room. Anyone who came to the house was seated, and there was always food on the table.

Until I was about six years old, we had a dairy. We had ten cows, all with girls' names, like Lillie and Tessie. I was my grandmother's favorite butter-maker, and I would also help her and my mother pick vegetables in our garden.

She raised us on vegetables. We grew our own peppers, and she would often use them to make lecso, which was a delicious vegetable side dish. She would also make wilted lettuce by rendering two slices of bacon and cooking two or three heads of romaine lettuce in the bacon fat until the lettuce wilted. Then she would add vinegar and salt and pepper. I loved it. For breakfast she often made us a big bowl of farina with raisins on top. She would put it in the middle of the table and we would all help ourselves. Sometimes, when she was really ambitious, she would toast bread on her coal stove, melt butter on top of it, smear it with garlic, and serve it with the cereal—farina and garlic bread.

Easter time was especially wonderful. Our table would be laden with food. There would be highly-seasoned sausages called kielbasi, smoked ham, and hard-boiled eggs. I would help her make the kielbasi. Sometimes she would make her special cabbage or apple strudel, which were so delicious that I make both of them to this day.

On Easter day, neighborhood boys would want to come into the house to get something to eat. It was a kind of tradition. But first they would have to sprinkle us with toilet water. That was the ritual. Those were such beautiful days.

—*Barbara Kovan*

98

Fruit Strudel

Strudel Dough*

6 cups all-purpose flour
2½ cups lukewarm water
Pinch of salt

1 tablespoon cider or white
    vinegar
2 tablespoons unsalted butter,
    softened

*This recipe makes enough dough for 12 strudels, each about 18 inches long. You may choose instead to use frozen prepared phyllo pastry, available in most supermarkets.

Fruit Filling

⅓ cup black raisins
1 pound apples, peeled and cored,
    or 1 pound peaches, pitted
3 tablespoons unsalted butter,
    melted
½ cup plain cookie crumbs
⅓ cup walnuts, chopped

Pinch of allspice or nutmeg,
    ground
Cinnamon sugar made of ⅔ cup
    sugar mixed with 3
    tablespoons cinnamon
Confectioners' sugar, for
    sprinkling

To make the dough, in a large mixing bowl, combine the flour, water, salt, vinegar, and 1 tablespoon of butter to make a stiff dough. Knead until the dough is smooth and firm, then divide into 12 pieces. Work with 1 piece of dough at a time, keeping the remaining ones covered with plastic. Pat the dough into a circle, then start gently pushing the sides all around using the heel of your hand. Work the dough, rolling it with a rolling pin and stretching it with your fingers, until it is paper thin and translucent—be careful not to let it tear.

Preheat the oven to 350 degrees.

To make the filling, soak the raisins in hot water until they swell, about 30 minutes. Meanwhile, slice the apples or peaches lengthwise into 6 or 8 slices per piece of fruit.

Brush the dough with the 3 tablespoons of melted butter and sprinkle it with the cookie crumbs. Spread the raisins and walnuts evenly over the dough, then carefully lay a layer of parallel fruit slices on top, piece by piece to prevent tearing the fragile pastry. Leave a margin at either end.

Sprinkle the pastry with the cinnamon sugar, and allspice or nutmeg. Roll into a long cylinder.

Grease the cookie sheet with the remaining tablespoon of softened butter, and place the strudel, seam side down, on the greased sheet. To fit, you may have to bend the strudel into a horseshoe shape. Bake for about 40 minutes. Sprinkle with confectioners' sugar before serving.

Makes 8 servings.

Lecso

1 pound tomatoes, peeled and
    seeded*
3 tablespoons unsalted butter
4 medium onions, peeled and
    sliced
5–6 green peppers, seeded and
    quartered

1–2 cloves garlic, peeled and
    mashed
½ teaspoon sugar
1 teaspoon salt
1 tablespoon paprika
Pepper to taste

Coarsely chop the tomatoes and set aside.

In a 10–inch heavy-gauge skillet, warm the butter and saute the onions until tender, about 10 minutes. Add the garlic and saute gently for another 5 minutes. Then add the tomatoes and sugar, lower the heat, and simmer for 15 minutes. Add the green peppers and simmer, uncovered, for an additional 15–20 minutes.

Makes 6 servings.

*To seed tomatoes, see Tomatoes St. Jacques on page 41.

Grandpa Conner's Oyster Stew

Jan (granddaughter): As a child, I always spent Thanksgiving in Guildford, Maine, on Grandpa and Grandma's farm. My brother Tom and I would huddle in the back of my Uncle John's MG in sub-zero temperatures, as we made the five-hour journey from Boston.

Emily (daughter): Jan was always stuck in the very back cubby hole because she was the tiniest. It was a wonder she had legs at all! One time she could hardly get out because she must have grown some as we were driving! Uncle John's eyes were sticking out of his head because it was so difficult to get her out. He felt sure she had been crippled. It was after that that Jan no longer had to ride in the cubby hole. For years after, though, Grandpa would say, "Oh Janice, you can get in there!" Typical Maine attitude: Nothing is impossible!

Jan: We'd drive up to the isolated farmhouse, and every window would be glowing with light from the fireplace, softened by the heavy frost on the windowpanes. Grandma and Grandpa would be waiting in the open door and we would scramble out of the car, our footsteps crackling across the frozen snow. I can see the sparkling white linen and china, meticulously set up with silverware, as clearly today as I could then. The aroma of Grandpa's stew wafted through the entire house. I'd run over and poke my nose right directly into the steam rising from the pot on the wood stove. The stew had mulled for hours, waiting for us to arrive, and all the while building flavor.

Emily: My mother used to feed all the delinquent and orphaned boys in town, and in return, they would cut firewood. She would spend three hours making biscuits and flapjacks, with real maple syrup, in order to feed them all. Can you imagine how much food boys from fourteen to nineteen years of age eat, especially after they've cut four or five cords of wood?

My mother was originally a Congregationalist, but when she moved up to Guildford, she had to switch over to being Baptist. No one was a Congregationalist in farm country. That was too liberal.

Jan: Grandpa was a champion dancer. Grandma didn't like to dance, so she sat there and knitted. Everybody sat there and knitted, who didn't like to dance. She always had the first waltz and the last waltz. In between, Grandpa capered all night. He never got tired. He used to fox trot in double time. That timing is exactly like the Texas two-step. He would have been one hell of a drummer. He couldn't carry a tune, but the man had a beat! The Baptists didn't like it that Grandma let Grandpa dance, but there was no stopping him. So she made up her mind that she was going to be there with him. The town had a lot to say about that, but they got used to it after a while.

—*Jan Giolito and Emily Sylvester*

Oyster Stew

2 pints oysters with their juice
1 quart milk
2 cups heavy cream

½ cup (1 stick) unsalted butter,
    softened
Salt and pepper to taste
Oyster crackers

In a small saucepan, poach the oysters in their juice just until their edges begin to curl.

Meanwhile, in a double boiler, heat the milk, cream, and butter until the butter is melted and the milk is hot. Add the oysters and their liquid to the milk mixture and keep warm for at least 1 hour. The longer the stew sits, the better the flavor. Season with salt and pepper. Serve with oyster crackers.

Makes 8 servings.

Baking Powder Biscuits

Emily: My mother claims her secret to the best biscuits in town is that she keeps the dough moist and handles it as lightly as she possibly can, not overworking the dough when she rolls it out.

2½ cups all-purpose flour
2½ tablespoons cream of tartar
1¼ teaspoons baking soda

¾ teaspoon salt
2 tablespoons shortening
¾ cup milk

Preheat the oven to 425 degrees.

In a large mixing bowl, sift together the flour, cream of tartar, baking soda, and salt. Work the shortening into the mixture, first using a wooden spoon, then your fingers, pastry blender, fork, or two knives. Stir in enough of the milk to make the dough very moist but not sticky—this is the secret to moist, puffy biscuits.

Turn the dough out onto a very lightly floured board. Knead it up to ten turns and then pat it into a flat circle. With a rolling pin, roll out the dough ½-inch thick. Cut into biscuits with a lightly floured 2-inch round cutter. On an ungreased baking sheet, place the biscuits about 1 inch apart for crispy-crust biscuits, closer together for soft-crust biscuits. Prick the top of the biscuits with a fork. Bake for 10–12 minutes, until golden brown. Remove from the sheet immediately and serve hot.

Note: To make drop biscuits, add a few more tablespoons of milk to the dough and drop by teaspoonfuls onto a greased baking sheet.

Makes 16 biscuits.

Easter Bread and Anisette Cookies

I remember my grandmother's kitchen. It was yellow and had bright lights. My grandmother and my aunts would stand there in colorful aprons—deep purples and greens that reminded me of fruits and flowers—and make my favorite macaroni. They used their thumbs to give the dough a special shape, which my cousin called "little hats." Around holiday times, there was always a flurry of activity. I loved being in the kitchen, and I would stand and watch them cook. I remember the really big pots that only got used on holidays and the smell of the sauce and the taste of it on the wooden spoons that were used to stir it. The spoons gave the sauce a very distinctive flavor.

At Christmas dinner there would be endless courses. Two long tables would be set up—one for the adults and a smaller one on the side for the children. Each child could have one "special dish," like extra sauce, or more macaroni, or more meatballs. After the antipasto and pasta, there would be meatballs, sausage, and rolled beef. The kids would always finish first, and not just because their portions were smaller, but because there were toys upstairs that they wanted to play with.

Easter dinner was at my aunt's house. My grandmother would bring each of us an Easter bread with a colored Easter egg baked inside. She would make twelve of them, one for each child, and also give each child a dollar. We would all wait on line to give her a kiss. She had long white hair that she always wore up in braids and combs. Then she would give us our gift. I would eat the bread immediately. It was very wonderful for my favorite cousin, Frances, and me—we would always share our eggs: I liked the white, and she liked the yellow.

—*Joseph Caputo*

Easter Bread

½ cup (1 stick) plus 2
   tablespoons unsalted butter,
   softened
2 cakes or 2 envelopes dried
   yeast
¼ cup warm water
1 cup scalded milk, slightly
   cooled
½ cup sugar
4 large egg yolks, slightly beaten

¾ teaspoon salt
2 tablespoons candied citron,
   slivered
1 tablespoon candied orange peel,
   slivered
¼ cup black raisins
4 cups sifted all-purpose flour
1 cup confectioners' sugar
1 teaspoon milk
1 uncooked colored Easter egg

With 2 tablespoons butter, lightly grease a baking sheet.

In a small mixing bowl, combine the yeast and water, and set aside. In a large mixing bowl, add the butter to the milk, and stir to melt the butter. Stir in the sugar, egg yolks, salt, citron, orange peel, raisins, and 1 cup of flour. Stir in the yeast mixture, then gradually add the remaining flour, 1 cup at a time, mixing until a firm dough forms.

Turn the dough out on a floured board and knead until it is smooth, about 5 minutes. Shape into a ball, return to the mixing bowl, cover with a dish towel, and allow the dough to rise in a warm place until doubled in bulk, about 1 hour.

Punch the dough down, knead again briefly, and shape into a flat round, reserving two small strips of dough. Place the dough on the prepared baking sheet. Make a depression in the center of the dough as a nest for the egg. Set in the egg, securing it with the two strips of dough. Cover and let rise again until doubled in bulk, about 45 minutes.

Preheat the oven to 350 degrees. Bake the bread for 45 minutes.

Mix together the confectioners' sugar and milk into a stiff glaze.

Remove the bread from the oven, let it cool for 15–20 minutes, then spread with the glaze.

Makes 1 large round loaf.

Anisette Cookies

Dough

3½ cups all-purpose flour
6 large eggs
8 teaspoons baking powder
½ cup sugar

½ cup (1 stick) plus 2
   tablespoons unsalted butter
1 teaspoon anise extract

Glaze

1 tablespoon hot water, or more
   as needed

½ cup confectioners' sugar
Colored sprinkles

Preheat the oven to 350 degrees. With 2 tablespoons of butter, lightly grease 2 baking sheets.

To make the dough, in a large mixing bowl, sift together the flour and baking powder, and set aside. In a saucepan, melt the butter and set aside. Beat the eggs until light. Stir in the sugar, 1 cup of butter, and the anise extract. Stir into the flour mixture. Knead well. Roll teaspoons of the dough into small balls and place them on the prepared sheets. Bake for 10–12 minutes, then cool the cookies on racks.

To make the glaze, stir the water into the confectioners' sugar. Add more water if too thick, more sugar if too thin. Glaze the cooled cookies and decorate with colored sprinkles.

Makes about 4 dozen cookies.

Grandma Lin's Taiwanese Tofu, Pork, and Mushrooms

My grandmother was a very special woman. She was beautiful. Everyone would ask,"Who is that?" and I would say, "That's my grandma!" She was so beautiful; like a Buddha. She was very smart, and very powerful: Everybody obeyed her. My grandfather was a nice, easy man. But everyone was afraid of my grandmother. Only I was her favorite. She died when she was ninety-three years old.

Chinese New Year, which comes in February, was a big holiday. On the last day of the old year, we would eat spinach, for long life. My grandmother would cook a whole fish, including the head and the tail. In Taiwan, it's traditional to have the whole fish. Without the head, it's no good; without the tail, it's no good. You also have to fill the entire table with food. If you do all that, you have lots of luck. On New Year's, no matter how expensive it is, you put plenty of food on the table. You don't have to finish all the food: If there is more food than you can eat, that means you'll have food during the coming year.

My grandmother had nine children. On New Year's, she would put money into rice balls wrapped in corn husk and go to each of her children's homes and give one to each of them. In America, on Christmas, you give presents. We don't. We use money.

My grandmother had had her feet bound when she was very small. It was the custom then. Her feet were only four or five inches long, and she couldn't walk alone. Every time she went walking, she had a son or grandson beside her, sometimes one on each side, to help her and see that she didn't fall. She could only walk very slowly.

I always experienced my family as very warm. The Taiwanese love to cook. They would rather eat than buy clothes. They'd rather put their money into food—education first, and then food! When you cook for someone, you want to show them how special they are, so you cook special food. That's what my grandmother did for us, and that is why my father, who loves to cook, does the same thing. Food tastes so much better when there's love in it . . .

—Joy Chen

Tofu, Pork, and Mushrooms

½ pound boneless pork loin, thinly sliced*
¼ cup light soy sauce
3 sheets flat, dried bean curd (available in Asian groceries)
1 cup water
1 cake deep-fried tofu (available in Asian groceries)
½ cup corn oil
3 strips dried, curly bean curd (available in Asian groceries)
½ cup soy sauce
1 cube yellow rock sugar, or 2 tablespoons granulated white sugar
1 can bamboo shoots
10 dried mushrooms, cut in half
¼ teaspoon five-spice powder, optional (available in Asian groceries or some supermarkets)
1 tablespoon sesame oil
3 tablespoons sesame seeds
2 scallions, cut into 1–inch pieces

In a large mixing bowl, marinate the pork in the light soy sauce for 1 hour. Break the flat sheets of bean curd into pieces about 1 × 2 inches, and soak them separately in one-half cup of water for 45 minutes. Cut the deep-fried tofu into 1–inch pieces and set aside.

Into a 4–quart pot, add the oil and heat over high heat. Drain the flat bean curd, pat it dry with paper towels, then add it to the hot oil. Stir-fry until the bean curd turns light brown, in 4–5 minutes. Pour the bean curd into a strainer, reserving the oil in a bowl for future use. Add 3–4 tablespoons of the reserved oil to the pot, add the curly bean curd, and stir-fry over high heat. Add the drained flat curd and mix together well. Cook for 3 minutes, then add the soy sauce, sugar, deep-fried tofu, and the remaining water. Mix well and add a few more tablespoons water, if necessary. Stir in the bamboo shoots, mushrooms, five-spice powder, marinated pork, and the sesame oil, and stir well. Cover and cook over low heat for 15 minutes, or until the pork is tender. Stir in the sesame seeds and scallions. Remove from the heat and serve immediately.

Makes 8 servings.

*This dish can also be made without meat.

Pork, Shrimp, and Rice Noodles

½ pound boneless pork loin, thinly sliced
¼ cup light soy sauce
5 tablespoons corn oil
2 scallions, cut into 1–inch pieces
2 tablespoons soy sauce
1 tablespoon sugar
1 dozen medium shrimp, peeled and cleaned
2 medium carrots, cut into julienne strips
½ cup water
½ pound bean sprouts
1 teaspoon salt
½ teaspoon pepper
1 package (1 pound) rice sticks (dry white noodles available in Asian groceries)

In a mixing bowl, marinate the pork in the light soy sauce for about 15 minutes. In a separate bowl, cover the rice sticks in warm water and soak them for 10–15 minutes.

Add 3 tablespoons of the oil to a wok, and, over the highest heat, swirl the oil around to coat the entire inside surface. When the oil is quite hot, add the pork and stir-fry until tender, about 4–6 minutes. Remove the pork to a plate, then add the scallions, soy sauce, sugar, and shrimp. Stir-fry until the shrimp turn pink, about 2 minutes. Remove the ingredients from the wok onto the plate with the pork, and set aside.

Add the remaining oil to the wok, and, over the highest heat, add the carrots. Stir-fry for 1 minute, then add the water, bean sprouts, salt, and pepper. Drain the noodles well, then add them to the other ingredients in the wok, and stir-fry for 3–5 minutes. If the mixture seems dry, add 1 or 2 tablespoons more oil. Remove from the heat and place in a large serving bowl. Arrange the pork and shrimp mixture over the noodles and serve immediately.

Makes 5 to 6 servings.

Sauerbraten and Beef Schlapp

The kitchen was the scene of constant activity in the house. I was always hungry, as are all kids, and whenever I would come in from playing outside, or I would come upstairs from practicing the clarinet, I would go into the kitchen to see what was cooking. In fact, I was nicknamed "the pot-cover lifter." I was always eager to have a job to do in the kitchen, like peeling onions or shelling peas. It made me feel I was part of an important process to help prepare the food.

Until I was six, we lived in a very rural area of New Jersey with my grandparents, Opa and Oma. We had a 104 × 104–foot vegetable garden. Living there, I got a great sense of continuity as I watched my mother cooking the vegetables we had grown in our own garden. When I was hungry, my mother would say, "Well, go outside and pick yourself a pepper." There wasn't the option to go down the street to a candy store or pizza parlor.

Opa and I were inseparable. He was a very warm man. We talked constantly and played a lot of games together. He would take me for rides around the countryside in his 1947 Chevy coupe.

After he and my grandmother died, we moved to Brooklyn. I often wish I could move back to that kind of rural life, but so much gets in the way.

My mother was the kind of cook who could take all kinds of scraps—bones, vegetables—left over from a meal, throw them into a pot with some water, onions, and carrots, and make a stock that she would use in the creation of the next dish. Then she would save the leftovers from *that* dish, add some flour and butter, and use this as a basis for the *next* dish. From her I learned how to look into a seemingly empty refrigerator and come up with a meal.

One of the dishes my mother made was a delicious kind of pot roast called sauerbraten. To make a good sauerbraten, she would, first of all, go to a German butcher and say, "I want a pot roast that I'm making as a sauerbraten." And so he would give her a really tough piece of meat. The reason is that you marinate it for three days in a mixture of red vinegar, onion, and juniper berries. By the time the meat gets to be sauerbraten, the marinade has tenderized it. In essence, it's a very inexpensive dish.

The last few years of her life, my mother was in the hospital a lot. She wrote out many of the family recipes and made them into a cookbook for me. It's really nice to have.

—*Gerhardt Koch*

Sauerbraten

Marinating

2–4 pounds beef rump or round
   roast
Wine vinegar to cover

1 large onion, peeled and sliced
10–12 juniper berries
1 bay leaf

Place the beef in a crock with a lid or a Dutch oven. Pour in vinegar to reach halfway, or a little more than halfway, up the roast. Add water to cover and stir. Add the onion, juniper berries, and bay leaf. Cover and turn daily for 2–5 days, depending on the size of the meat. You do not need to refrigerate. Drain the meat well and pat dry.

Cooking

4 tablespoons shortening
1½ cups boiling water
8 whole allspice
3 peppercorns

2 medium onions, peeled and
   halved
4–6 ginger snaps

Over a high heat, seer the meat in the shortening in a crock or a Dutch oven. Then add 1½ cups of boiling water, the allspice, the peppercorns, and the onions. Place the ginger snaps on top of the meat. Cover the meat, lower the heat, and simmer slowly 2–3 hours. Then stir down the ginger snaps to thicken the gravy. Heat through and serve.

Makes 4 to 8 servings.

Beef Schlapp

2–3 pounds shin beef, with
   marrow bone
6–8 cups water
7–8 medium potatoes
4 bunches kohlrabi, or 2 medium
   heads Savoy or white cabbage

6 tablespoons unsalted butter
3 tablespoons all-purpose flour
½ cup water
¼ cup beef stock
Nutmeg, freshly grated, or
   caraway seeds, to taste

Place the meat in a Dutch oven or other heavy pot with a lid. Pour in the water to cover two-thirds of the meat. Cover the container, bring the water to a boil, then lower the heat and simmer for 1 hour.

Cook the potatoes in boiling water. Meanwhile, if using kohlrabi, discard the tough parts of the leaves and tear the rest of the leaves loosely. Pare the skin from the bulbs and cut them into julienne strips. If using cabbage, cut each head into 8 wedges. Drain the potatoes, peel, and set aside.

Add the kohlrabi or cabbage to the meat and cook until tender, about 15–20 minutes. Remove the meat and the bones and set aside. Using a potato ricer, rice the potatoes and add to the vegetable.

In a heavy-gauge skillet, melt the butter and then stir in the flour. Gradually add a half cup of water and the stock, stirring constantly, and cook until thickened and smooth. Stir into the vegetable mixture and simmer for 15 minutes. Return the meat to the mixture and stir well. Heat thoroughly before serving, then sprinkle with freshly grated nutmeg, or caraway seeds, to taste. This dish tastes particularly good served with thick slice of dark bread.

Makes 8 servings.

Anna May's Corned Beef and Cabbage

My great-grandmother, Mary Ellen O'Donnell, and my grandmother, Anna May O'Donnell, were amazing women. My great-grandmother owned the first phone company in Averill Park, New York. She later sold out to Bell Telephone. And then my grandmother owned the first telephone exchange in Albany. It was a kind of answering service.

There is a line of strong women in my family. My grandmother was born on the day that my great-grandfather died. So Anna May grew up without a father. Soon after she married, *her* husband left her, so *my* mother grew up without a father. That makes two generations of women who were the sole support of their families.

My grandmother was not the more usual domestic type of grandmother. She liked order; she was a business-woman. She treated us like "people," even when we were very young. We always had fun with her, but she was a very strict woman.

She lived in Albany, in an old-fashioned brownstone. The stove was in the back of the kitchen. We loved to stay with her, because in the morning she would allow us to have corned beef hash and coffee. Later she would make us chicken and dumplings. Neither my mother, nor her mother, nor her mother's mother, ever wrote down their recipes. My mother wrote these recipes out for me and said "Both of these Irish ladies cooked from memory, as I also do today."

—*Kristin Corman*

108

Corned Beef and Cabbage

2–4 pounds corned beef brisket
6 quarts water

5–6 small white pototoes, peeled
1 head cabbage, sliced into 6 sections

In a large pot, over medium heat, boil the corned beef in water to cover for 4–5 hours. During the last half hour of cooking, add the potatotes and cabbage. Bring to a boil, then lower the heat and simmer until the meat is tender. Remove the meat and vegetables. Slice the meat across the grain and arrange the meat and vegetables on a serving platter.

Makes 4 to 5 servings.

Chicken and Dumplings

Chicken

1 5–pound stewing hen, cut into serving pieces
4 quarts water

2 onions, peeled
3 carrots, peeled

Dumplings

2 cups all-purpose flour
4 teaspoons baking powder
1 teaspoon salt

1 tablespoon shortening
1 cup milk

To cook the chicken, in a large saucepan, over medium heat, simmer the chicken in water to cover with the onions and carrots until tender, about 1½ hours.

To make the dumplings, in a large mixing bowl, sift together the flour, baking powder, and salt. Cut in the shortening until the mixture resembles coarse corn meal. Add the milk and stir quickly to make a soft dough.

During the last 20 minutes of cooking the chicken, drop the dough by small teaspoonfuls on top of the simmering chicken. Cook uncovered for 10 minutes, then cover and cook an additional 10 minutes.

Makes 12 dumplings, 6 servings.

Mamabebe's Fried Apple Pies

One thing I've noticed is that my grandmother doesn't make her fried pies as often as she used to. Now it seems like she only makes them because my aunt and uncle from Ohio are coming, or somebody else is visiting, and that's usually around holiday time. She'll go all out, then. She's a real bustler in the kitchen and she has her own way of doing things too. You know how pie crust is ruffled and crumpled around the edges? Well, she does it with her own little wrist action to get it just so.

There's a counter in the kitchen, and in the center of it she always has something freshly baked on a plate, covered with waxed paper. That's the treat of going out there, to see what it's going to be. I eat her pies cold. I'm sure they would be good heated up, and I have taken one or two with me thinking, "Mmm! This would be good for breakfast tomorrow with coffee. I'll heat it up." But it never lasts that long.

The tricky part of making the pies is in the frying. She uses Crisco. It shouldn't get too hot, but it should be heated until it's bubbling—just like when you fry chicken. It's beyond me how she can make them taste the same way every time.

Everyone in the family wants one of these pies. There are about a dozen pies in each batch, and it takes quite a while to make a dozen. If Rob and Merle and Brad and Brian are there, and Allen and Mary Ann and Kirk and Glenn come, and then my mother and my daddy and myself, and Sally and Connie—you see, you've already got fifteen people. So sometimes you don't manage to get one. What happens if you don't get one? You just hear about 'em. They say, "Yeah, there were some pies...but they're no more. They're gone!" And that's that!

—*Lu Ellen Huntley*

Fried Apple Pies

Apple Filling

4 cups dried sliced apples
4 cups water
Sugar to taste

Allspice to taste
Cinnamon, ground, to taste

Pastry

4½ cups all-purpose flour
1 teaspoon salt
1 tablespoon baking powder
⅓ cup shortening

¼ cup milk
1½ cups flour for dusting
Vegetable oil for frying

To make the filling, in a large saucepan, place the apples and water, and simmer until tender (the time varies with each batch of apples). Remove from the stove and cool. Mash well, then add the sugar, allspice, and cinnamon to taste. Place the mixture in a bowl, cover, and refrigerate overnight.

The next day, to make the pastry, in a large mixing bowl, stir together 4½ cups of flour, the salt, and the baking powder, and cut in the shortening, using a fork, pastry blender, or two knives. Add enough milk to form a stiff but moist dough. Mix lightly until all the ingredients are blended. Refrigerate for at least one hour.

Line 2 cookie sheets with wax paper.

With a rolling pin, on a lightly floured surface, roll out the dough ⅛–inch thick, and, with a floured 4-inch round cookie cutter, cut the dough into circles. Place about 2 tablespoons of the apple mixture in the center of each of the circles. Moisten the edges with water, then fold the pastry in half and press the edges together, sealing the edges tightly with your fingertips. Place the turnovers on the prepared cookie sheets. Brush off any excess flour. Work as rapidly as possible to keep the dough firm.

In a heavy-gauge saucepan, over medium heat, heat 1 inch of oil to a temperature of 375 degrees. The oil is ready when a piece of dough browns evenly. Using 2 large spatulas, gently lift one pie at a time off the cookie sheet and slip it into the hot oil. Cook two pies at a time. When one side browns, turn to brown the other side. Do not turn more than once. With a slotted spoon, remove the cooked pies to a rack to cool. Continue to cook the remaining pies in the same manner.

Do not stack the pies until they are cool.

If excess sediment accumulates in the bottom of the saucepan, pour off the oil, wipe out the saucepan with a paper towel, and return the oil to the pan, adding more if necessary.

Makes 12 to 15 pies.

Winter Soup

10 cups water
4 or 5 beef ribs
2 15–ounce cans tomatoes
4–6 medium white onions, peeled and chopped
5–6 stalks celery, quartered
Kernels from 3 ears of corn, uncooked

1 small potato, peeled and diced, or ⅓–½ cup rice, uncooked
10–ounce package frozen butter beans
1 tablespoon sugar
Salt and pepper to taste
1 fresh basil leaf, or ⅛ teaspoon dried basil

In a stock pot, over medium heat, add the water and ribs, and bring to a boil. Lower the heat and simmer until tender, about 2 hours. With a slotted spoon, remove the ribs from the broth. When they are cool enough to handle, cut the meat off the bone, and remove the fat and gristle. Reserve the bones for another soup. Dice the meat and return to the stock pot. Remove any hard cores from the tomatoes and add them to the stock. Add the onions and celery, and simmer for at least 2 hours. Then add the corn kernals, the potato or rice, butter beans, sugar, salt, pepper, and basil, and simmer 30–40 minutes more.

Makes 8 to 10 servings.

Uncle Mike's Rabbit Stew

My family were all avid sportsmen, so I grew up with my father and my uncle going off to hunt. I used to just walk along with them while they hunted, until finally I got old enough to have my own gun. I was still a little kid when I got my first buck. The legal age to hunt was twelve, and I don't think I was licensed yet, but we were hunting in a desolate part of the woods.

Even today, when I see a deer in the woods, my heart starts going boom, boom, boom. When you're a little kid, you don't get macho, like "me killum rabbit." You're excited to be able to pull the trigger, to be coordinated enough to do it. People think that hunting is like shooting fish in a barrel, but it's not at all. The game has the distinct advantage. Most times when I hunt—why, I see more guns miss than I see make.

My uncle is a naturalist. He's the kind of person you could put out in the woods and he'd be okay. He's a hearty kind of guy. And he grows things: he's a flower arranger. He manicured his garden so that it looked like something out of a magazine. He enjoys being outside and seeing the beauty in things. To him, hunting was a kind of tradition, a part of growing up. When I started hunting, we had a celebration with candles and a little glass of wine. It was a celebration of my being one of the guys.

It was the Friday before Thanksgiving. I was nine years old and not of the legal age to hunt, but my uncle took me out in the woods and gave me a shotgun that was bigger than I was. There was a thick row of trees on my left and a power-line cut on the right. He said, "Why don't you go out and stand by the power lines, and I'll walk through these woods, and maybe some bunny will come bopping out into the open air and you'll get him." It was very exciting to get my first rabbit. I think I got two that day.

—*Scott Nedrow*

112

Stewed Rabbit with Red Wine

1 rabbit, cut into serving pieces*
½ cup all-purpose flour, or more
   as needed
2 tablespoons unsalted butter
Salt and pepper to taste
1 cup onion, peeled and sliced, or
   ½ pound pearl onions, peeled
1 cup carrots, peeled and sliced
¾ cup mushrooms, sliced
1 bay leaf
1 teaspoon sage

1 teaspoon savory
1 teaspoon marjoram
2 teaspoons garlic, peeled and
   minced, or 1 teaspoon garlic
   flakes
2 cups dry red wine
1 cup water
2 tablespoons brown sugar
A few sprigs of parsley, to
   garnish, optional

Dust the rabbit pieces with flour. In a 10–inch heavy-gauge skillet, heat the butter over medium heat until bubbly. Add the rabbit pieces and brown them on all sides, adding salt and pepper to taste. This should take about 10 minutes. Add the onions, carrots, mushrooms, bay leaf, sage, marjoram, garlic, and 1 cup of the wine. Simmer until the vegetables are crisp-tender. Transfer the contents of the pan to a flameproof casserole with a lid and add the rest of the wine, the water, and the brown sugar. Cover the casserole and simmer over low heat for 30–45 minutes, stirring as necessary. Remove the bay leaf, and garnish with parsley, if desired, before serving.

Makes 4 servings.

*Prepackaged rabbit parts are available in some supermarkets.
 Otherwise, a specialty butcher can dress and cut into serving pieces a
 freshly killed rabbit.

Thea Iphigenia's Rice Pudding and Egg-Lemon Soup

Thea means "aunt" in Greek, and Iphigenia is my great-aunt who lives in Athens. She's a very lively woman. She's never been to America; she's afraid to ride on an airplane. She wears hornrimmed glasses and always has her hair up in a bun. She lives in a two-story house. It has a garden out in the back yard where she keeps a few chickens, and there is a circular iron stairwell leading from the garden up to the second floor. Whenever we came to Iphigenia's house, she would make rice pudding because she knew we liked it. We would have it for breakfast or lunch, because we would usually go out for dinner. The pudding is sort of like yogurt; it has a very creamy consistency—not like the rice pudding you have here, which has so much rice in it and is chunky and not very tasty.

Lunch in Greece is a big deal. You'd sit down at a table with a plastic tablecloth and have menestra, a type of pasta shaped like little grains of rice, and meat. There would be wine and a lot of bread, and everyone would eat very intently, while Thea Iphigenia would make jokes. She'd call everyone *kamadimou,* which means "my dear." Meanwhile, the rice pudding would be waiting in the fridge. She would make the pudding without the cinnamon, and then add the cinnamon on top and put it in the fridge until we were ready to eat it. It gets very hot in Athens, so after lunch, everyone would take a nap.

Thea Iphigenia doesn't speak any English, but when we were young, my brother and I visited her in Greece and taught her a few English words— "Thank you very much," "son of a bitch," and "shut up." She *knows* what they mean, but to this day she'll run the three together. People will be speaking English, so she'll say the only English she knows—"Thank you very much, son of a bitch, shut up." Her side of the family is very witty and humorous. They're all practical jokers, and Iphigenia likes to tell stories and jokes. I always had to get her jokes second-hand, because of the language barrier.

—*Tom Soter*

114

Greek Egg-Lemon Soup

1–1½ quarts chicken stock
  (recipe follows)

1 large egg
Juice from 1 lemon

In a large saucepan, over medium heat, warm the chicken stock until just to a boil. Meanwhile, in a small mixing bowl, beat the egg until light, gradually adding the lemon juice. When beaten, take a ladle of broth and gradually pour it into the egg mixture, stirring constantly. Doing this gently heats the egg, preventing it from scrambling when you add it to the hot stock. Add 2 more ladlefuls of stock to the egg, then pour the egg-stock mixture into the large saucepan of stock, stirring thoroughly. Remove from the heat immediately, and serve.

Makes 5 to 6 servings.

Chicken Stock

4 quarts water
Salt to taste
4 pounds chicken necks and
  backs
2 large onions, peeled and
  quartered
2 carrots, peeled and cut into
  sections

2 stalks celery
1 parsnip
1 turnip
6 sprigs parsley
1 teaspoon thyme
6 peppercorns

In a large soup kettle, over medium heat, add the water, salt, and chicken parts, and bring to a boil. Skim off any scum that forms on the surface. Cover the pot, reduce the heat, and simmer for 1 hour. Add the onions, carrots, celery, parsnip, turnip, parsley, thyme, and peppercorns, and taste for seasoning, then cover again and simmer for 1½ hours. Strain the stock through cheesecloth or a strainer into a heatproof container. Cover and refrigerate until ready to use.

Makes 2 to 2½ quarts.

Rice Pudding

1 quart milk
½ cup hot water
⅛ teaspoon salt
⅓ cup long-grain white rice,
  uncooked

2 large eggs
¼ cup sugar
½ teaspoon vanilla extract
Ground cinnamon for sprinkling

In a large saucepan, over medium heat, scald the milk. Meanwhile, in a second saucepan, bring the salted water to a boil, and add the rice, parboiling it for 5 minutes. Drain the rice into a colander, then add it to the scalded milk. Simmer until the rice is tender, about 15 minutes.

Meanwhile, in a large mixing bowl, beat the eggs until light and lemon-colored, then slowly add the sugar. Remove the milk and rice mixture from the heat and, to prevent curdling, slowly stir in the egg mixture, mixing well. Replace over the heat and cook for 5 minutes, stirring constantly. Remove from the heat once more and stir in the vanilla extract. Pour into individual bowls or molds, sprinkle with cinnamon, and allow to cool before serving.

Makes 8 servings.

Granny Wilhoit's Cinnamon Milk Rolls

My Granny's name is Mary Ruth Wilhoit. She grew up in Sequatchet County, Tennessee. Her father was a schoolteacher and a prominent man in the county. They lived in a big old house up on a mountain. They had a fair amount of land but they lost it all during the Depression. By that time my grandmother was grown and had five kids of her own. They had moved to Chattanooga and she worked in the school system as a cook. It was then that she started making these cinnamon rolls for the programs they had organized to feed the poorer children.

One day the supervisor came by and was sort of bent out of shape. He said, "What is this? Why are you baking cinnamon rolls for these kids?" It seemed that the school got surplus bread from a local store and could buy cinnamon rolls as well. But then the supervisor tasted Granny's rolls. They were so good that it became clear she should continue baking them. The recipe started getting passed around to the other cooks in the other schools, and soon enough it became a standard recipe throughout the school system. It's a basic biscuit dough that you roll out and put the cinnamon and butter mixture over. Then you roll it up, cut it into lengths, put it in a pan, and cover it with enough milk to come up the sides of the pan. That was Granny's own part. I will always remember how Granny pulled them out of the oven, and they were all brown and bubbly.

Granny also makes a nice, fresh salad with onions, fresh tomatoes, and fresh green peppers. It's got a relish on it that makes it a spicy little side salad. The relish mixture gets even better the second day you eat it, because everthing kind of marinates and the juices just slop around. She pulls all of the vegetables right out of her garden.

My grandmother's garden is thirty by fifty feet. She always does summer squash, okra, and tomatoes, bell peppers (both green and red), and hot chili peppers. Some years she's done potatoes, though her land is pretty low, and it tends to stay wet. I think my grandmother maintains her garden because it's something she can still do for herself. She can no longer do the plowing or the weeding, but it's a connection with something she had from the time she was a little girl. Her garden is a big part of any conversation. And even my mother, who's holding down a full-time, high-powered job, still has her own garden. In the last few years, I have felt the pull myself. The sooner I get where I can spread out a bit, the better things will be.

—*Jacob Young*

116

Cinnamon Milk Rolls

Dough

2 cups all-purpose flour
¼ cup shortening

¾ cup milk

Filling

½ cup (1 stick) plus 2
    tablespoons unsalted butter,
    softened

1 cup sugar
1 tablespoon cinnamon, ground
Milk

To prepare the dough, in a mixing bowl, cut the shortening into the flour until it is the consistency of coarse cornmeal. Slowly stir in the milk. A little more flour may be needed to to make the dough firm enough to handle. With a rolling pin, roll the dough into a rectangle roughly ¼–inch thick.

Preheat the oven to 400 degrees. With 2 tablespoons of butter, grease an ovenproof 9 × 9–inch baking dish.

To prepare the filling, in a mixing bowl, combine the sugar, the softened butter, and the cinnamon; the resulting paste should be the approximate color of brick. Spread the mixture evenly onto the dough.

Roll the dough up jelly roll fashion into a long sausage shape. Cut individual rolls about ¾–inch wide and place them in the greased baking dish. Pour in milk to reach about half-way up the rolls.

Bake for about 30 minutes, or until all the milk has been absorbed and the rolls are bubbling hot. Serve immediately.

Makes 6 to 8 servings.

Fruit Cobbler

¼ cup (½ stick) plus 1
    tablespoon unsalted butter
1 cup milk
1 cup all-purpose flour
1 cup sugar

3 cups apples or peaches (fresh
    or canned), peeled and sliced
1 teaspoon cinnamon, ground
1 teaspoon lemon juice, optional
Sugar to taste, optional

Preheat the oven to 350 degrees. With 1 tablespoon of butter, grease a 2–quart baking dish.

In a small mixing bowl, combine the milk, flour, and sugar to make a thick dough. In a separate bowl, combine the fruit with the cinnamon, lemon juice, and sugar to taste. In the baking dish, starting with the fruit, alternately layer the fruit and the dough to make four layers. Dot the top with the remaining butter cut into small pieces. Bake for 1 hour, or until golden brown and bubbly. Serve hot.

Makes 4 servings.

Ozark Vegetable Soup and Lemon Fluff Pie

My family was really big on desserts and we have a lot tales that center around them. My mom had a wonderful recipe for a lemon meringue pie that she got from her aunt Nan Dixon Graves. In it she would take at least one-half the meringue that would normally go on top of the pie and whip it into the lemon portion, so the lemon would be very, very high, like a cream pie. She called it Lemon Fluff Pie.

My brother Don was a real pie lover, and he always asked my mother to make a pie on special occasions, like birthdays and graduations. The day before Don was to turn twelve years old, he requested a Lemon Fluff Pie for his birthday. So, late at night, my mother secretly stole into the kitchen to make the pie. She knew that my brother would check in the cupboard the next morning to see if the pie was there. The next morning he did just that and said, "Where's my pie?" She said, "Well, we'll have our celebration in the evening time." He said, "But you're going to work all day." And she said, "Don't worry about it." He became very quiet because he knew she was working two jobs, and he figured she didn't have time to make the pie.

We walked to school together as usual, and I remember him complaining to me, "She's forgotten. She hasn't made the pie, blah blah blah..." After school we usually hitchiked home together, but my brother didn't show up. I asked his friends, and they said he took sick and went home. I thought, "Oh, my God, he is so disillusioned over the fact that he thinks mom's not going to make the pie, he's doing sort of a number..."

So I traveled home, wondering where Don was. When I got home, there he was, sitting on the porch, with a sort of smile on, looking very friendly. I said, "What are you doing here?" He said, "I wasn't feeling very well, so I came home. But I'm all right now." I really didn't think about it anymore. We had to go take care of our paper route.

When we got home, my mother had a big dinner waiting. She had made spaghetti and meatballs. But I noticed that Don didn't eat much, and I thought, "He knows he's going to get the pie, and he's waiting for it." My mother's a big woman; she goes for a lot of whooping and hollering. She talks with her hands. Everytime she would speak, it was like she was getting ready to sing an aria. So she said, "Now we're ready for the big part of the evening." My brother was looking very antsy, sort of squiggling in his chair, and sometimes giggling. My mother was getting more and more enthusiastic, and finally she climbed up on a ladder to the top shelf, where she normally kept things like dish towels, and she pulled out a box and said, "Don, here is your present!" She put the box down, lifted up the lid, and there was an empty pie tin. My mother was fit to be tied. She looked at me and said, "You ate this pie." I said, "I didn't eat the pie." Finally, my brother admitted that he had snuck home from school, searched the whole house, and ate the whole pie!

—*Bruce Kaiper*

118

Ozark Vegetable Soup

Bruce: My mother was an Ozark Mountain gal. She had learned an incredible recipe for vegetable soup from her great-aunt Mim. In the soup she would use essentially either a beef or pork stock and then she would add everything—from okra to corn to onions to green beans. It would be a catch-all for everything. This vegetable soup was very rich and thick. We would eat it every Saturday; it was like a ritual. My mother loved to sing opera. She had convinced herself she should be an opera singer. As she cooked, she would listen to the Metropolitan Opera on the radio and she would sing along. She loved all the Verdi operas. She would sing "Amore, amore" from *Aida* as she went about making this soup.

12 cups water, or more as needed
1 beef soup bone
3 onions, peeled and sliced
4 stalks celery, diced
4 potatoes, peeled and sliced
3 large tomatoes, quartered
6 fresh okra, sliced into rounds

1 green pepper, seeded and diced
2 carrots, sliced into rounds
½ pound green beans, trimmed
1 cup corn kernels, uncooked
½ cup parsley leaves, chopped
Salt and pepper to taste

In a large stock pot, over medium heat, add the water and soup bone and bring to a boil. Lower the heat and simmer for 2 hours.

Remove the soup bone from the stock. When the bone is cool enough to handle, remove any meat and return the meat to the pot. If any water has simmered away, add enough water to bring the stock back to the 12–cup level. Add the onions, celery, potatoes, tomatoes, okra, green pepper, carrots, green beans, corn kernels, and parsley to the stock. Add salt and pepper to taste, and simmer for 45 minutes.

Makes 8 to 10 servings.

Lemon Fluff Pie

3 large eggs, separated
1 cup sugar
1 tablespoon cornstarch
½ teaspoon salt
1½ cups hot water
Grated rind and juice of 1 lemon

2 tablespoons unsalted butter
¼ cup sugar
¼ cup all-purpose flour
9–inch pie shell, baked (see pie pastry recipe on page 127)

Preheat the oven to 325 degrees.

Beat the egg yolks lightly and set aside.

Sift together three-quarters cup of sugar, the cornstarch, and the salt. Place them in a saucepan and stir in the hot water. Over low heat, simmer until the mixture begins to thicken. Add in the egg yolks, stirring constantly, and cook for another minute. Stir in the lemon rind, lemon juice, and butter. Remove from the heat when the mixture is thickened.

Beat the egg whites until foamy. Gradually beat in the remaining quarter-cup of sugar and beat until stiff but not dry. Fold half of the egg whites into the lemon custard and pour into the baked pie shell. Spread the remaining egg whites over the top and brown in the oven, about 10 minutes.

Makes a 9–inch pie.

Bread-and-Butter Pickled Tomatoes

Grandma made pickled tomatoes that she called bread-and-butter pickles. They're sweet, but they're not too sweet. They're not dill, either. She used to cook them up in the summer. I was in second grade the last time I saw her on the farm. Then my grandad died, and Grandma was robbed, so she moved into town—Harrisonville, Missouri. But on the farm they had cows and lots of acreage. From the kitchen window you could see a big tree with a rope swing that we'd swing on. We used to go into the house through the back door and come right into the kitchen, to where all the pickle jars were lined up on the shelf. The kitchen had an old linoleum floor, little cafe curtains, and big old pans. I have my grandmother's recipe box, with all these faded old clippings and old, old recipes. That's about all that's left now; my grandmother died two years ago.

In the last few years of her life, she and I started making pickles together. I knew that I wanted to learn how to make them before she was gone. It was just a matter of cutting and boiling them. They smelled like onions and herbs while they were cooking. And of course, the longer they sat in the jar, the tastier they'd get. We'd seal the jars like regular canning jars, with heat to sterilize them. She'd serve the pickles with bread. They were always gone by the end of the year. She always made sure I got some pickles because she knew I loved them. I would take some to college and pass them out to my friends. I guess it got to the point where she was making them just for me.

My grandmother's name was Fannabel Emmons. She was a schoolteacher in a one-room schoolhouse. I guess one of the best things she ever taught me was the value of a rubber spatula. If you have a jar or pan of anything liquid that you want to get the last drop out of, always use a spatula. Sure enough, you can get ten more cookies, or a dozen more spoonfuls of anything.

—*Karen Emmons*

Pickled Tomatoes

8 quarts green tomatoes, thinly
  sliced
1 cup salt
4 onions, peeled and thinly sliced
1 tablespoon cloves, ground
1 tablespoon allspice, ground

1 tablespoon peppercorns
1 cup brown mustard seed
1 pound brown sugar
4 green peppers, finely chopped
3 quarts cider vinegar

In a stainless steel or enamel soup pot, place a layer of tomatoes. Sprinkle them with salt, then cover them with a layer of onions and sprinkle with more salt. Continue alternating layers of tomatoes and onions, sprinkling them with salt. Let them stand overnight and drain them in the morning. Place the mixture in a preserving kettle and stir in the cloves, allspice, peppercorns, mustard seed, brown sugar, and peppers. Pour in vinegar to cover. Over medium heat, bring the mixture to a boil and cook for 30 minutes. Pack into sterilized pint–sized canning jars, seal them, and let them sit for at least a week before eating.

Makes about 10 pints.

Cookie-Sheet Cake

Cake

1 cup plus 1 tablespoon
  shortening
1/4 cup cocoa
1 cup cold water
2 cups all-purpose flour
2 cups sugar
1/2 cup buttermilk

1 teaspoon baking soda
1/4 teaspoon salt
1 teaspoon white vinegar
1/2 cup milk
1 teaspoon vanilla extract
2 large eggs, slightly beaten

Icing

1/2 cup (1 stick) shortening
1/4 cup cocoa
5 tablespoons milk

1 teaspoon vanilla extract
1 cup nuts, chopped
1 pound confectioners' sugar

Preheat the oven to 375 degrees. With 1 tablespoon of shortening, grease 2 cookie sheets.

To make the cake, in a large saucepan, mix together the shortening, cocoa, and cold water, and bring to a boil over medium heat. When the shortening has melted, remove from the heat. Meanwhile, sift together the flour and sugar. Pour the hot mixture over the flour mixture and stir well. Add the buttermilk, baking soda, salt, vinegar, milk, vanilla extract, and eggs. Mix well, then pour the batter onto the prepared cookie sheets. Bake for 20 minutes.

To make the icing, in a large saucepan, mix together the shortening, cocoa, and milk, and bring it to a boil. Stir in the vanilla extract, chopped nuts, and confectioners' sugar, mixing until the sugar is fully incorporated, and pour over the warm cake. When cool, cut the cake into bars or squares.

Makes about 16 servings.

Grandma Rose's Challah and Original Grandma Cookies

Ann (daughter): My mother's name was Rose. I didn't know any of my grandparents. My mother was an orphan, and my father's parents died during the First World War. So as a child, whenever I saw a man with a beard and a little girl or boy holding onto his hand, I envied them because I never had a grandma or a grandpa.

Jason (grandson): Whenever I went to visit Grandma Rose, I would come home with a brown paper bag filled with wonderful cinnamon Grandma Cookies. She had an enamel-topped table and used to roll out the dough on a dishtowel. I would sit at the side of the table and watch her cut the cookies into circles and squares and diamonds.

Ann: I learned to cook from my mother. I would go to the market with her, and she would pick out a live chicken. The *shochet,* a person trained in ritual slaughter, would kill it, and we would pluck the feathers, open it right there, and throw away what we weren't going to use. It was the same thing with fish. My mother would bring the whole fish home and put it in the bathtub to let it swim around. Later we would kill it, scale it, and then cut it up. Then we'd chop onions, and cry over them, and then cook everything.

My mother used to make her own noodles. You did the best with what you had and tried to make the food interesting. For instance, you'd take potatoes and you'd *make* something

with them, not just mashed potatoes. You'd fry an onion or put in a little chicken fat, called schmaltz. Nobody died of chicken fat. *Now* if you eat it, it's poison! So my mother used to put these things together. If chicken was eighteen cents a pound at the live market, well, she would buy a rooster. They were big and they were cheaper. But look, if you had nothing else, you ate it. If my mother gave us a piece of bread with schmaltz and a little salt, and a cup of tea, it was out of this world. Especially if the bread wasn't fresh bread but was stuck in the oven for a couple of minutes and got a little toasted, and you rubbed the crust of the bread with garlic. It left a lousy taste in your mouth, but it was delicious!

Jason: Even though I was a finicky eater when I was a child, I would eat anything my grandmother gave me— things I would never dream of eating at home! But my main memory of her cooking has to be those wonderful cookies. I don't know if my grandmother was a good or bad baker. For instance, these cookies were hard as rocks. To this day, I don't know if that's the way they were supposed to be or if they were overdone, but they were absolutely delicious, and a bagful would last me a week. Finally tracking down this recipe has been a great pleasure. I can't wait to bake a bagful and give them to *my* daughter!

—*Ann Berkowitz and Jason Shulman*

Challah

1 tablespoon unsalted butter
3–4 cups all-purpose flour
2 cakes or 2 envelopes dried
   yeast
2 tablespoons sugar

1 teaspoon salt
1 cup water
1/3 cup vegetable oil
4 large eggs
1 egg yolk

Lightly grease a large bowl with 1 tablespoon of butter, and set aside.

Sift the flour, and combine with the yeast, sugar, and salt. Pile the flour on a board and make a "well" in the center into which you place the other ingredients. (This can also be done the "modern" way: in a bowl.)

In a saucepan, combine the water and oil, and warm gently. When lukewarm, remove from the heat and stir in 4 eggs. Pour this liquid into the flour well, and fold in to form a sticky dough. As you mix, add more flour until you have a dough that doesn't stick to your fingers. Transfer the dough into the greased bowl, and turn to coat it all over with oil. Cover it with a kitchen towel and let it rise in a warm place until doubled in bulk, about 30–60 minutes.

Punch down the dough and knead on a floured surface to release the air bubbles. You may have to add a little more flour to make the dough smooth and pliable. Put the dough back in the bowl and let it rise again for 30 minutes. Then divide the dough in half. Roll each half into a long loaf. Place the loaves on a baking sheet and make a slit down the middle of each loaf, about ½–¾ of an inch deep.

Preheat the oven to 400 degrees. Let the dough rise one more time for 10–20 minutes in a warm place.

Bake the bread for 20–25 minutes. The bread should sound hollow when tapped. Five minutes before removing from the oven, brush the top of each loaf with the egg yolk.

Makes 2 loaves.

Cinnamon Cookies

Anne: My mother used to shape these cookies with tin cookie cutters that my brother made when he worked at the Brooklyn Navy Yard.

¾ cup sugar
1 cup shortening
2 large eggs
½ cup water or orange juice

4 cups all-purpose flour
2 teaspoons baking powder
¼ cup sugar mixed with ½
   teaspoon cinnamon, for rolling

In a mixing bowl, cream together the sugar and the shortening, then beat in the eggs, and the water or orange juice. Mix well. Stir the flour and the baking powder together and gradually add them to the sugar-butter mixture, blending well. The dough should be soft. Cover with wax paper and refrigerate for 1 hour.

Preheat the oven to 350 degrees.

With a rolling pin, roll out the dough ¼-inch thick on a pastry board or cloth. Cut out the cookies with a cookie cutter, then dip each cookie into the cinnamon-sugar mixture. Place the cookies on baking sheets, and bake for 10 minutes.

Makes about 6 dozen cookies.

Honey Cake

1 cup honey
1 cup black coffee, seltzer, or
   club soda
2 cups all-purpose flour
2 teaspoons baking powder

1 teaspoon baking soda
1 cup sugar
2 large eggs
½ cup vegetable oil

Preheat oven to 350 degrees. Lightly grease a 5 × 9–inch loaf pan.

In a large bowl, mix together the honey, and the coffee, seltzer, or club soda. Blend the flour, the baking powder, and the baking soda. Stir the sugar, the eggs, the oil, and the flour mixture into the honey mixture. Mix well and pour into the prepared loaf pan. Bake for 1 hour.

Makes one loaf.

Muti's Wiener Schnitzel

I was the first grandchild, and my grandparents always loved to take care of me. When my brother and sister—the twins—arrived, my parents were really busy with them, so I got to spend even more time with Vati and Muti. Vati means father, and Muti means mother in German, and that's what we called them. We used to spend school breaks and summers with them when my father was stationed in Germany.

Vati and Muti had a large old house, and they owned a restaurant and guest house. When the guest house was full, Muti was always in the kitchen, cooking. She cooked all the food for the restaurant-bar where people would come for a quick meal, like schnitzel, sandwiches, wursts, and other meats. People would sit around, eat and drink and play cards, and sing old German songs.

Muti and Vati lived in a small town, and I got to know everybody there. When all the relatives showed up, Vati and Muti would set up separate tables in the guest house for each of the families, and Muti would make us her schnitzel. She was a wonderful cook. I've eaten other schnitzel a number of times, but it's never as good as when she cooked it. Even though I had some trouble communicating with her because I couldn't speak German so well, I loved talking to her. If I could, I would talk with her for hours. When we moved to the United States, I must have cried all the way over, I missed her so much. Whenever I eat schnitzel here, it brings back the memories of sitting in the kitchen with Muti watching her cook.

—*Uwe Gordon*

Wiener Schnitzel

Salt and pepper to taste
4 thin veal cutlets or boneless
*   pork loin (1½ to 2 pounds*
*   total)*
½ cup all-purpose flour

1 large egg, beaten
1 cup plain breadcrumbs
1 cup vegetable oil
1 lemon, sliced, for garnish,

With a wooden mallet, pound the salt and pepper into the veal cutlets. Then dredge them in the flour, dip them in egg, and coat them with breadcrumbs. Let the breaded veal sit for about an hour to firm up the crust.

In a heavy-gauge deep skillet, over medium-high heat, warm the oil until very hot. Add the veal slices, and pan-fry for 8–12 minutes, or until the meat rises to the surface. Remove from the skillet, drain on paper towels, garnish with lemon slices, and serve immediately.

Makes 4 servings.

Rolladen

6 strips bacon
6 thin slices top round steak
*   (about 2 pounds total)*
3 tablespoons prepared mustard
Salt and pepper to taste
1 medium onion, peeled and
*   finely chopped*
1 large carrot, grated

3–4 tablespoons dill pickle,
*   chopped*
3 tablespoons parsley, finely
*   chopped*
1½ cups beef broth
½ cup dry red wine
2–2½ tablespoons all-purpose
*   flour*

Preheat the oven to 325 degrees.

In a heavy-gauge skillet, fry the bacon until crisp, then drain it, reserving the bacon fat, and crumble the strips.

Rub the beef slices with the mustard, then sprinkle them with the salt and pepper. Spread the bacon, onion, carrot, and dill pickles evenly over the meat slices. Sprinkle with the parsley. Roll up each slice and fasten with toothpicks. In the same skillet, heat the reserved bacon grease and brown the rolls in it. Transfer to a casserole. Stir together the beef broth and wine and pour over the meat. Cover and bake for 1½ hours, basting occasionally.

Remove the rolls from the oven and transfer them to a warm platter. Spoon a few tablespoons of the liquid into a small bowl or saucer, and stir in the flour to make a thin paste. Stir the paste into the pan juices and cook on the stove just long enough to thicken the gravy. Spoon the sauce over the rolladen and serve immediately.

Makes 6 servings.

Grammy's Pineapple Pie and Sugar Cookies

My paternal grandmother's name is Laura Alice Worrell Stevenson. I remember our visits to her in Memphis, Tennessee. The whole house always smelled a certain way, and Grammy always had this wonderful grandmother smell, almost like baby powder, and her cheeks were always soft and she had white, white hair. She is a big woman, and I can picture her standing in the kitchen in a flowered dress and those black lace-up grandmother shoes, making a type of cookie she calls Divinity. They are fluffy white cookies made out of egg whites and corn syrup and they melt in your mouth. I have a couple of her recipes. One is Grammy's pineapple pie, and that's *really* good. It's made with cream cheese and crushed pineapple and whipped cream. Now, my maternal grandmother has the best recipe for pie pastry. I've never had a recipe from Betty Crocker or anything else that comes out as good. Grammy's pineapple pie filling tastes great in my other grandmother's pie crust!

Grammy will be ninety-seven this year and she is really amazing. She has a constitution that just does not quit. She says it's because she "never had a draw on a cigarette and alcohol has never touched these lips." She's always been as strong as an ox. When she shakes your hand, you feel like she's rubbed your knuckles together. I remember that when she would come and visit us, the cat would hide under the bed because Grammy was so strong that she would pet him down to the ground!

I remember this story about when she lived in Tennessee. She'd hired a couple of men to do some housepainting or something. Well, this one guy had left a pair of brass knuckles up on a bookshelf, and Grammy found them and, of course, kept them. And then the guy came back and said, "Mrs. Steve," (people used to call her Mrs. Steve) "Mrs. Steve, I think I left something here." But she wouldn't give the brass knuckles back. She wanted to carry them in her purse so she would be ready when someone came to "knock off the old lady," as she'd say.

She's always had a strong character and her own way of doing things. When she was in her eighties, she used to do volunteer work to help the elderly—who were twenty years her junior! When she traveled she would carry a cane, even though she didn't need it, so that she would get special attention at the airport and be able to board the plane first. She loved it! She also had this big blue Oldsmobile. It was a 1956 model, and she drove it up until 1980 when she broke her hip. Even then she would get out and drive it up and down the driveway. Right now she's in the Texarkana Nursing Center in Texas, still going strong. She makes the morning announcements over the PA and plays the piano in the rec room.

—*Nancy Stevenson*

Pineapple Pie

Pie Pastry

2 cups all-purpose flour
¾ teaspoon salt

⅔ cup shortening
4–5 tablespoons cold water or milk

To make two pie shells, sift together the flour and salt. Using a fork, pastry blender, or two knives, cut in the shortening until the mixture is the consistency of coarse meal. Add the water or milk, pressing the dough together with a fork. Divide the dough in half, cover with wax paper, and chill for at least an hour. The dough can be frozen for future use.

Makes two 8 or 9–inch pie shells.

To bake a pie shell, preheat the oven to 450 degrees.

Using a rolling pin, roll out the dough for one pie shell to ⅛–inch thickness on a floured board or cloth so the dough is slightly larger than the size of the pie pan. Place the dough in the pie pan, trim the edges, and bake for 15 minutes. Remove it from the oven and allow it to cool.

Filling

8 ounces cream cheese, softened
1 cup sugar
1 can (8–11 ounces) crushed pineapple, drained

1 pint heavy cream, whipped
1 pie shell

To make the pineapple filling, blend the cream cheese and sugar thoroughly, then add the drained pineapple to the mixture and stir well. Fold in the whipped cream and pour into the cooled pie shell. Chill for a minimum of 4 hours. If possible, make it a day in advance.

Makes an 8 or 9–inch pie, 8 servings.

Sugar Cookies

1 cup (2 sticks) unsalted butter or shortening, softened
1 cup confectioners' sugar
1 large egg

2 teaspoons vanilla extract
½ teaspoon salt
2½ cups all-purpose flour

Preheat the oven to 325 degrees.

Mix together the butter or shortening, the confectioners' sugar, the egg, the vanilla extract, and the salt. Gradually add the flour, mixing well after each addition. Drop the dough by teaspoons onto a cookie sheet. Flatten slightly with the bottom of a glass or the heel of your hand. Bake for about 7 minutes, until set.

Note: The dough may be kept in a covered bowl in the refrigerator until you are ready to bake. It can also be rolled, after chilling, to a thickness of about ¼–inch and cut with a cookie cutter. The baking time remains the same.

Makes about 5 dozen cookies.

Grandpa's Linguini with Anchovies

We used to spend all the big holidays—Christmas, New Year's, and Easter—with my father's parents. My father's father was from Sicily. His mother was from Calabria. They had a table so long you never saw the end of it. And they would have their eight children there, plus husbands and wives and all the grandchildren—so there had to be at least sixty people. My grandfather made fruit soaked in liqueur and gave it to the kids as a treat. And at his table, you could be a month old or 105, but you had to have wine. He felt it was healthy. If the parents objected, he would put in a little soda. But you had to have the wine; it was part of your meal.

I think my grandfather enjoyed cooking. He took over for my grandmother because she had so many children. He had been a merchant marine before coming to this country, and I think that's where he learned to cook. Most merchant marines are very good cooks. My grandfather knew how to prepare pigeon and turtle. He knew how to pick wild mushrooms and bread them and fry them like veal cutlets. And he also cooked lamb's head. When he put a lamb's head out, it was like hamburger to his kids. These were the things my grandfather enjoyed eating, so his kids were brought up on them.

It was a lot of fun being with all my cousins, aunts, and uncles. On Sundays, we always ate at my grandparents' house. It was like a commandment: You had better be there on Sunday! My grandparents had a tremendous house on Cropsey Avenue in Brooklyn. For a small crowd, they used the formal dining room. But if we were a large crowd, we ate in the basement. We used to have a sit-down dinner no matter how many people there were.

My grandfather used to serve the meals and he was the last one to sit down. He sat at the head of the table. If there was nothing left over after serving everyone, he didn't eat. He made sure the whole family had their food first. I thought that was a beautiful thing. And don't forget, there were twenty or twenty-five people at the table. My grandfather loved the company.

—*Mary Ellen Parisi*

Linguini with Anchovies

3 tablespoons vegetable or olive
   oil
2 cloves garlic, peeled and chopped
½ cup Italian-style breadcrumbs
2 cans anchovies, drained
4 quarts water
1 pound linguini

In a 10–inch heavy-gauge skillet, heat the oil. Add the garlic and saute gently for 2–3 minutes. Add the breadcrumbs and toast them, stirring constantly, until browned. Stir in the anchovies.

In a large saucepan, bring the 4 quarts of water to a boil. Add the pasta and cook until *al dente*. Drain the pasta and place it in a large bowl. Top with the breadcrumb and anchovy mixture. Serve with Italian bread.

Makes 4 servings.

Chicken Baked in Vinegar and Oil

1 3–pound chicken, cut into
   serving pieces
¾ cup olive oil
½ cup red wine vinegar
2 cloves garlic, peeled and finely
   chopped
1 onion, peeled and finely
   chopped
2 tablespoons water

Preheat the oven to 350 degrees. Lay the chicken pieces in a foil-lined pan and place in the oven.

Mix together the olive oil, vinegar, garlic, and onions, and baste the chicken with this mixture every 10 minutes. When the chicken is brown, after about 30 minutes, remove the chicken from the pan. Add 2 tablespoons of water to the pan to deglaze it, scraping up the drippings with a spoon. Put the pan over medium heat and stir until the basting sauce has reduced to form a thin gravy. Arrange the chicken pieces on a serving platter and pour the sauce on top.

Makes 4 servings.

Edna Goble's Beef Steaks in Ale and Yorkshire Pudding

My father lives in Holland, where he is a market-gardener, which means he grows vegetables, fruits, and flowers to sell in marketplaces all over the Netherlands. He took the business over from his father when he was eighteen.

With all the greenhouses and four children, my father would get tired of taking care of everything, but there was never any time to get away. Each summer would pass and he would say, "Maybe next year we'll be able to go on holiday," but that time never seemed to come around. Finally, when my father was exhausted, he asked my mother if she would mind if he took a short break, a vacation in England by himself. My mother knew he needed the rest, so she agreed. That autumn, he found a nice farm in Surrey where he could spend a week. He liked the farm, the farmer and his wife, and their little boy. After the first year, my father was so pleased with his little vacation that he couldn't wait to get back to the farm again. He's gone for a week every autumn since.

When we girls grew up, my father took all of us to England to visit with the farmer and his wife, Mr. and Mrs. Goble. These days, my parents take the two youngest of my sisters to visit England in the spring, summer, and autumn, and the Gobles have come to our home in Holland. Two years ago, we all went to the wedding of the Gobles' son.

It has been twenty years since my father first started visiting Surrey and raving about Edna Goble's cooking. My father is very fussy about his food, but he loves everything that Edna Goble cooks for him. Last year, he finally persuaded her to allow him to bring back some of her recipes. I must tell you something else: My father eats everything that Mrs. Goble cooks him, but when he is back in Holland, he eats only Dutch food!

—*Yvonne de Jong-Eÿgenraam*

Beef Steaks in Ale

*4 pieces rump steak (about 2
   pounds total)*
1¼ cups ale or beer
1 onion, peeled
3 sprigs fresh thyme
3 sprigs fresh parsley

1 teaspoon salt
Pinch of pepper
Pinch of nutmeg, grated
1 tablespoon unsalted butter
1 teaspoon all-purpose flour

To tenderize the steaks, beat them with a rolling pin. In a large skillet, place the steaks with the ale or beer. Bring to a boil slowly. Lower the heat, then cover and simmer for 10 minutes.

Meanwhile, slice the onion, and chop the thyme and parsley. Add them to the steaks and season with the salt, pepper, and nutmeg. Cut the flour into the butter to form a paste. Stir into the meat juices, cover, and cook gently for 45 minutes.

Makes 4 servings.

Roast Beef
and Yorkshire Pudding

5–pound beef sirloin roast
Black pepper to taste
1 cup all-purpose flour
½ teaspoon salt

2 large eggs, beaten
1¼ cups milk
1 tablespoon water

Preheat the oven to 450 degrees.

Season the meat with pepper, then place the meat on a rack in a roasting pan and cook for 15 minutes. Lower the heat to 300 degrees and cook for 75 minutes (15 minutes per pound).

In a large mixing bowl, combine the flour and salt. Make a well in the flour. In a mixing bowl, stir together the eggs and milk, then stir this into the flour, mixing quickly but thoroughly. Stir in the water. After the roast has been cooking for an hour, pour the batter into the roasting pan on the drippings (the roast is still cooking on the rack above the drippings). Cook the pudding for 30 minutes. When puffy and brown, remove the roast and pudding from the oven, and serve immediately.

Makes about 8 servings.

Margarita Anastasiou's Pastitsio and Greek Walnut Cake

Everyone calls me Greta, but my full name is Margaret. That's important because it's my grandmother's name too. She was born in Cyprus, in a small mountain village called Lefkara. Now the population of the village is maybe one-tenth of what it was when my grandmother lived there. It is a beautiful village and it smells of jasmine. In Lefkara they're famous not for food but for making lace. Tourists go up there to buy lace, and the old women are still tatting in the streets. My grandmother makes lace. She's very good with her hands. In fact, years ago, I took a picture of her hands because I was so impressed with how articulate they were, very creative and always in use. She is still alive, and turns eighty-one this August. She is spry and youthful.

When she was around eighteen, she came over to the States. She had married my grandfather and they came together. They were turned away because of the immigration laws of the day and had to spend a year in Paris and then reapply. She had her first child in Paris, but he died because they were so poor that they didn't even have enough to feed themselves.

She cooks a lot of Greek food, but she is very experimental. She adapts a lot of Greek cooking to American needs. She makes the dishes less heavy, and has incorporated some things that were not available in Greece, and vice versa. She is still experimenting. I remember that she always had a jar of Greek twisted butter cookies with sesame seeds on top. They were twisted in a very unusual fashion. In fact, there is one that was twisted like the columns on the Acropolis. She would cook spinach pie, and traditional Greek moussaka, and lamb and beef Greek style, with tomato sauce, lots of herbs, and spices like cinnamon and cloves. What amazes me is that I have always felt I had the best of both worlds in my grandmother's life. I always felt that she kept what was best of the culture that she came from, but she never failed to open herself up to the American culture that she took on in her new land. It was like the doors were open at both ends, and this was reflected in her cooking. She is a great American cook as well.

We used to go to her house every Sunday. It would start out with her immediate family—my mother, my brother, and my uncle, who was also a marvelous cook. They used to spend hours together in the kitchen, screaming and yelling at each other about the cooking. Then the bell would ring and another cousin would come over. Every Sunday there would end up being about thirty people at the dinner table, and she would just know how to add and improvise to expand; she understood that there were always going to be people coming to the door. I think the one word I could use to describe my grandmother would be "open." I love her and I'm glad I have her name and spirit.

—*Greta Mavromatis*

Pastitsio

Baked Macaroni

½ gallon milk
3 large onions, peeled and finely
   chopped
1 cup (2 sticks) unsalted butter
2 pounds beef, ground
3 tablespoons parsley, chopped
Salt and pepper to taste

1 pound macaroni
8 cups water
5 tablespoons all-purpose flour
6 large eggs
1 cup grated Romano cheese
1 cup breadcrumbs

In a large saucepan, scald the milk. Meanwhile, in a 10–inch heavy-gauge skillet, heat 4 tablespoons of the butter and fry the onions until they are golden brown. Add the meat, stirring well to make a fine mixture, then add the parsley. Season with salt and pepper to taste. Set aside.

Preheat the oven to 350 degrees. In a large pot bring water to boil and cook the macaroni according to the package directions, then drain.

Meanwhile, in a large saucepan melt the remaining butter, add the flour, and stir until smooth. Gradually add all but 1 cup of the milk, stirring continuously. When the sauce begins to thicken, remove it from the heat. Beat 5 of the eggs and add the remaining cup of milk. Stir this mixture into the white sauce. Mix half of the sauce with the drained macaroni. Spread half of the macaroni mixture in a 9 × 13–inch baking dish. Sprinkle with half of the grated cheese, then spread the meat mixture and the rest of the cheese over the macaroni and cheese, and top with the remaining macaroni. Pour the remaining sauce over the top. Beat the last egg and pour it over the sauce.

Sprinkle with the breadcrumbs and bake for 30 minutes. Cut into squares to serve.

Makes 8 to 10 servings.

Greek Walnut Cake

Cake

1 pound plus 1 tablespoon
   unsalted butter
1 cup sugar
10 large eggs
2 cups walnuts, coarsely chopped

1 tablespoon baking powder
1 teaspoon cinnamon, ground
1½ cups all-purpose flour
1 cup farina, uncooked

Syrup

2 cups sugar
2½ cups water
2 or 3 whole cloves

1 stick cinnamon
1–1½ tablespoons orange peel,
   grated

Preheat the oven to 375 degrees. Grease with 1 tablespoon of butter and flour a 14 × 10 × 2½–inch baking pan.

To make the cake, in a large mixing bowl, cream together the butter and sugar until light and fluffy, then beat in the eggs. Add the walnuts, baking powder, cinnamon, and 1 cup of the flour, mixing well. Stir in the farina and the remaining flour.

Pour into the prepared pan and bake for 30 minutes. Reduce the heat to 350 degrees and bake until the top is browned.

Meanwhile, prepare the syrup. Combine the sugar and water, and bring to a boil. Add the cloves, cinnamon, and grated orange peel. Cook for an additional 5–10 minutes. Strain and cool slightly. Pour the warm syrup over the cake as soon as you remove it from the oven. Cut the cake diagonally into diamond-shaped pieces.

Makes 1 sheet cake.

Grandma Bühler-Rüegsegger's Carnival Cookies and Apple Fritters

I remember my grandmother in 1945 and '46. In the days during the War, sometimes the sirens would go off when a foreign plane flew overhead, and at night we had blackouts. And all during the War, rationing. I don't remember my grandmother ever complaining about it. In those days you did whatever you could with whatever you had.

We had rationing until 1949. I guess the Swiss wanted to be independent after the War, and only use whatever resources they had. My grandmother kept chickens. That was where we got our eggs. Every day she would go and feed her chickens, as you can see in the picture. Some of them were so tame that they knew her when she came

around. They would sit down on the ground and wait for her to pet them. Every time I look at this picture, that's what it reminds me of. She had names for them, but I don't remember them.

Once, my father brought home a white bread. I had never seen a white bread before, and I had no idea even what it was. My father was stationed someplace that was near a farm, and the farmer was the one who still had white flour. It was against the law to bake anything from white flour during the War, because it was considered wasteful. The government wanted people to use whole wheat flour and not throw away half of it to make white flour.

There was this one particular thing she made called Fastnacht Küchli, or "Carnival Cookies." Instead of rolling all the dough out fully on a table, she would do it halfway and shape the rest on her knees. She would take a clean towel, put flour on it, put it on her knee, shape the thing until it was the right size, then fry it in a pan. She'd call them "kneepad cookies." I remember that very distinctly because I used to sit and watch her do it.

I left Switzerland in 1960, when I was twenty-two, and came to America. My grandmother lived well into her eighties, in Switzerland all her life.

—*Yvonne Mayer*

Fastnacht Küchli

Carnival Cookies

This dish is traditionally served at carnival time, just before Lent.

4 cups all-purpose flour
1 teaspoon salt
3 tablespoons milk
6 tablespoons unsalted butter,
   melted

3 large eggs
Oil for frying
Confectioners' sugar for dusting

In a large bowl, combine the flour (adding it by the spoonful), salt, milk, butter, and eggs. Beat thoroughly with a wooden spoon, then let the dough rest for 30 minutes.

Cut the dough into 20–24 pieces. With a rolling pin, roll out each piece on a floured board or cloth into a paper-thin round about 8 inches in diameter.

In an 8–inch heavy-gauge skillet, heat about 1 inch of oil and quickly fry the dough, one or two pieces at a time, until lightly golden on both sides. Drain the pastries on paper towels and dust with confectioners' sugar.

Makes 20 to 24 pastries.

Apple Fritters

½ cup all-purpose flour
⅓ cup water
⅓ cup milk
Pinch of salt
2 large eggs, separated

Vegetable oil for frying
5 apples or pears
Sugar to sprinkle
Cinnamon to sprinkle

In a large mixing bowl, place the flour and form a well. Combine the water and milk, and pour into the flour well. Beat the egg yolks with the salt, then add into the flour well. Mix well until smooth. Beat the egg whites until stiff, then fold them into the flour mixture.

In a deep fryer, place 4 inches of oil and heat.

Meanwhile, core and peel the apples or pears, then cut crosswise into rings. Dip each ring in the batter. When the oil is hot, with tongs, gently place 5 pieces of fruit at a time into the oil. Turn them when brown on one side. When brown on the other side, with a slotted spoon, remove the fruit pieces and place them on paper towels to drain. Sprinkle with sugar and cinnamon.

Makes 8 servings.

Sittoo's Lebanese Doughnuts

My grandmother was called Sittoo; that's Lebanese for "grandmother." My family lived with Sittoo, and the house was always full of relatives, food, and laughter. I remember when all the relatives would come over and talk Arabic and play Lebanese drums and sing and dance. They would hug and kiss you, and the good-byes would last an hour! Sittoo would always impress on my mom and dad and sister and me how important it was to carry out the traditions until the children were old enough to remember them themselves.

From her, I learned Lebanese customs I might not have known about, having been born in the United States. One of my favorite times was twelve days after Christmas, when we would make Epiphany Doughnuts. According to tradition, on the eve of Epiphany Christ would pass over at midnight and bless all of those who were awake and eating the doughnuts. We got to stay up late, and all the relatives would come over and it would get real loud. It was always a fun time.

As Sittoo was making the doughnuts, she would tell us how the cows bowed their heads and the trees bowed all the way down in reverence to Christ. I remember that story from the time I was real little. She would also sing a little song as she made the doughnuts and they puffed up in the oil. She'd sing, "While mama goes tish, tish, papa goes lish, lish." The doughnuts made the tish-tish noise as they hit the hot oil, and the lish-lish was supposed to mean "delicious." We would always say that the doughnuts looked like animals or letters because they took on all different shapes when they puffed up.

When Sittoo died, things weren't quite the same. We continued the traditions because we knew she would want us to, but everybody wasn't into it as much. Since I was around her when I was growing up, the traditions were a lot stronger with me. I always remember them, every time that time of year rolls around.

—*Karen Elias*

Ul-Way-Mat

Epiphany Doughnuts

3 cups all-purpose flour
1 cake or 1 envelope dried yeast
    dissolved in ½ cup warm
    water with 1 teaspoon sugar
½ teaspoon salt
1 teaspoon finely pulverized
    mahleb seeds (available in
    Middle Eastern groceries)
½ teaspoon finely pulverized
    miskee (available in Middle
    Eastern groceries)
1½ cups water
1 small potato, peeled
Vegetable oil for dipping and
    frying
2½ cups itir (recipe follows)

Oil a piece of wax paper large enough to cover a large mixing bowl.

In a large mixing bowl, place the flour and stir in the dissolved yeast, salt, pulverized mahleb, pulverized miskee, and water. Mix well, then cover with the wax paper, oiled side down. Set the bowl away from any draft and cover it with two or three heavy towels or a light blanket. Let the dough rise until doubled in bulk, about two or three hours.

In a deep heavy-gauge skillet or pot, heat 4 inches of cooking oil until it is just at the smoking point and the surface shimmers.

Meanwhile, in a small bowl, pour a half cup of oil. Dip your left hand in the oil, take a piece of the dough in the same hand, and gently squeeze it between your thumb and forefinger to form a small walnut-size ball. Dip a teaspoon in the oil and scoop the balls from your hand into the heated oil. Cook until golden brown, then remove the balls with a slotted spoon and drain them on paper towels. Dip the drained balls into the cold syrup. Serve them warm.

Makes about 4 dozen doughnuts.

Itir

Basic Syrup

2 cups sugar
1 cup water
½ fresh lemon
1 teaspoon rose water, or orange
    blossom water, or both

In a saucepan, combine the sugar and water. Squeeze the lemon juice into the pan, then add the lemon itself. Over medium heat, bring the mixture to a boil, stirring constantly with a wooden spoon. Cook for 10–15 minutes before adding the rose and/or orange blossom water. Bring the syrup to a full boil again, then remove from the heat. Remove the lemon and allow the syrup to cool.

Makes about 2½ cups.

Tabuli

1 cup cracked wheat
4 large ripe tomatoes
1 or 2 bunches parsley, stems cut
    off
1 bunch scallions
Juice of 2 lemons
2 tablespoons mint flakes, ground
    to powder
½ cup vegetable oil
½ teaspoon allspice, ground
Salt and pepper to taste

Wash the wheat until the water runs clear. Let it stand 30 minutes in cool water, then put the wheat in a colander and squeeze out the water.

Chop the tomatoes, parsley, and scallions, including the tops, very finely. Put the ingredients in a mixing bowl and add the wheat. Stir in the lemon juice, mint flakes, vegetable oil, allspice, salt, and pepper. Chill thoroughly before serving.

Makes 4 servings.

Bubbie's Tzimmes and Tayglach

My grandmother, an Orthodox Jew, was from a small town called Donkera, outside of Riga, in Latvia. When she was only eighteen she had her own dry goods business. My grandfather was a "drummer"—a travelling salesman. For six years he sold merchandise to my grandmother. Finally the business relationship changed to a romantic one and they became engaged. I once asked Bubbie—my grandmother—why it took so long. She said that he wrote her business letters for six years and love letters in the seventh year. The reason my grandfather chose her was that she was the only woman he ever knew who cared about world affairs.

Bubbie was a remarkable woman. She did all sorts of good works during the Depression of the 1930s, when everyone was having a hard time. My grandmother had a reputation for her kindness and generosity. Hoboes would often come to our door for a meal. They'd say, "Mrs. Schlossberg, I heard that you might give me something to eat." These men would sit down at the table with us. She drew no racial lines, and she treated blacks and whites the same. And this was the Depression South. Bubbie said, "Everyone eats at the same table in our house." She was very proud to be in a democracy. She would say, "I'm good enough to talk to the President! Nobody's better, and nobody's worse!"

Her attitude had a profound effect on me. After she died, many people I didn't know told me of the kind things she had done. One little old lady came by and said, "I'm sorry to hear about your grandmother. I just wanted to tell you she was a good Christian woman!"

Bubbie's cooking was a combination of traditional Jewish cooking with bold and imaginative use of spices and inventive cooking methods. I remember fondly her gefilte fish, her pirogena and her wonderful pot roast with carrots, prunes, and sometimes potatoes, called tzimmes.

Bubbie was a woman who was always interested in gadgets and modern things. She should have been born in the twenty-first century! Once she heard about a new invention called the pressure cooker and got herself one. She then made a confection called tayglach, which has a syrup of honey and water. Bubbie set to making her tayglach syrup in the new pressure cooker. But she didn't know how the thing worked. The syrup plugged up the vent and the top blew off. It took the whole family to scrub the mess off the ceiling!

She specialized in long and slow cooking. She would say, "Heninka, put this in the oven, with just a little bit of water, a very low oven, cook it very slowly, and be patient. Let it take care of itself." When it was done she would say, "Now look at it!" She was always so proud of her cooking.

—*Cinde Nissen*

Tzimmes with Chuck Roast

1 large onion, peeled and diced
1 large stalk celery, diced
1 large carrot, peeled and diced
1 clove garlic, peeled
3–5 pounds chuck roast, bone in
2 tablespoons vegetable oil
2 large stalks celery with leaves
¼ cup water
Pepper to taste
3 medium potatoes
2 medium sweet potatoes
6–8 medium carrots
½ pound pitted prunes
Brown sugar to taste
Salt to taste
Grated rind and juice of 1 orange
Horseradish for serving

Preheat the oven to 300 degrees.

In a Dutch oven, prepare a bed for the roast by spreading diced onion, celery, carrot, and garlic on the bottom of the roasting pan.

In a heavy-gauge skillet, over high heat, add oil and sear the roast on both sides. Then, place the roast on the vegetables. Put the celery stalks with the leaves on each side of the meat. Pour one-quarter cup of water around the meat. Sprinkle pepper on the roast to taste. Cover tightly, and place the roast in the oven.

One hour later, peel the potatoes and carrots and cut into chunks. In a large saucepan, cook the vegetables and the prunes in boiling water until they are fork-tender. Note: Since these items cook at different rates, put the carrots in the boiling water first, wait about 5 minutes, then put in the potatoes, wait another 5 minutes, and then the sweet potatoes and prunes.

After an hour and a half, remove the roast from the oven. Arrange the vegetables and prunes on top of the roast. Sprinkle a modest amount of salt and brown sugar over the top, then moisten with orange juice and scatter the grated rind. If the pan juices are drying out, add one-quarter cup of water. Cover and continue cooking for one-half hour. Turn off the heat and remove the cover. Let the roast rest in the oven for about one-half hour (with the door closed). Remove the celery stalks before serving and serve with horseradish and fresh challah (see challah recipe on page 123).

Makes 6 to 8 servings.

Tayglach

Dough

3 large eggs
1 tablespoon sugar
3 tablespoons unsalted butter, softened, or vegetable oil
2 cups all-purpose flour, sifted

Syrup

1½ cups honey
1½ cups sugar
2½ teaspoons ginger, ground
¼ teaspoon cinnamon, ground
1 cup warm water, as needed

To make the dough, in a large mixing bowl, beat the eggs with 1 tablespoon of sugar and the butter or vegetable oil. Add the flour and mix to form a soft dough. If the dough is sticky, add a small amount of flour.

Divide the dough into 36 small pieces. Flour the board, then gently roll the dough into pencil-sized lengths. Make a loop and bring one end of the pastry through it until the loop is almost closed. The pastry will be about ¾–inch wide. Nip the excess dough off the ends and secure by lightly pressing the ends to the loop. This process takes some time, so have good company to entertain and/or help you.

To make the syrup, in a heavy, wide pot, over medium heat, bring the honey, sugar, ginger, and cinnamon to a boil.

Stir enough warm water into the syrup to dilute it slightly. This will help keep the tayglach soft and prevent them from sticking together. Drop the pastries into the syrup. Cover the pot, lower the heat, and simmer for 30 minutes. The tayglach are finished when they are cakey inside, not doughy. Fish them out with a spoon and store them in a jar.

Makes about 3 dozen tayglach.

Mumzie's Maine Fish Chowder and Strawberry Shortcake

We called my grandmother Mumzie. Her name was Gladys Ricker Crocker. I believe that she was born in Maine. She met my grandfather in Maine, and they got married when she was about twenty and he was about twenty-three. My grandfather worked on the Maine Railroad, but then lost his job because of the Depression. They went to live on his parents' farm in Maine for the rest of the Depression.

They had only one child, and that was my mother. My grandmother nearly died when she had my mother. I don't know why, but there were complications. In fact, they told her that if she had the baby, she *would* die, and she said, "I will have this baby." So she had the baby, and neither one of them died.

She had a lot of courage. Finally my grandfather got a job as a salesman in Massachusetts. He would be out of town for about three weeks out of the month, so she was alone a lot. It was a hard time for her.

We lived far away from my grandmother, but some of my fondest memories are of the times we were together. My grandmother was a very beautiful person, very sweet and loving. My grandfather was very irrascible. He was "Get me this! Do that!" and she was just the opposite. It was always said that there was only one woman in the world who could get along with my grandfather, and that was my grandmother. I guess opposites really do attract!

Whenever she had family over, she would make huge meals. My mother hated to cook, so Mumzie would do it all. She used to make strawberry shortcake, New England style, with homemade biscuits and homemade whipped cream. She made molasses cookies all the time. They were individual little cakes that melted in your mouth. Sometimes my grandfather and I would bring back perch that we had caught, and she would make the greatest fish chowder you ever tasted. I've never had anything like it anywhere else. She loved to cook, and even had special plates she used when we were together. She was always giving.

—*Steven Landrum*

140

New England Strawberry Shortcake

Shortcake

2 cups all-purpose flour
2 teaspoons baking powder
½ teaspoon salt
⅔ cup plus 3–4 tablespoons
    sugar

¼ cup shortening
1 cup cold milk
1 quart strawberries, washed and
    hulled
Butter for spreading

Whipped Cream

⅔ cup heavy cream
2 teaspoons sugar

½ teaspoon vanilla extract

Preheat the oven to 425 degrees.

To make the shortcake, mix the flour, baking powder, salt, and 3 tablespoons of sugar. With a knife or wire mixer, cut in the shortening. Add the milk and mix to form a soft dough. Gently roll the dough into a ball on a lightly floured board. Knead 8–10 times, then roll out the dough ½–inch thick. Cut out 6 circles of dough with a 3–inch floured cutter. With your fingertips, gently pat the top of each shortcake with milk to moisten it. This aids in browning. Bake them on an ungreased cookie sheet until golden brown for 12–18 minutes.

Reserve 6 of the largest strawberries for garnishing; sprinkle them with a little sugar. Slice or crush the remaining berries and stir in the rest of the sugar. Let them stand in a warm place until the sugar dissolves.

Just before serving, slice each warm shortcake into two layers and spread them with butter. Cover the bottom layer with the crushed berries, and set the top layer in place. Pour any remaining crushed berries over the top.

In a large bowl, whip the cream until slightly thick. Then add the sugar and vanilla extract, and whip until stiff. Cover the shortcakes with whipped cream and garnish with the reserved berries.

Makes 6 servings.

Fish Chowder

2 pounds cod or haddock fillets
2 cups water
1½–inch cube salt pork, diced
1 large onion, peeled and
    chopped

2 large or 3 medium potatoes,
    peeled and diced
1 quart milk
2 tablespoons unsalted butter
Salt and pepper to taste

In a large saucepan, bring the water to a simmer and poach the fish in the water for 7–9 minutes. Remove the fish, skin and flake it, and set it aside. Reserve the fish broth. In a 6–inch heavy-gauge skillet, render the salt pork, then remove the browned pieces, or cracklings, from the skillet. Set aside. Cook the potatoes and onion in the fat until tender, about 15 minutes, stirring frequently. Add the potatoes and onions to the fish broth, then add the milk, pork cubes, and the fish. Heat until very hot but not boiling. Stir in the butter and season to taste.

Makes 8 to 10 cups.

Shumsky's Meat Knishes

Rita (granddaughter): My grandfather was born in Russia. I'm not sure of the town, but I believe it was someplace near Minsk. The reason he left Russia is the same reason I think every Jewish man about that age was leaving—to avoid conscription into the Czar's army.

First he went to London, where he became a peddler on Petticoat Lane. Then he came to the United States.

Where he got the idea to open a restaurant in the 1920s in Atlantic City I have no idea. It was small; one room that had been divided into two. It was originally called "Shumsky's Rumanian Restaurant," even though none of the family came from Rumania! The food was a combination of Hungarian, Russian, and Rumanian. My grandfather put together the menu of all the things he liked to eat, like kishka, pickled herring, and sweet and sour cabbage. The restaurant was famous for knishes and cheese cake.

Until I was married, I used to eat dinner in the restaurant every night. It served a seven-course meal—an appetizer, soup, an entree, dessert, relishes (like pickles and cole slaw), and bread. Everything was included in the dinner.

Ron (grandson): Rita's father—my Uncle Jimmy—came into the business a few years after our grandfather started it, sometime in 1929. At one time he was both the waiter and the cook. He would get the order from a customer, run back in the kitchen and yell, "Two soft-boiled eggs!" go over to the stove and make them, and then come out and serve them. My uncle was a jovial man who always had time to spend a few minutes with me if I stopped by. He was one of my nicest uncles, and I had many of them!

Rita: It was an interesting place because the waiters were so crazy. There was "John the Sheriff," "Little Abe," Otto, who was a big tall lanky guy, and "Jimmy the Greek." They were all gamblers, and they were all very colorful.

By the time I got to know my grandfather, he was older and commanded a lot of respect from his four sons, who all worked in the restaurant. He was sick later on, but he always came to work. He was diabetic then, but that never stopped him from sneaking into the back and having a piece of cake.

Ron: The restaurant and its characters created a world of romance for me as a kid. It was a popular public place, and there were always lots of people around. Seeing Uncle Jimmy was exciting because he was involved with this restaurant and everything that went with that. Uncle Jimmy was a terrific guy who loved people and was the perfect host and perfect restaurateur. I loved him.

—*Rita Shumsky Fogel and Ron Lieberman*

142

Meat Knishes

Dough

2 cups all-purpose flour
2/3 cup shortening
1/2 teaspoon salt

1/3 cup cold water, or more if
  necessary
2 tablespoons butter for greasing

Filling

2 tablespoons unsalted butter
1 medium onion, peeled and
  chopped
1 clove garlic, peeled and minced

1 large egg
1 pound beef, ground
Salt and pepper to taste

To make the dough, in a large mixing bowl, combine the flour, shortening, and salt by rubbing them together until the dough resembles coarse corn meal. Add the water, one tablespoon at a time, and stir it into the dough. When all the water has been added, press the dough into a ball, cover with wax paper, and refrigerate for 1 hour. Divide the dough in half, then, with a rolling pin, on a lightly floured board, roll out each half into a rectangle.

Preheat the oven to 400 degrees. With the butter, grease a baking sheet.

To make the filling, in a mixing bowl, combine the onion and the garlic. Stir in the egg, the ground beef, and salt and pepper to the mixture. Mix together well. Take half of the meat mixture and place it in the center, lengthwise, of one of the dough rectangles. Fold the dough over lengthwise and seal the edges to form a cylinder of meat and dough. Slice the roll into 8 sections. The repeat the filling and rolling step with the other half of the dough and meat mixture. Pull the dough around each exposed end and crimp closed. Place the knishes on the greased baking sheet.

Bake for 20 minutes, or until the crust is golden brown.

Makes 16 knishes.

Almond Toast

2 tablespoons unsalted butter
6 large eggs
1 cup sugar
1/2 cup vegetable oil
1/2 teaspoon vanilla extract
Juice and rind of 1 lemon

3 cups all-purpose flour
3 teaspoons baking powder
3/4 cup almonds, shelled
Pinch of salt
Cinnamon to taste

Preheat the oven to 350 degrees. With the butter, grease two 8 × 4–inch loaf pans.

In a large mixing bowl, beat the eggs lightly, then fold in the sugar, oil, and vanilla extract. Add the lemon juice and grate the rind into the mixture. Add the flour, baking powder, almonds, and salt to taste, stirring to combine well.

Pour the mixture into the loaf pans and bake them for 45 minutes. Remove the pans from the oven. When cool, slice the loaves and sprinkle the slices with cinnamon.

Makes 10 to 12 servings.

Mama Boyd's Sweet-Potato Pie

My grandmother and grandfather had a farm in Orangeburg, South Carolina, in back of South Carolina University. They had about 700 acres of farmland. I'll never forget the way the scenery would change as we rode down to South Carolina from New Jersey. It would change from the suburban sights of New Jersey to fields, and the earth would become an orange color, and I'd know that I was getting closer and closer to my grandmother's farm. We would go through all these back ways and country roads, get lost a few times and get thirsty and tired. Then I could smell the scent of *farm*. I could see flies all over the place and a couple of hogs and chickens running around the yard and past the tires of our car. Finally, we would come to the house.

Next to the house was my grandmother and grandfather's grocery store—a very small country store, where they sold things they made on the farm, like their own homemade sausages, chickens, corn, canned goods, and baked goods. People would come from all over the county to shop at the store. If my grandmother was in the house, they'd call out, and she would yell back, "Just a minute, I'll be right there!" And it would usually take her twenty minutes or a half-hour to get out there, because she was busy doing something else at the time. They all took their time in the South. My grandmother used to say, "All you folks from the North live in the fast life!"

When my grandmother smiled, she had a mouth full of gold teeth. All of her teeth were fully rimmed in gold. She always wore an apron. Always! And she was always busy—up at five-thirty in the morning and trying to get us up, telling us we were lazy. She would have breakfast ready at six-thirty, with sausage and a meat "pudding." She called it pudding, but it was like a sausage. She would have biscuits and fresh butter and bacon they had smoked themselves.

She would make sweet-potato pie, and apple pie and ice cream. Everything. And the amazing thing was that cooking seemed to be a pastime thing to do. Making a pie was like relaxation for her. She made her own peach cobbler, strawberry jams, and did all kinds of canning. Everything was homemade and fresh. Eating an egg there was different; the eggs were so yellow and they tasted different than what you buy in the stores now. My grandmother was sweet, innocent, very religious, and very hard working. She represented everything that makes a home to me.

—*Donald Jones*

Sweet-Potato Pie

Pastry shell for a single-crust pie
(see pie pastry recipe on page
127)
1½ cups (about 4 medium) sweet
potatoes or yams, cooked and
mashed
2 tablespoons unsalted butter or
shortening, melted
1 teaspoon grated orange or
lemon peel
½ cup firmly packed brown
sugar

1 teaspoon cinnamon, ground
½ teaspoon ginger, ground
½ teaspoon nutmeg, grated
¼ teaspoon cloves, ground
½ teaspoon salt
2 large eggs, beaten
1½ cups milk, scalded
1 cup heavy cream
1 tablespoon white sugar
2 tablespoons chopped pecans

Preheat the oven to 450 degrees.

In a large bowl, place the sweet potatoes or yams, and stir in the melted butter and grated orange or lemon peel. Combine the brown sugar, cinnamon, ginger, nutmeg, cloves, and salt, and beat into the sweet potato mixture. Gradually beat in the eggs. Stir in the scalded milk, blending well. Pour into the prepared pastry shell.

Bake for 10 minutes, then reduce the temperature to 350 degrees and bake for an additional 30–35 minutes, or until a knife or toothpick comes out clean when inserted halfway between the center and the edge of the filling.

Cool the pie on a wire rack. When ready to serve, whip the cream with the sugar and spread it over the pie. Sprinkle the top with chopped pecans.

Makes one 9–inch pie.

Southern-Style Gold Cornbread

1 cup all-purpose flour
4 teaspoons baking powder
¼ cup brown sugar
½ teaspoon salt
1 tablespoon nutmeg (or more, to
taste), ground

1 tablespoon ginger (or more, to
taste), ground
1 cup yellow corn meal
1 cup milk
1 large egg
¼ cup plus 1 tablespoon
shortening

Preheat the oven to 425 degrees. Grease an 8–inch baking pan with 1 tablespoon of shortening.

In a large mixing bowl, sift together the flour, baking powder, brown sugar, salt, nutmeg, and ginger, and then stir in the corn meal.

In a separate bowl, beat the egg and then beat in the milk and shortening.

Pour the liquid ingredients into the dry, stirring well. Pour the batter into the prepared pan and bake for 25–30 minutes.

Makes 9 servings.

Mary Bobich's Potato Soup

My mother's mother lived in Jacob Creek, Pennsylvania, about two miles from where she was born. The town had about 200 people and everyone knew everyone else. She lived on her own farm right into her seventies. The farm used to be self-sufficient; she used to sell some crops. She had corn and beans, eggs, and cherries from the trees that were around, and wild raspberries. She had a huge house with a porch and a swing and lots of room to store things.

She married a man who was a teacher in Russia, but when he came over here, he had to work in a coal mine. He had an accident in the mines and became paralyzed. He went to have an operation and didn't make it through. So, during the Depression, she had to run the farm, feed five kids, and take care of this huge house by herself.

I would visit her on holidays. The atmosphere of the house was always cheery, with lace curtains and plants and the aroma of coffee perking. She would be making eggs. She would beat the eggs with cream and salt and pepper and saute the bacon in slabs. Then she would take homemade bread, slice it, dip it in egg, and flip it over, so that the bread would be in with the eggs and bacon. She had a stove that was half coal and half electric. It was always on, so there was a warmth that constantly exuded from the oven.

She cooked a lot of Slavic dishes. Her big dish was potato soup, which is not like vichyssoise, but made with sour cream. She made kielbasa, and the best bread. You think that Arnold's bread is yellow? Hers makes theirs look white!

She also made good chicken soup. She would buy the chicks and raise them into chickens. One time, she had these two roosters that were constantly fighting for dominion over the hens. She said, "I'm going to make chicken soup." First she made the noodles, and then she said, "I have to go get the chicken," and I said, "Oh, where are you going to get the chicken?" She just took a knife, went outside, got one of the roosters, and whacked his head off. The soup was delicious.

She was a very strong-willed person, very fiesty and bold in her tongue. Not mean, but honest. Because she didn't have much of an education, she had her own words to describe certain things. She would decribe a feeling that touched her heart as "I feel real funny inside." She had a childlike quality to her. She enjoyed the simple things, like flowers and birds. There was one cardinal that she'd trained to come to the banister, where she fed it bread. She had a chicken coop, and in the winter she would go down to the coop to look in the window and see how the chickens were warming themselves in the sunlight. These were the kinds of things she liked to do.

—*Athena Coroneos*

Potato Soup

6 medium potatoes, washed,
  peeled, and cubed
½ teaspoon salt, or more to taste

½ gallon milk
1 cup sour cream

In a large pot, place the potatoes and add salted water to cover. Bring to a boil and cook for about 30 minutes, or until the potatoes are fork-tender and some of the water has boiled off. Add the milk and sour cream, and stir until smooth. Gently reheat the soup. If the soup is too thick, you may thin it with water.

Makes 6 to 8 servings.

Baked Cottage Cheese

1 tablespoon unsalted butter
6 large eggs
2 pounds small-curd cottage
  cheese

1 cup sugar
2 teaspoons vanilla extract

Preheat the oven to 350 degrees. With the butter, grease a 2–quart ovenproof casserole.

In a large mixing bowl, place the eggs and beat them lightly, then stir in the cottage cheese, sugar, and vanilla extract, blending well. Place the mixture in the casserole and bake for 1 hour. Cool slightly before serving.

Makes 6 to 10 servings.

English Groom's Cake

As soon as my grandmother found out that we were getting married, she sent me a letter about the Groom's Cake and its history. The bride was supposed to make it herself. It's a dark wedding cake, and in the old days it would be packed in little boxes for the guests to "take home and dream on," you know, to dream of your husband-to-be. That was the old English tradition. My mother had one at her wedding, and of course my grandmother and *her* mother had had theirs too. So she sent a whole package with the recipe and the citrons and raisins and nuts, everything that was supposed to go into the Groom's Cake.

It's a funny old recipe because it says things like "fill the milk pan." Now, I don't know what a milk pan is. And then it says, "Add an apple when you put it away," and "one wine glass of brandy." You've got to use your judgment. The original recipe called for almonds, but my grandmother lives down in Oklahoma, so she sent me and my sister pecans for our cakes. A few months before the wedding, I made it, stuck it in a tin, and put it in the pantry down in the cellar to age—and forgot about it, and I mean *forgot* about it!

We had the reception at home. The day of the wedding everyone was running around. It was a chaotic day. When it got time to do the cake, people realized that the Groom's Cake wasn't there. So my cousins ran downstairs, found the cake, and whipped up some frosting and frosted it just in time to bring it out to be with the white cake. It really looked lovely. There was a Groom's Cake at my sister's wedding too, only she used bourbon instead of brandy because she got married in Louisville, Kentucky.

My grandmother's name is Mary Buckbee Riggs. The Riggses came over in 1630. They landed in Roxbury, Massachusetts. The wedding dress I wore has been passed down in the Riggs family. My great-grandmother made the dress. My great-great-grandfather, Samuel Hynes, worked on the railroad out West. His family lived with him in a private railroad car. He befriended an Oriental family who gave him a silk tablecloth with long, 10–inch fringes. Each of his four daughters was given a quarter of the cloth to make her wedding dress. My grandmother's dress has a bustle and a high neck, it's draped and embroidered. It's really beautiful. My mother and sister and aunts have all worn it for their weddings, and I wore my grandmother's veil at my wedding, too.

—*Maryanne Dawson*

Groom's Cake

Maryanne: This recipe, dating back to 1897, makes enough to fill an old fashioned milk pan—equivalent to two modern angel food cake pans. This cake was served at the following weddings:

Florence Day and John Buckbee, November 1897
Mary Buckbee and Samuel Riggs, June 1923
Mary Riggs and F. Robertson Dawson, June 1950
Susan Riggs and David Reed, October 1954
Susan Dawson and Richard Dunning, May 1976
Maryanne Riggs Dawson and Jeffrey Persons, August 1981

4 cups all-purpose flour	*1 cup dark molasses*
1 teaspoon baking powder	*1½ cups (3 sticks) unsalted*
2½ pounds black raisins	* butter*
2 pounds dried currants	*2 cups brown sugar*
1 pound candied citron, chopped	*¾ cup red wine*
½ pound pitted dates	*¾ cup brandy*
¼ pound almonds, sliced	*1 tablespoon mace, ground*
10 large eggs, separated	*1 teaspoon cinnamon, ground*
1 teaspoon baking soda	*1 teaspoon cloves, ground*

Preheat the oven to 300 degrees. Line two 10–inch angel food cake tube pans with brown paper or wax paper.

In a large mixing bowl, sift the baking powder with 1 cup of the flour, then dredge the raisins in this mixture. Sprinkle the currants, citron, dates, and almonds with the remaining flour. Beat the egg yolks lightly. Stir the baking soda into 3 tablespoons of the molasses.

Cream together the butter and sugar. Beat in the egg yolks, the remaining molasses, and the baking soda-molasses mixture. Stir in the flour gradually. Add the wine, brandy, spices, and the fruit and nuts, stirring well to incorporate. Fold in the egg whites. Pour into the prepared pans and bake for 2 hours. Test by inserting a clean broom straw or a sharp knife in the middle. If it comes out clean, the cakes are done. If not, bake for an additional 30 minutes or until it tests done. Store in tightly closed tins for 2–3 months, if possible—the cake improves with age.

Makes 2 tube cakes.

Hot Mustard Sauce

Maryanne: Another of my grandmother's real family recipes is her mustard sauce. I give it as Christmas presents every year. We all love it. It's very good on sandwiches of cheese, ham, or other meats, or even as a dip. It has a nice sweet-tart taste to it.

2–ounce can mustard powder	*1 large egg*
½ cup white vinegar	*½ cup sugar*

In a small mixing bowl, combine the mustard and vinegar, then cover with foil and leave overnight.

The next morning, beat together the egg and sugar. Stir into the mustard mixture and cook in a double boiler until the mixture thickens. Cool the sauce, then refrigerate it in a tightly closed container.

Makes about 1½ cups.

Oma Schreck's Red Cabbage and Plum Cake

My great-grandmother on my mother's side was named Antonia Klara Marie Butler Schreck. When she and my great-grandfather, Fritz, came over from Germany in 1926, they already had a sixteen-year-old daughter, who was to become my grandmother. They all moved to Cohoes, New York, where my great-grandfather worked for the Delaware and Hudson Railroad.

We called my great-grandfather Opa. He was a very quiet man. I don't remember a lot about him, except that sometimes I used to sit on his lap, and he would read me a Classic Comic Book. He would pretend to read it to me, but really he was making up the words to go along with the pictures because he couldn't read English.

My great-grandmother, Oma Schreck, was the matriarch of the family. Even though she was only four foot eleven, she had a lot of power. This woman ruled with an iron first. If people needed money, or some kind of counsel, they would go to Oma, not Opa. She was never afraid to lay down the law; she was never afraid to say what she thought. But Oma could also be very soft-hearted. She would always help someone if they needed it.

Up until the time I started school, I used to spend the whole day at Oma and Opa's because both my parents worked. My father would drop me off on his way to work. I remember the meals because Oma was always cooking; there was food all the time. I think that's how I began my battle with slight plumpness! For breakfast there would be half a grapefruit, a soft-boiled egg, cereal, toast, and coffee, which was really only half coffee and half milk. And no sooner was breakfast over than it seemed time for lunch.

Oma served a European lunch that was more like our dinner. It was always a big, hot, heavy meal—chicken livers and noodles, and chicken soup that was thick like a lentil soup. In it were klossen, which are like matzoh balls the Germans make from stale hard rolls instead of matzoh meal. I used to see her sitting in the kitchen by the window with this huge bowl, mushing up hard rolls and eggs, making them into little balls, and then adding them into the chicken soup. For dessert, she used to give me a farina-like mixture with raspberry sauce on top, served cold, or her wonderful plum cake. Dinner was called *Abenbrot,* which means "evening bread" and was more like our lunch, with open-faced sandwiches of ham or turkey and Swiss cheese. Sometimes we would have her great green-bean soup, and a very good and tangy red cabbage. You would never see hamburgers and hot dogs at Oma's. She knew how to cook.

—*Paula Bachinsky*

Red Cabbage

2–pound head red cabbage
1 teaspoon salt
6–8 slices bacon, chopped
3 apples, peeled, cored, and
    chopped

2 bay leaves
5–6 peppercorns
½ cup vinegar
¼ cup granulated or brown
    sugar

Shred the cabbage. In a large saucepan, over medium heat, bring salted water to a boil and cook the cabbage for about 10 minutes, or until almost tender. Pour off the water. In a heavy-gauge skillet, cook the bacon until fairly crisp, then add the bacon and drippings to the cabbage. Stir in the apples, bay leaves, peppercorns, and enough hot water to cover the cabbage. Stir in the vinegar and sugar, cover, and simmer for about an hour.

Makes 6 servings.

Plum Cake

Cake

1 cake or 1 envelope dried yeast
¼ cup lukewarm water
½ cup milk
⅓ cup sugar
1 teaspoon salt
2 tablespoons shortening

2½ cups all-purpose flour
2 tablespoons unsalted butter
1 large egg, lightly beaten
4 cups Italian plums, sliced
¼–⅓ cup sugar
½ teaspoon cinnamon, ground

Butter-Sugar Topping

½ cup flour
½ cup sugar
½ cup (1 stick) unsalted butter

½ cup almonds, ground, with 2
    teaspoons cinnamon, optional

To make the cake, in a small mixing bowl, sprinkle the yeast into the warm water and set aside until bubbly, about 10 minutes. In a saucepan, scald the milk. Stir in the sugar, salt, and shortening, and pour into a large mixing bowl. Cool to lukewarm. Stir in enough of the flour to form a thick batter. Add in the yeast and the egg, beating well, and stir in the remaining flour to form a stiff dough. Turn out on a lightly floured board and knead until the dough is smooth and satiny.

With 2 tablespoons of butter, grease a large bowl. Place the dough in the bowl and turn to coat all sides. Cover the dough with a clean kitchen towel and let rise until doubled in bulk, about 1½ hours.

Meanwhile, make the butter-sugar topping. In a large mixing bowl, stir together the flour and sugar, then cut in the butter until the mixture resembles coarse crumbs. Stir in the ground almonds mixed with cinnamon, if using.

Preheat the oven to 350 degrees.

Punch down the dough and let it rest for 10 minutes. With a rolling pin, roll out the dough on a floured surface and fit it into a jelly roll pan. Combine the plums, sugar, and cinnamon, and spread the plum mixture over the surface of the dough. Spread the butter-sugar topping over the entire surface and bake for about 30 minutes.

Makes one 10½ × 15½–inch cake.

Jennie Appleby's Ranch Pudding

My grandmother's from Salisbury, Connecticut. Her family comes from southern Connecticut, and as far as I know they have always lived there.

My mother ran a little restaurant and tearoom in the 1930s, and my mother and grandmother worked together in the kitchen. My mother made the cakes, and my grandmother made all the homemade pies and the other foods. I had my own restaurant for a number of years, and I was fortunate that my mother was still alive when I started it.

She passed on all the recipes that she had used, mainly desserts and some of the basic entrees, and, of course, along with those, my grandmother's recipes.

Grannie Appleby lived with us. In addition to running the restaurant, we took in guests, and there was a room in the guest house where Grannie slept. She was alone when I knew her and so was my mom. But they had each other and the business. When they had the restaurant, Grannie's recipe for apple pie was legendary. She used lard. I did too, in my restaurant. I definitely feel that lard makes the best pastry. Even though it's an animal fat, it makes the lightest, most delicate flaky-dough crust. That's half the secret of an apple pie. And she used to stand there with these two knives and just keep cutting through the dough until it was totally coated with the lard. Now, when *we* made the same recipe in the restaurant, we used the modern knife, which is a Cuisinart! You put the ingredients for her pie crust in a Cuisinart, and in a matter of six or seven seconds a ball of dough suddenly appears and you stop it immediately. I would say that we really accomplished the same thing my grandmother did, only much quicker.

Another recipe I used was her original Ranch Pudding. It was the biggest hit of the restaurant, and the customers kept asking me for the recipe, which I considered to be a trade secret. In fact, a number of customers contacted us with a view to publishing the recipe in *Bon Appetit* and *Gourmet* magazines. At that time I declined because I was still in business, and I considered that recipe unique. I'll tell you something funny about the Ranch Pudding: If you've never made it before, you would swear you had made a horrendous mistake, because what comes out of the oven is so different in appearance and texture from what goes into the oven; it's incredible.

Grannie Appleby lived until she was about eighty. She had a terrific sense of humor. You see, I knew her all during the Depression—very tough times. Everyone would be sitting there, quiet and depressed. Suddenly, she would say the funniest thing right out of the blue and just break everyone up. She was the one, by the way, from whom I got the word "pissant." She never said much about people, but once, she was very annoyed at somebody and she said, under her breath, "That *pissant!*" I've used it ever since.

—*Roger Appleby*

Ranch Pudding

8 cups (3½ pounds) brown sugar
½ cup (1 stick) unsalted butter
10 cups water
4 cups black raisins

5 cups instant biscuit mix*
1 tablespoon vanilla extract
3 cups walnut pieces
2 cups milk

Preheat the oven to 375 degrees.

In a saucepan, over medium heat, stir together 4 cups of the brown sugar, the butter, and the water, and bring to a boil. Cook for 5 minutes. This makes a caramel sugar mixture.

Meanwhile, in a large mixing bowl, stir together the raisins, biscuit mix, vanilla extract, walnut pieces, and milk.

Pour the caramel sugar mixture into 2 9 × 13–inch pans. Pour the batter into the center of the pans: *Do not spread*. Bake for 30–40 minutes.

Makes 24 servings.

Jennie always used Bisquick.

Potato Leek Soup

10 cups water
8–10 potatoes, peeled and
  quartered
1½ cups (3 sticks) unsalted
  butter
1 or 2 leeks, well washed and
  chopped
1 large onion, peeled and
  chopped

¾ cup all-purpose flour
2 cups heavy cream
Salt and white pepper to taste
4 egg yolks
Toasted almonds to garnish
Chopped parsley to garnish
Light cream or half-and-half to
  serve

In a big pot, bring the water to a boil, and add the potatoes. Cook for 10 minutes.

Meanwhile, in a large heavy-gauge skillet, heat the butter, then saute the leeks and onions until soft. Set aside one-third of the leeks and onions. To the remainder, add the flour and stir to form a creamy roux. Then thin it with a little of the pototo water and stir it into the potatoes. Cook until the potatoes are soft, about 30 minutes. Puree in a blender or food processor and return to the pot. Add the reserved leeks and onions and then add the cream, and salt and pepper to taste. Allow the soup to cool. Whip the egg yolks and combine with a little of the lukewarm soup. Stir the egg yolk mixture into the cooled soup and reheat gently. Garnish with almonds and parsley, and serve with light cream or half-and-half, if desired.

Makes 6 to 8 servings.

Granny Stella's Pirogis

I guess you could make veggie ones, but you have to remember that I'm of European descent, and meat is a very important part of the diet. Meat is more than just a food: it's status, and it always has been.

My favorite one of Granny's dishes is her pirogis. She fills them with a mixture of mashed potatoes and cheddar cheese, or sometimes with just sauerkraut. Sometimes instead of boiling the pirogis, she fries them. The dough gets a little more hard and crispy that way. Her pirogis are always right on.

When I got older, she used to have me cook them. We'd have two frying pans going at once. She's great in the kitchen. She's one of those grandmothers who loves to talk. She asks me if my wife cooks: "Does Ellen cook?" I say, "No, of course not. I do all the cooking." Then I say, "No, I'm joking. We split it," which she finds very interesting.

Most of her female grandchildren won't cook. They are just not interested. But I wanted to learn, and the best way was sitting there and watching her. Although I have her recipe for pirogis, mine come out a lot different from hers. The family goes crazy over *her* pirogis. And you don't ask twice about who wants the last one. You say, "No? Okay, fine. Thank you!"

—*Rick Telman*

My grandmother was born in the old country. In her time it was questionable whether you came from Poland or Russia or Lithuania. She's not really sure, because the borders kept changing. And either she doesn't remember or she doesn't want to: She's happy here.

Granny cooked for us on holidays. And she cooked for me anytime I was there. She was the kind of grandmother who would always say, "Have some more."

She was always trying to put more food on your plate. If she was having ten guests over, she would prepare seventy-five pirogis, a lot more than were needed. She also made galumkis. Galumkis are stuffed cabbage put in a big pan with tomato sauce and baked. When I was a kid, I used to hate cabbage, so I would unroll the galmukis and eat just the insides. They finally got me to eat the whole thing by putting ketchup on: "Oh, put some ketchup on it, you'll like it!" Now I don't eat meat.

Pirogis

Potato Dumplings

Dough

6 cups all-purpose flour
2 large eggs, lightly beaten
2 cups water

2 teaspoons salt
2 tablespoons vegetable oil

Potato Filling

4 or 5 potatoes, peeled and
    quartered
8 cups water

1 teaspoon salt
½ pound American cheese, cubed
2 tablespoons unsalted butter

Topping

3 tablespoons vegetable oil for
    frying
2 tablespoons unsalted butter

3 large onions, peeled and
    chopped

To make the dough, place the flour in a large bowl. Make a well in the center and add the beaten eggs, water, salt, and oil. Mix well and place on a floured board. Knead until smooth, about 5 minutes. Divide the dough into two equal parts. On a floured board roll out one half of the dough to a thickness of ¼ inch and cut with a round cookie cutter or glass.

To make the filling, place the potatoes in a pot with the water and salt. Bring to a boil and cook over moderate heat for about 30 minutes, or until tender. Drain and mash the potatoes, and add the cheese and butter. Stir well to combine.

Bring a large pot of salted water to a boil. While the water heats, fill the pastries: Place a teaspoon of filling in the center of each pastry round, and fold the edges together, sealing well using the tines of a fork. Drop the pirogis in the boiling water and cook for 5–10 minutes. Drain and rinse in cold water.

In a 10–inch heavy-gauge skillet, heat vegetable oil and brown the pirogis on all sides. Remove from the skillet and drain on paper towels.

To make the topping, in the same skillet, melt the butter, add the chopped onion, and saute until tender. Arrange the pirogis on a serving platter and pour the onions on top.

Variations: Instead of mashed potatoes, use prunes, cottage cheese, or sauerkraut to fill the pirogis.

Makes about 6 dozen pirogis.

Galumkis

Stuffed Cabbage

2 medium heads cabbage
8–10 cups boiling water
1 pound beef, ground
½ pound pork, ground
½ teaspoon salt
Dash of pepper
1 teaspoon dried parsley, crushed

3 cups rice, cooked
2 tablespoons butter or
    shortening
¼ cup white vinegar
¾ cup water
32–ounce can crushed tomatoes

Cut around the core of each cabbage head to loosen the leaves. Place the cabbage in a kettle, cover with boiling water, and simmer for 12–15 minutes, turning occasionally, until the leaves are soft enough to roll.

Meanwhile, mix together well the beef, pork, salt, pepper, parsley, and rice.

Preheat the oven to 325 degrees.

Remove the cabbage from the kettle. Peel off the large outer leaves, reserving 10 for wrappers and 6 for covering. Shred the remaining cabbage cores and sprinkle over the bottom of a Dutch oven or roasting pan. Place a tablespoon of filling in the center of each of the 10 wrapper leaves. Turn in the sides and roll each leaf into a packet. Place the rolls in the Dutch oven or roasting pan on top of the shredded cabbage. Dot the top layer with butter or shortening. Pour the vinegar, water, and tomatoes over the cabbage rolls, and arrange the leaves for covering on top. Cover with foil and the lid of the Dutch oven or roasting pan. Bake for 2 hours.

Makes 10 galumkis.

Kim Chee and Fiery Beef

My grandmother was very refined and reserved, and didn't show her emotions. She was educated in China, which was not common for Koreans in those days. My grandfather was a preacher, and my grandmother was a businesswoman. She was very determined and enterprising. She owned and ran a hotel that had 250 rooms, and is considered something of a landmark in Korea today. Guests in the hotel were served small meals, upon request, in their rooms. My grandmother ran the kitchen and made a great deal of the food herself. She also ran our household and cooked the majority of the meals.

After the morning meal at the hotel, she would walk across town to our home to take care of me, my two sisters, and my six cousins. We were raised during the war, and food was scarce. One of the biggest treats was black-market American candy. My grandmother would give us each two candies a week, which was quite a lot.

The most wonderful dinners my grand-mother made were the ones for festivals. There was a dinner for the Chinese New Year, for the August Moon Festival, and, of course, birthdays. At the dinners, my oldest cousin was treated like a king. He was always served first and got the best quality food because he was the eldest boy.

I remember a special meal that my grandmother made on United Nations Day. My mother went to the Army base and said she wanted to invite soldiers who had no place to go to dinner. Fifteen soldiers came to dinner. My grandmother cooked for three weeks in advance so that the meal would be perfect. She hired a pianist and a violinist, and the celebration lasted all day. Though the food was wonderful, the ambiance wasn't exactly a child's dream. My grandmother and my uncle thought that one shouldn't talk at dinner, that only barbarians did that. The attitude was, eat in silence and be grateful. All of the children wished my uncle wouldn't come to dinner so that we could talk and giggle. But he always came.

I never saw my mother and grandmother eat, so I wasn't sure if they *ever* ate, until I was a bit older. Lack of food was a big issue when we were growing up, and I later learned that my grandmother and mother wanted to make sure we all had enough to eat first, so they used to eat very simply, later.

—*Choan Kim*

Kim Chee

Pickled Cabbage

2–pound head Chinese cabbage
½ cup coarse or kosher salt
3 tablespoons water
2 tablespoons red pepper flakes
3 cloves garlic, peeled and finely minced

2 tablespoons fresh ginger, peeled and finely minced
1 tablespoon sugar
3 scallions, finely diced
2 tablespoons marinated small shrimp (available in Korean groceries), optional

Core the cabbage, then rinse and drain it. Sprinkle it with the salt, and add the water. Let the cabbage stand in a stock pot for 8 hours. Stuff the red pepper, garlic, ginger, sugar, scallions, and shrimp into the core of the cabbage. Put it in a tightly sealed glass container or a crock. Let it stand at room temperature for 2 days in warm weather or 4 days in cold weather, then refrigerate. Slice thinly and serve as a relish.

Makes about 10 to 12 small servings.

Ginger Tea

1 inch fresh ginger, peeled and thinly sliced
1 quart cold water

1 cinnamon stick
Sugar or honey, as desired

In a small saucepan, place the ginger and the water, and heat until just at the boil. Add the cinnamon stick. Bring to a boil, lower the heat, then simmer for about 15 minutes. Serve hot with sugar or honey to taste. This is particularly good during cold weather.

Makes 4 1–cup servings.

Bulgogi

Fiery Beef

2 pounds flank or sirloin steak
1 tablespoon sesame seeds, powdered*
3 scallions, finely chopped
3 cloves garlic, peeled and finely chopped

2 tablespoons fresh ginger, peeled and grated
2 tablespoons sesame oil
¼ cup sugar
½ teaspoon black pepper
⅓ cup soy sauce

Slice the steak against the grain into strips ⅛–inch thick. In a large mixing bowl, stir together the scallions, garlic, ginger, sesame oil, sugar, and pepper, and add the beef. Cover the beef with the marinade and let it soak overnight in the refrigerator.

Thirty minutes before cooking time, stir the soy sauce into the marinade. Turn on the broiler, arrange the meat slices in a pan, and broil the meat for 30–60 seconds. You can, if you wish, grill the meat over a hot fire.

Makes 4 servings.

*If you cannot find powdered sesame seeds, toast 1–1½ tablespoons of the seeds in a dry, heavy-gauge skillet until they turn golden brown. Allow them to cool, then grind them in a mortar and pestle, a food processor, or a blender.

Grandmother Campbell's Granite-Pan Burnt Sugar Cake

I lived with my grandparents. My grandfather's father built the house I grew up in. It had been a stagecoach stop on the Oregon Trail. In the back of the house were some garages, but originally they had been stables for the horses. Stagecoaches would come through on the Oregon Trail, and my great-grandparents, who ran the stage-coach stop, would feed all of these people that came in. So we had a kitchen that was as big as my apartment in New York is today.

My grandmother was a wonderful cook, and she trained our housekeeper to cook her way, which was to just throw things in until it was the right consistency. That's the way people always used to learn, and that's the way I cook. I follow recipes, but I seldom have a mistake, because I can tell if the batter is a little too thick or too thin. I'm great with pie crusts and pastry batters and pizza dough and things like that—noodles and spaghetti, because I learned very early what the consistencies were and how they should feel, and how sticky they should be or how moist or dry. My grandmother could always determine the right oven temperature—her oven had no gauge—by sticking her hand in. And that's really what the old-fashioned kind of cooking is based on, textures and feelings.

She did use recipes, but almost all of the preparations of different kinds of meat and things like that I think she did more "by guess and by Gosh." Some of her recipes are really hard to read. The books of hers that I have—one of them was published in 1913—have a blank page every couple of pages where you would write down your own recipe. She put in a lot of them, and most of them were desserts. I'm putting these recipes in modern-day terms because I know that when they say "sour cream," they mean you put the milk on the shelf and let it sour. When they say "teaspoon," they took a heaping eating spoon; they didn't have measuring spoons.

Like with this burnt sugar cake—you're supposed to put the sugar in a granite pan. Now, I don't know *who* has a granite pan. I use an aluminum pan because it doesn't stick.

My grandmother always had a lot of handy hints. For instance, she'd always say that if you wanted vegetable soup to be good, you should add an apple—just cut up an apple and put it in to give flavor. That's one of her most handy hints. I always do that when I cook vegetable soup. In fact, I make everything from scratch in my kitchen, just the way she did, and most everything I do I learned from her.

—*Jerald Stone*

158

Burnt Sugar Cake

Cake

½ cup (1 stick) plus 1 tablespoon
   unsalted butter
1½ cups sugar
2 large eggs, separated
1 cup water
2½ cups sifted cake flour

1 tablespoon caramel syrup
   (recipe follows)
1 teaspoon vanilla extract
2 teaspoons baking powder
Rum glaze, optional (recipe
   follows)

Preheat the oven to 350 degrees. Grease with 1 tablespoon of butter, and flour 2 layer cake pans or a bundt pan. Beat the egg whites until stiff and set aside.

To make the cake, in a large mixing bowl, cream together the butter and sugar until light and fluffy. Beat in the egg yolks and water. Gradually add 2 cups of the flour, beating after each addition. Beat for 3 minutes. Add the caramel syrup, vanilla extract, and the remaining flour. Beat again until well incorporated. Stir in the baking powder and fold in the egg whites. Pour into the prepared cake pans and bake for about 30 minutes if using 2 pans, about 50 minutes if using a bundt pan.

To test the cake, carefully open the oven door after about 25–30 minutes for layer cakes, 45–50 minutes for a bundt cake, and insert a clean broom straw, sharp knife, toothpick, or cake tester in the middle. If it comes out clean, the cake is done.

Makes 1 two-layer 8 or 9–inch round cake, or 1 bundt cake.

Caramel Syrup

½ cup sugar

½ cup boiling water

In an enameled or stainless steel saucepan, over medium heat, place the sugar, stirring constantly, until the sugar is melted, brown, and begins smoking. It really must darken. Have the boiling water at hand. Protect your hands and arms with oven mitts or dish towels, then remove the pan from the heat and immediately and rapidly stir in the water, which will splatter and steam. Return the mixture to the heat and allow to boil. Remove from heat, and allow to cool thoroughly, then bottle and store for future use.

Makes enough syrup for 3 cakes.

Rum Glaze

2 teaspoons caramel syrup

1 cup rum

To glaze, pierce the top of the cake repeatedly with an ice pick or sharp knife while still warm and in the pan(s). Stir together the caramel syrup and rum and pour over the cake.

German Coffee Cake

½ teaspoon baking soda
1 cup thick sour milk or
   buttermilk*
1 large egg, beaten
1 cup sugar
2 cups all-purpose flour

1¾ teaspoons baking powder
½ teaspoon cinnamon, ground
½ teaspoon nutmeg, ground
¼ teaspoon salt
½ cup (1 stick) plus 1 tablespoon
   unsalted butter, melted

Preheat the oven to 350 degrees. Grease with 1 tablespoon of butter, and flour a 9 × 5–inch loaf pan or an 8–inch square pan.

In a large mixing bowl, combine the baking soda and soured milk or buttermilk, then stir in the beaten egg and the sugar.

Sift together the flour, baking powder, cinnamon, nutmeg, and salt. Sift into the milk mixture, stirring well to incorporate. Add the melted butter and mix well. Spread in the prepared pan and bake for 50–60 minutes.

Makes one 9 × 5–inch loaf or an 8–inch square cake.

*If you don't have any soured milk or buttermilk, add 1 teaspoon of lemon juice to 1 cup of milk and let stand for 5 minutes.

Mama Lizzie's Shrimp Gumbo and Salmon Croquettes

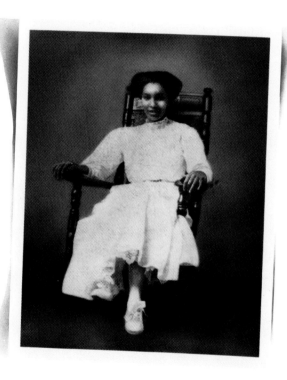

My great-grandmother was named Mama Lizzie, and I'm named after her. She lived in Kentucky, but her ancestors came from the West Indies. One of her ancestors was Alexander Hamilton. I don't know how it happened, but it happened. My great-grandfather was a British subject. I also have some Irish and some American Indian blood on Mama Lizzie's side, and I think there's some German in there, too. Mama Lizzie had six children, and one of these six was my grandmother Mabel.

These salmon croquettes were passed down a fair ways through the family. My grandmother Mabel made them in the thirties and forties because fish was cheap at the time, and she wanted something quick and substantial enough to feed six children. I don't know if it was the taste I loved so much or the warm and loving atmosphere that she created when she cooked. I really loved my grandmother a lot. She was always talking and cooking, and she was always teaching me stuff. She was a musician, and she would tell me all these stories about when she used to play in theaters, when the movies first came out. She would tell me what it was like on road trips with her group, and how they played throughout the South. They would always worry if they were going to get paid or not, because they'd be playing for a lot of white people, and sometimes, they just wouldn't pay them; you know, they would just run them out of town. She was a very good piano player, and her son played with Louis Armstrong. There's a lot of musical talent in my family, none of which I have.

My grandmother lived up in Harlem with my aunt, and she practically raised me. My mother was working two jobs, but my grandmother always had time for me. She was working for the Penn Central Railroad, but she still cooked all the meals, ran the house, and played with me. She was so full of energy! She lived in a five-story walk-up—that's ten flights of stairs—and she would always beat me up those steps. I could never figure it out. That was my last vision of her before I went into the Air Force—she could still get up those steps faster than me, and be talking all the way up. She had long beautiful hair, and I used to sit sometimes and just brush it. She was the person I turned to, much more so than my mother, more than anybody in my life. She died on my birthday.

—*Elizabeth Cespedes*

160

Quick Shrimp Gumbo

2 tablespoons vegetable oil
2 medium onions, peeled and
   diced
1 large green pepper, chopped
1 pound okra (fresh or frozen),
   sliced

28–ounce can tomatoes
1 pound medium-size fresh
   shrimp, shelled and deveined
White rice (recipe follows)

In a 6–inch heavy-gauge skillet, heat the vegetable oil and saute the onion and pepper until tender.

Meanwhile, in a saucepan, cook the okra in water almost to cover, for 10 minutes. Drain and set aside.

In a large soup pot, over low heat, heat the tomatoes. Add the onion, green pepper, and salt and pepper to taste. Simmer for about 10 minutes. Then add the okra and simmer for 30 minutes. Add the shrimp about 8 minutes before serving, but do not let them overcook. Serve over white rice.

Makes 6 to 8 servings.

White Rice

4 quarts water
2 tablespoons salt

2 cups long grain white rice

In a large saucepan, add the salt to the water and bring to a boil. Gradually add the rice, half a cup at a time, making sure the water continues to boil. Cook the rice uncovered at a boil for 20 minutes, then drain in a colander.

Makes 6 to 8 servings.

Salmon Croquettes

16 ounces canned salmon
1 tablespoon vegetable oil
1 medium green pepper, chopped
1 medium onion, peeled and
   diced

1 large egg
Garlic powder to taste
Salt and pepper to taste
1 cup seasoned breadcrumbs for
   coating
Oil for frying

Drain the salmon and set aside. In a 6–inch heavy-gauge skillet, over medium heat, warm the oil, and saute the onion and pepper until tender. Stir in the salmon and egg, and season with garlic powder, salt, and pepper to taste.

Form the mixture into 6 croquettes. Dip into the seasoned breadcrumbs to coat.

In a 10–inch heavy-gauge skillet, over medium heat, warm about an inch of oil until very hot. Add the croquettes and brown on both sides for about 10 minutes.

Makes 6 croquettes.

Bessie Budgen's Oatmeal Tarts and Harvest Home Grape Pie

My grandmother Bessie was born in Avon, New York, in 1893, while her parents were in the U.S. to visit relatives, but she was brought back to England before she was five and was brought up southeast of London, in the county of Kent. She married her cousin Jack Budgen during the First World War. They emigrated to Canada in the 1920s, and my grandmother landed a job as a servant in the kitchen of the Mellons, the American millionaires, at their summer estate in Muskoka, Canada. After she finished working for the Mellons, she and Jack bought a farm west of Toronto.

Jack was a very stubborn man who considered he had gained the wisdom of the world. He would often end an argument with Bessie, or anyone, for that matter, by saying, "Aw, yew cahn't tell me nuffin', Ah seen it awl before!"

My grandmother's cooking was definitely British. And I don't know that there was ever a time that there wasn't a pot of tea brewing. During her later years, my grandmother owned a little budgie bird, which she named Skipper, in honor of my grandfather's days in the merchant marine. The bird's only two phrases were "Time for tea!" and "Put the kettle on!" He said both with an accent, unmistakably my grandmother's.

It's Sunday dinners that I most vividly recall. We'd always arrive early in the afternoon: time for tea. She would always serve tea with cookies, or maybe some of the oatmeal tarts she'd made on Saturday, baking day. Dinner was at five and it was big. If it wasn't roast beef, it might be roast pork, or young lamb—always served with a mint sauce that she would make from the wild mint she had gathered from the yard.

The other vivid memory I have is of Christmas. It was the tradition, back in England, to put sixpences into the Christmas pudding batter for people to find. In Canada, my grandmother substituted dimes for sixpences, and even during the Depression, she always managed to find a couple of dimes for the children. The only problem was making sure you didn't crack a tooth on a piece of money in your pudding! Without a doubt, Bessie's Christmas pudding was always one of the favorite parts of Christmas dinner, and seeing who found money added a certain element of suspense to dessert!

—*David Eden*

Oatmeal Tarts

Pie pastry for 8 3–inch tart shells
(see pie pastry recipe on page
127)*
4 tablespoons unsalted butter
½ cup sugar
½ teaspoon cinnamon, ground
¼ teaspoon salt

½ teaspoon cloves, ground
½ teaspoon vanilla extract
1 cup corn syrup
3 large eggs
1 cup rolled oats
½ cup black raisins

To prepare the pastry for the tart shells, follow the procedure described in the recipe on page 127 up to the point where the dough is divided in half. Instead of dividing the dough, cover it with wax paper, and chill it for at least an hour. Then roll out the dough to ⅛–inch thickness, and cut out 8 rounds of dough 4 inches in diameter. Place the rounds snugly into muffin tins or tart shell molds, and pierce each several times with a fork.

Preheat the oven to 350 degrees.

Blend together the butter and sugar until light and fluffy. Add the cinnamon, salt, cloves, vanilla extract, and corn syrup. Add the eggs, one at a time, beating well. Stir in the rolled oats and raisins. Distribute the mixture among the pastry shells. Bake for 20–25 minutes, until a knife inserted in the center of a tart comes out clean.

Makes 8 servings.

*David: Bessie's secret for making any pastry recipe flakier and lighter is
to add some lemon juice in place of a bit of the water in the recipe.

Harvest Home Grape Pie

1½ pounds (4 cups) blue Concord
grapes
¾ cup sugar
2 tablespoons all-purpose flour

1½ tablespoons lemon juice
Pie shell for a 2–crust 9–inch pie
(see pie pastry recipe on page
127)

Preheat the oven to 425 degrees.

Slip the skins off the grapes, and set them aside. Put the pulp into a large saucepan. Over medium heat, bring the pulp to a boil until the seeds are loosened. With a spoon, press the pulp through a colander into a large mixing bowl.

Add the reserved skins to the pulp. Stir in the sugar, flour, and lemon juice until all ingredients are well combined. Pour the mixture into an unbaked pie shell. Cut the remaining pie dough into strips and arrange them in a lattice-work fashion over the top. Bake the pie for 25–30 minutes. When the crust is brown, remove the pie from the oven and cool it on a rack. Serve warm or cold.

Makes 6 servings.

Grandma Frances's Jewish Caviar and Hamantashen

My grandmother was born in Rumania. She came over when she was about three years old, so she grew up in this country. She had an apartment in our house, which she loved, and we loved having her with us. She always kept active. She was involved with senior citizen groups, and late in life she took up sculpting. She did busts that looked very much like the people she was sculpting: Albert Einstein, Lenin, President Kennedy, and my father.

My father gave her a cassette machine, and she started taping an auto-biography. She loved the idea. Her tapes are really a pleasure to listen to. One of her stories was about being one of the first California hippies. She and my grandfather were involved in the first union organizing and they used to picket. And long before there were even decent roads, she and my grandfather used to drive back and forth from New York to California every now and then, in a Dodge truck that was a forerunner to a camper van. My grandfather was

sort of a Jack-of-all-trades, and he'd just decide, "Well, I want to go to California. Maybe I'll buy a cart and sell fruit." So he would do that, and the whole family would go. Since my grandmother was a nurse, she could find work to help support the family. She was very dedicated.

I used to watch her make eggplant. She'd make it for the whole family. It was sort of a staple with her, and she always liked to have some of it around. That's probably because she remembers her mother making it. She had a troughlike wooden bowl and a single-bladed chopper with a wooden handle that her mother had used to make the eggplant. She also had a brass mortar and pestle; she'd use that to mash the garlic. That was also from her mother. She called it a *shtasel*. It was all banged up, but it was still functional. She'd even pound nails in with the pestle part of it, and also use it to grind spices.

Recently I made the eggplant when I was up at Saranac Lake for a choir convention. I made it for a potluck dinner, and one of the men there was Rumanian and he could not believe that I had made it, because he had not had decent eggplant in years. He said, *"Where* did you learn to make this?" He was so shocked that I knew how. My grandmother used to call it the Jewish caviar!

—*Jonathan Pickow*

164

Rumanian Eggplant Salad

1 large eggplant
1 medium onion, peeled and
  diced
1 large clove garlic, peeled and
  minced
6 tablespoons oil

3 tablespoons white vinegar
1 tablespoon lemon juice
1 green pepper, seeded and diced
Salt to taste
10 black Greek olives

Preheat the broiler to 500 degrees.

With a knife, pierce vents in the unpeeled eggplant. Cook the eggplant under the broiler, turning it until soft when tested with a knife. Slice the eggplant in half and let it cool. Scrape out the eggplant pulp and chop finely. Mix together the diced onion, garlic, oil, vinegar, lemon juice, green pepper, and salt with the eggplant pulp. Arrange the eggplant on a serving dish, garnish with the olives, and chill.

Makes about 6 cups.

Hamantashen

Prune Pastries

Dough

⅔ cup (1⅓ sticks) unsalted
  butter
½ cup sugar
1 large egg

3 tablespoons milk
¾ teaspoon vanilla extract
3 cups all-purpose flour, sifted

Filling

½ cup (1 stick) unsalted butter
2 cups walnuts, ground
1¾ cups sugar
1 cup prune butter
½ cup black raisins
4 figs, diced

2 large egg whites, slightly
  beaten
3 tablespoons lemon juice
2 tablespoons rum
1 teaspoon vanilla extract
Cinnamon, ground, to taste

To make the dough, in a large saucepan, over medium heat, melt the butter. Remove from the heat, and mix in the sugar, egg, milk, and vanilla extract. Stir in the flour gradually, mixing well. Divide the dough in two, cover or wrap it in plastic wrap, and chill overnight.

To make the filling, in a large saucepan, over medium heat, melt the butter. Remove from the heat and stir in the walnuts, sugar, prune butter, raisins, figs, egg whites, lemon juice, rum, vanilla extract, and cinnamon to form a thick filling.

Preheat the oven to 375 degrees. Grease baking sheets.

With a rolling pin, roll out half of the dough into a circle ⅛–inch thick on a floured board. Cut into 3–inch circles with a water glass. Place a teaspoon of the filling in the center of each round, pull the edges up, and pinch the dough into a triangle. Repeat with the remaining dough and filling. Bake the pastries for about 12 minutes, until light golden in color.

Makes about 36 pastries.

Grandpa's Ginger Snaps and Lace Coconut Cookies

My grandfather makes billions of dollars. But he also makes cookies. He bakes every Sunday, and has for the last thirty years. It's true. He's made his own recipes, and he's refined them. As his friends get older, he tries to make cookies with less fat and lower cholesterol. They used to be all sugar and butter, but no more. Now he puts margarine instead of butter, and uses molasses instead of white sugar.

I tell you, he's so funny. You can just imagine this executive type—from six o'clock till noon he's in the kitchen, baking. He makes lace coconut cookies, oatmeal raisin cookies, and the all-time family favorite, Bakeless Cookies. My grandmother's maiden name was Bakeless, and the recipe comes from her family. They are ginger snaps. They're so good because he rolls them up into the shape of a little bar, and then he chills the bar so he can cut the cookies really thin. He cooks them up so they're black around the edges and really crispy.

At our old place in Nassau, he used to shred his own coconut and bring it back and freeze it. When he sold the place, part of the deal was that he retained "coconut rights." The new owners have to have their gardener shred the coconut and ship it off to my grandfather in St. Louis!

He also makes cheese-dollars that he gives to all his business associates. They think he's a great guy. He's eighty-six, works about a hundred hours a week, and still has time to bake cookies! At this point, his business is himself. He runs a hospital, he's on the board of a bank, and he still has his own corporation. It's a Fortune 500 company, even after all these years. He's got so many associates around the world, and they love it when he bakes cookies. He takes cookies to parties and gives them as gifts. It's like a tradition. You really know you've made it when L.Z. Francis brings you a bag of his homemade cookies!

—*Nina Francis*

166

Lace Coconut Cookies

1 cup (2 sticks) plus 2 tablespoons unsalted butter or shortening, melted*
6 tablespoons light corn syrup
6 tablespoons light cream or half-and-half
2 teaspoons vanilla extract

1½ cups all-purpose flour
1½ cups sugar
1 teaspoon baking powder
1½ cups quick-cooking oatmeal
1 cup English walnuts, chopped
1 cup coconut, grated

Preheat the oven to 375 degrees. With 2 tablespoons butter or shortening, grease baking sheets (even non-stick ones) well.

In a large mixing bowl, combine the remaining butter or shortening, corn syrup, cream, and vanilla extract. Sift together the flour, sugar, and baking powder, and stir into the butter mixture. Stir in the oatmeal, walnuts, and coconut.

Drop the dough by heaping teaspoonfuls onto the prepared cookie sheets. Bake for 6–8 minutes, or until lightly browned. Allow to cool briefly before transferring to racks to cool.

Makes about 12 dozen cookies.

*Nina: These days, my grandfather uses margarine and vegetable oil spray to keep the cholesterol content low.

Ginger Snaps

4½–5 cups all-purpose flour
2 teaspoons baking soda
1 teaspoon ginger, ground
1 teaspoon cinnamon, ground
1 teaspoon cloves, ground
¼ teaspoon salt

1 cup (2 sticks) plus 2 tablespoons unsalted butter or shortening
1 cup sugar
1 cup dark molasses
1 tablespoon white vinegar
1 large egg, beaten

In a large mixing bowl, sift together the flour, baking soda, ginger, cinnamon, cloves, and salt.

In a separate bowl, place 1 cup of butter or shortening and 1 cup of sugar. In a saucepan, heat the molasses to a boil, then remove from the heat and pour over the butter and sugar. Add the vinegar and stir until the ingredients are well blended. Stir in the beaten egg. Stir in the flour mixture gradually, mixing well after each addition. Cover the bowl with foil, wax paper, or plastic wrap and chill several hours or overnight. The dough can be frozen for up to 2 weeks.

The next day, remove the dough from the refrigerator and allow it to sit at room temperature for about 2½ hours to soften.

Preheat the oven to 350 degrees. With 2 tablespoons of butter or shortening, lightly grease baking sheets.

Divide the dough into thirds. Roll each piece into a roll about 14 inches long and 1¼ inches in diameter. Slice off cookies about ⅛-inch thick. Place on baking sheets and bake for 9–10 minutes. Allow to cool for a minute or two before transferring to racks to cool.

Each roll makes 8 to 10 dozen cookies, about 300 cookies total.

Chocolate-Mocha Almond Cake and Headache-Cure Cookies

Budapest before the War: The quality of the food was so wonderful, so fresh and delicious! One totally outstanding thing we had was a big New Year's family party. We'd have a turkey galantine, made by taking out all the bones and turkey meat, leaving the skin as intact as possible. Then the meat was mixed with rice and mushrooms, stuffed back into the empty skin, sewn up, and roasted. Can you imagine what a production it was?

Everybody had their favorite cake. My sister Lydia's favorite had chocolate in the batter and walnut cream in between the layers. My favorite was a grillage cake. The batter was made of blanched almonds (instead of flour), The *grillage* was burnt sugar with almonds, ground up and sprinkled on the coffee cream between the layers. Totally incredible! In fact, for a while, my daughter Marina baked these traditional Hungarian recipes professionally.

Some of my mother's recipes were really old. My mother kept a book of all the recipes she used, each labelled with the name of the person who had given her the recipe. One recipe was for an apricot-filled cookie. Once, a pharmacist friend who came over had a headache. We offered him some of these cookies and all of a sudden he said his headache was gone! From then on we called them "Aspirin Cookies" and my mother listed them that way in her cookbook. It's really a very simple cookie, but it's probably the proportions that make it so delicious.

—*Judith Garai Saly*

Apricot Sandwich Cookies

3 cups all-purpose flour
1 heaping teaspoon baking
   powder
½ cup (1 stick) plus 1 tablespoon
   unsalted butter

½ cup sugar
2 large egg yolks
Juice of 1 lemon
Apricot jam for sandwiching

Stir together the flour and baking powder in a large mixing bowl. Cut in the butter using a fork, pastry blender, or two knives until the mixture resembles coarse corn meal. Knead in the sugar, egg yolks, and lemon juice, and form the dough into a ball. Divide the dough in half, cover with wax paper, and refrigerate the dough for about 30 minutes.

Preheat the oven to 350 degrees. Grease 2 cookie sheets lightly.

Using a floured rolling pin, roll out one half of the dough very thinly on a lightly floured pastry board. Leave the other half in the refrigerator while you work. Cut the dough with a cookie cutter and, using a thimble, cut out the center of each cookie. Roll out the other portion of dough, cut the dough with a cookie cutter, but do not cut out the center of each cookie.

Place the cookies on the prepared cookie sheets, and bake them for about 10 minutes, or until the cookies are light brown. Remove the cookies from the oven. With a spatula lift the cookies off the sheets almost immediately, and transfer them to racks to cool. When cool, spread apricot jam on the bottom (holeless) cookie halves, and place the holed halves on top to make sandwiches.

Makes about 3 dozen sandwiches.

Chocolate Balls

8 ounces (8 squares) semi-sweet
   chocolate
7½ tablespoons unsalted butter
3 large egg yolks
3½ tablespoons confectioners' or
   extra fine sugar

2 heaping tablespoons cocoa
1 tablespoon dark rum
4 tablespoons hazelnuts, shelled,
   roasted, and finely ground*
Chocolate sprinkles

Melt the chocolate over a low flame, then let it cool. Beat the butter until creamy. Add the yolks, one by one, to the butter while beating. Beat in the sugar, cocoa, and rum. Add the cooled chocolate to the butter mixture. Hazelnuts are the last thing to be added to the mixture.

Leave the mixture at room temperature until it starts to thicken. Wet your hands and form the thickened chocolate into 1–inch balls. If the mixture is too runny, wait until it becomes the proper texture to roll into balls. Roll balls lightly in sprinkles.

Makes about 3 dozen chocolate balls.

*To roast hazelnuts: Heat a grease-free frying pan over a moderately high heat. Add the hazelnuts and stir constantly until lightly brown all over. Rub the hazelnuts between two towels to remove the skins. Cool, then grind the hazelnuts finely.

Hungarian Chocolate-Mocha Almond Cake

This cake tastes best when made 1 day in advance. Store it wrapped in foil in the refrigerator, but bring it to room temperature before serving.

Cake

4 ounces (4 squares) semi-sweet chocolate

2½ tablespoons strongly brewed coffee

8 large eggs, separated

½ cup sugar

4½ ounces (about ¾ cup) almonds, finely ground

Filling

½ cup (1 stick) unsalted butter

3 ounces (3 squares) semi-sweet chocolate

2 tablespoons strongly brewed coffee

1½–2 tablespoons sugar

Few drops vanilla extract

2 large eggs yolks

Grated semi-sweet chocolate for decoration

Preheat the over to 350 degrees. Lightly grease a 9 × 12–inch cake pan and dust it with flour. Set the pan aside in a cool place. Cover a pastry board with wax paper.

To make the cake, place the chocolate and the coffee in a small heavy saucepan and cook over low heat until the chocolate melts. Remove from the heat and cool the mixture to room temperature.

Whip the egg whites until stiff, but not dry, and set aside. Beat the egg yolks, gradually adding the sugar, until the mixture is pale yellow and creamy. Stir in the melted chocolate mixture and the ground almonds, then fold in the whipped egg whites. Mix well and pour into the prepared pan. Bake for 30 minutes. Remove from the oven and let stand for 5–10 minutes. Turn out onto a pastry board covered with wax paper. Let cool.

To make the filling, beat the butter until soft and creamy. Combine the chocolate, coffee, and sugar in a heavy saucepan over low heat until the chocolate is melted. Remove from the heat, add the vanilla extract, and mix well. Let stand until cool. When the mixture is cool, beat in the egg yolks one at a time. Pour the chocolate mixture into the butter and beat until very smooth.

Cut the cake into two layers. Spread the bottom layer of the cake with half of the filling, then place the other layer on top. Cover the top and sides of the cake with the remaining filling. Sprinkle the top with grated chocolate for decoration.

Makes 8 servings.

Photographs

Alphabetical Index

Category Index